WITHDRAWN

Related titles

Great Thinkers A–Z – Julian Baggini and Jeremy Stangroom

The Greatest Educators Ever

Frank M. Flanagan

TOURO COLLEGE LIBRARY
Kings Hwy

continuum
LONDON • NEW YORK

KH

Continuum International Publishing Group
The Tower Building
11 York Road
London SE1 7NX

15 East 26th Street
New York
NY 10010

www.continuumbooks.com

© Frank M. Flanagan 2006

All rights reserved. No part of this publication may be reproduced or transmitted in
any form or by any means, electronic or mechanical, including photocopying, recording,
or any information storage or retrieval system, without prior permission in writing from
the publishers.

British Library Cataloguing-in-Publication Data
A catalogue record for this book is available from the British Library.

ISBN: 0-8264-8467-0 (hardback) 0-8264-8468-9 (paperback)

Library of Congress Cataloging-in-Publication Data
A catalog record for this book is available from the Library of Congress.

Typeset by Aarontype Limited, Easton, Bristol
Printed and bound in Great Britain by Antony Rowe Ltd, Chippenham, Wiltshire

9/19/06

Contents

Introduction

At the start of the twenty-first century the universal accessibility of primary and secondary schooling in industrialized countries is taken for granted. Schools, qualified teachers, curricula, systems of assessment and evaluation, additional supports for learners with specific difficulties, are integral features of the cultural landscape. This is a far cry from the situation in many underdeveloped nations where educational access is restricted, often available only to the children of an economic or political elite, and poorly developed in terms of facilities, curricula and teaching expertise. It is a far cry too from the situation which prevailed universally at the dawn of modern Western civilization in the city states of Greece in the fifth century BC. Then, as now in underdeveloped states, education was a haphazard and fortuitous experience: it was not available at all to women or to the poor, much less to those in that unimaginable state of non-being called slavery.

How this situation developed to what we know today is a long and complex story and not one which any single volume can even attempt to relate. It is a story of economic growth and associated technological development, a story of growing political freedoms and conceptions of individual rights, a story of the development of human understanding, as well as an appreciation of the social, cultural and economic power of learning and teaching.

The evolution of educational thought and practice which is an integral part of this story, and itself part of the reason for the story itself, did not happen by accident. It happened because of the vision and commitment, the passion and sacrifice of countless people, men and women, rich and poor, exalted and humble. The vast majority of these educational pioneers lived and died in obscurity, their lives spent in significant and selfless service to the children of their communities and neighbours, studying, teaching, establishing and running schools, striving to improve the common lot of their communities through the advancement of learning. As Oliver Goldsmith described one such:

> There in his noisy mansion, skill'd to rule,
> The village master taught his little school;
> ...
> Yet he was kind, or if severe in aught,
> The love he bore to learning was in fault.[1]

Their motivation was not just love of learning, but much more, a love of humanity embodied in specific communities, specific children and specific historical circumstances.

But not all of those responsible for the growth of education have been forgotten: many names stand out as beacons in the long journey towards enlightenment, people who, whether their motivation was spiritual, political, cultural, humanistic, or a combination of some or all of these, created something new, something which changed the way their contemporaries and/or their pedagogical descendants saw the world, saw the significance of the education of the young, and undertook the practical task of combating ignorance.

The chapters of this book provide an introduction to some of these pioneers of Western educational thought and practice, their ideas and, where appropriate, their methods. The teachers and thinkers included here are among the most eminent causes of the growth and development of education and, alongside revolutionary politicians, innovative scientists, inventive technologists and progressive healers, created the world we know and which we are pleased to consider civilized.

The essays are intended to provide a simple and, I hope, accessible introduction to the ideas of these great pioneers in the history of Western education. None of the essays is intended to be a comprehensive account of its subject. At best each chapter will, it is hoped, provide a purchase on the thinking and teaching of the individual involved, a base camp, so to speak, from which further exploration can proceed. Neither should the essays be read as collectively expressing any kind of overarching theory or interpretation. Insofar as it is possible each should speak for itself and only for itself.

Education and society

Of course the attentive reader will discern common themes. This should not surprise; all of the people involved are, after all, writing about the same thing, or about the same kind of thing: how any society should approach the task of educating its young. What this means in individual cases cannot differ too much, or too radically. There are children and young people who are becoming adults, and there is a culture to be transmitted; for whatever else it may do, education must propagate the identity of the community in which it is operative and which sustains it. Education in human society is neither a natural phenomenon nor a random activity, it is the systematic attempt by human societies to safeguard their continuity. Children, new human beings, must be changed from egoists who are concerned only with their own self-regarding imperatives to social individuals who can respond in non-egotistical modes such as duty, loyalty and compassion for the good of the collective. In short, the demands of social life must be given priority over personal gratification if any society is to survive, much less flourish. Since the earliest ruminations of the Greeks, education has been recognized as the process of inculcating the necessary discipline and self-control, transforming the utterly self-regarding infant into the socially conscious and morally aware citizen. Society cannot subsist in anarchy, however benign: in order to survive human societies must generate a foundational consensus regarding central values and beliefs. How this may happen and who will cause it to happen is a central issue for educational policy and practice.

This was recognized in modern times by the great French sociologist Émile Durkheim, but had also been the central concern of Plato's educational theories more than 2,000 years earlier: the task of education is to ensure the stability of the just society. This is why the state has an abiding and compelling interest in education: its very survival depends on the adequate transmission to the young of the basic principles of its common life. The state must ensure that the schools transmit the necessary principles and values to the young. It must, in Durkheim's words, 'see to it that nowhere are children left ignorant of (the necessary principles and values), that everywhere they should be spoken of with the respect which is due them'.[2]

So in one view the teacher becomes the functionary of the state: the transmission of crucial beliefs and values is the teacher's central task. Teachers are not allowed to teach their own idiosyncratic convictions. Where, from time to time, individual teachers themselves are less than fully committed to the orthodox beliefs and values which they are expected to inculcate, they are forced to conform or be dismissed. If they are to be subversive of the prevailing order they must be so in very subtle ways or establish an alternative school as A.S. Neill did or an alternative system of education as Maria Montessori. In general, however, teachers' unaffected commitment to the central beliefs and values of the prevailing order translates into a way of life and a personal projection of these beliefs and values (their embodiment in the teacher's own behaviour) that presents the child with a model of personal life and a vision of the prevailing moral order. Education must be, within constraints of personal style, the same for all.

Progress

But, clearly, if education were the same for all there would be nothing but a repressive, static political system in which change would not only be unlikely but impossible: for, if all are acculturated to accept the status quo and to think alike, where will change, growth and development come from? This is the significant difference between Plato and John Dewey, for example. Plato wanted a state in which the received certainties would be fully accepted and proofed against change. Once the perfect state was established (according to Plato's principles) then every effort would be made to ensure that it did not change, for any change from perfection is deterioration. Dewey, on the other hand, realized that without change there is stasis and death: change is life, growth.

So each new generation must, at one and the same time, be acculturated in such a way that each individual becomes a stable and reliable member of society but somehow simultaneously retains the necessary creativity (that is to say, rebelliousness, unconventionality) to provide for change. This gives education two contradictory aims: the protection of the status quo and the promotion of individual creativity.

But this does not provide a full account of the perennial struggle for education. For the people whose ideas are dealt with here were not, for the most part, state functionaries although they might, collectively, be understood as contributing to the evolution of the idea of the state through their educational efforts. To illustrate the further dimensions of the education project it might help to look briefly at the situation which arose at the dawn of Western civilization.

The shadow of the Greeks

Following the chaos of the Peloponnesian War in the fifth and fourth centuries BC, Greece was riven by profound intellectual uncertainty. A decline of faith in the traditional gods, a growing mistrust of absolute answers and a consequent erosion of moral values had driven philosophers to question certainties which hitherto had been buttressed by belief in divine authority. The philosophers sought answers based on human reason and human purpose. Man became, as Protagoras, one of the leading teachers of the era, is reputed to have declared, 'the measure of all things'. This was a rather shocking thing to assert in a society which, up until then, had depended largely on the authority of tradition and relied on belief in the central guidance of divine forces in human affairs.

The most notable group to exploit the decline of traditional beliefs were the Sophists. The word 'Sophist' comes from the Greek word 'sophos' meaning 'wise', from which, together with the word 'philos' meaning 'loving', we get the word 'philosophy'. The Sophists were considered 'wise' in the sense of having a knowledge of the skills necessary for success in the world of practical affairs. Individual Sophists, such as Protagoras and Gorgias, travelled from town to town instructing young men of wealth and family in preparation for their role in public life. These young men, the sons of the upper classes of Peloponnesian society, were expected to fulfil their civic duties as legislators, jurists, advocates, administrators or military officers. As belief in divine authority and absolute values degenerated many of the Sophists argued that, since laws and moral codes were of human origin, they were therefore imperfect and unreliable as a guide to human behaviour. Since there were no absolute values or standards in human affairs, either at the level of individual morality or at the level of government, everything became a matter of expediency. The one who could best turn circumstances to his advantage would succeed best.

In their instruction the Sophists therefore concentrated on public speaking or rhetoric, the arts of persuasion. The ability to address and sway large groups of people was of crucial importance because in the city states of Greece all decisions of public policy were made by assemblies of adult male citizens. Rhetoric was an essential element, perhaps the most important element, in the formation of young men for public service. In a free society only able orators would be able to mould and change opinion and policy by entertaining, informing and persuading their listeners. It is not too fanciful to assert that the Sophists' role in ancient Greece was similar to that of image consultants who currently provide media training for politicians and others.

The skills which the Sophists taught were instrumental, that is they were intended to achieve some end beyond themselves. They were not necessarily associated with truth or virtue: the Sophists taught the skills, it was a matter for the individual to decide how to use them, whether for good or ill. In other words, what the Sophists promised was a strictly utilitarian technical education unaffected by issues of morality or human goodness. The Sophists charged for their services and, since they were effectively the only educational opportunity available, many of them became wealthy as a result of their instruction.

Socrates was a part of this ethos but he is not generally considered a Sophist; he was not an itinerant teacher, he never charged a fee and in fact he opposed the values and methods of the Sophists vigorously. He did not accept that the only alternative to divine intervention in human affairs was an arbitrary human standard, or that the principal method of public policy should be emotive persuasion through rhetoric. Socrates taught, on the contrary, that ignorance could be dispelled and objective truth discovered by means of rational argument, or dialectic. This difference between the Socratic approach to education and that of the Sophists resurfaces every time we question whether the primary concern of education should be the pursuit of knowledge and truth (i.e. be humanistic or liberal) or whether it should emphasize method and skill (i.e. be a technical preparation). Both of these positions can be set against a third tradition which is in fact the first historically: the orthodoxy against which both Socrates and the Sophists rebelled: the pre-eminence of established, conventional beliefs defended and promoted by those who held power in society and which constituted the core of education.

These three traditions can be found, to varying degrees, not only in most educational philosophies but generally in the ethos and principles of a culture, whether it is dominated by an authority (human or divine), by a technology or a class of technocrats, or by the free individual pursuit of truth and happiness. Many of the great educational controversies of the past can be understood as conflicts between alternative visions based on the ascendancy of one or other of these three components.

All educational systems or philosophies will embody some mixture, some balance of these perspectives and their attendant values. They represent, as it were, the primary colours from which the vast variety of human cultures and political organizations can be formed. Each system presents a unique profile based on the way in which authority, technology and individual liberty are blended or on whether any one is present in an extreme form: totalitarianism, technocracy or anarchism. Each of the thinkers and practitioners dealt with in this book can be evaluated in these terms using three simple questions: to what extent does each of them support and attempt to promote a particular existing form of authority, or propose reform or more radical change in the social or political order? Second, to what extent does each promote a particular technical solution to perceived social, human or economic problems? Last, to what extent does each promote the freedom of choice of the individual? Each response is a matter of proportion; a matter of blending power, technique and morality.

The teachers and thinkers

The first three thinkers are located in a century-long period between the fifth and fourth centuries BC: a brief period in the history of the Peloponnese, the location of modern-day Greece. No account of the history of educational thought can begin without paying tribute to Socrates, for he is the beginning and even yet the principal inspiration of the vocational conception of teaching; the view that teaching is divinely inspired, committed to truth and yet somehow subordinate to the civic order. Then comes Plato with a magisterial blueprint for education as an instrument of statecraft – a view which has lost none of its relevance two and a half millennia later. Aristotle continued Plato's concern with the relationship between education and the governance of the community. How can people be educated to submit to government and, at the same time, be prepared to govern as the occasion demands: a crucial question even today for contemporary liberal democratic systems.

Next in chronological order comes Jesus Christ of Palestine. Is there a connection with the Greeks? Only in retrospect: we can perceive from the perspective of the twenty-first century how the Greek conception of man as the ultimate measure of value and the Christian celebration of the moral status of the individual merged to create the contemporary conception of rights-based individualism.

Quintilian was the epitome of the teacher/educator of the Roman era. Through the application of Greek technique in rhetoric and Greek philosophical principles he sketched a vision of an education which could be practically useful without compromising moral integrity. His principal contribution to educational thought was his recognition of the importance of the early education of the individual learner. Until now the priority had been the education of the late adolescent or the adult.

St. Augustine redirects attention from the objective of education to the method, and to the importance of epistemology – how knowledge is acquired. In effect, he challenges the Socratic pre-occupation with verbal definition by challenging the pre-eminence of the verbal over the experiential, especially the experience inspired by divine illumination. With Augustine, God becomes an agent in human knowledge.

A thousand year lacuna does not mean that there were no educational activities or developments. There were, of course, the rise of the universities and the contributions of such as Abelard and Erasmus, but in general such developments as there were were no more than elaborations of what had gone before: the thought of Aristotle – lost and returned to Europe through the agency of Arab philosophers – and Augustine, for example, systematized by the methodical brain of Thomas Aquinas.

The next real educational developments were the rights-based educational proposals of John Amos Comenius. The reformed religions had tossed a new challenge into the educational arena: if salvation is a matter of individual engagement with the truth of Scripture then each and every individual, irrespective of social, economic or political status, is entitled to, that is must have, an appropriate education.

Comenius' influence, for whatever historical reasons, was not immediate. We find John Locke, the prophet of political freedom, preoccupied with the educational requirements of the sons of gentlemen and relatively unconcerned with the educational requirements of the masses.

And then there was Rousseau.

Jean-Jacques Rousseau is to education as Copernicus is to cosmology. After Rousseau educational thought and discourse were irredeemably changed. He switched the focus of educational thought from the immediate needs of the social order, the orthodoxy, to the needs of the individual in the first instance; the needs of the man came before the needs of the subject or the citizen. Rousseau forged the re-conceptualization of education, especially in relation to the education of young children, which would influence thinking about education and redirect practice over the next three centuries.

It is important to remember that Rousseau was not operating in a vacuum. The process of establishing religious and secular educational systems throughout Europe had already begun and the educational struggle in the next two or three centuries would be between the demands of educational systems for social conformity and ideological orthodoxy and the drive towards individual developmental freedom as outlined by Rousseau and his successors. In simple terms, the tension would be between the Romantic conception of the autonomous individual and the requirements of the social and economic order.

Rousseau introduced a paradigm shift in our thinking about education and, like Thomas Kuhn's account of the history of scientific thought,[3] Rousseau's successors can be seen as simply teasing out the implications of the new perspective: how to apply Rousseau's radical insights to practical educational situations.

The political demand for universal education which followed the political revolutions of the seventeenth and eighteenth centuries and the Industrial Revolution from the eighteenth century onwards meant that educators had to address the problems of education for the masses. Pestalozzi, for example, sought a conceptualization of human thought which could be replicated in a method of teaching which would allow for the education of the masses in conformity with Rousseauist principles, without reliance on the individual talent or inspiration of individual practitioners. Froebel, through the medium of German idealist philosophy, continued this programme. Between them, Pestalozzi and Froebel sowed the seeds of what would grow to be educational psychology. But Froebel also made a singular contribution. With his conception of early childhood education as a necessary prerequisite for conventional, curriculum-centred education he introduced into educational discourse two of the most influential ideas of the past 200 years: the idea of the kindergarten with all its ramifications, and the sustaining metaphor of organic growth which places the teacher in the role of the attentive gardener.

The educational philosophy of John Henry Newman returns to many of the preoccupations of the Greeks: the education of the young men (and later, happily, women) of the community/state. Like the Sophists, but with more regard for the truth, Newman wanted the young prepared for whatever occupational demands society would make of them: education in the first instance is a preparation for life, not for earning a living. But, like Quintilian, Newman insisted that education must be conducted with due regard for truth and moral rectitude.

With John Dewey and Maria Montessori we reach the confrontation of the romantic with the scientific. Intuition, metaphor or cultural inspiration are no longer sufficient. Scientific theory (evolution, psychology) and scientific practice (detached observation, experimental method) require systematic, structural conceptions of human development. From Pestalozzi and Froebel we inherit the idea that there is a developmental pattern which determines how children learn, when they learn particular kinds of knowledge, and how, as a consequence, they should be taught. Montessori and Dewey took these insights into account in forging more scientific approaches to education.

When these kinds of preoccupations took hold of education, particularly at the level of early childhood education, it became necessary to sound a note of caution. The great Jewish philosopher Martin Buber warned that children are not just learning organisms operating out of a force for self-expression. Young human beings, as well as a predisposition for self-expression, have a predisposition for communion: education is not just about opportunities for self-expression but, more importantly, about opportunities for cooperative, communal and interpersonal life.

Meanwhile, it is important to note that, however influential the influence of Rousseau might have been, it was no more than one influence. The work of A.S. Neill manifests another, Freudian psychoanalysis. As the development of psychology and psychiatry progressed it would be expected that they would exert more and more influence on educational theory and practice. What is surprising is that theories like Freudianism, which had such a major influence on the mainstream arts of painting, literature and cinema, had, apparently, so little influence on mainstream education. Neill was one of the very few to take its educational significance seriously.

By the 1960s formal, state-mandated education had become an object of radical dissent. Illich and Freire articulate reservations regarding the social and cultural preoccupations and predispositions of conventional education systems. By the second half of the twentieth century, in their view, education systems promoted or underwritten by the state had themselves become part of the problem of the quality of education.

The thinkers and teachers dealt with here approach the problems of education within the constraints of their own time and culture; they can do no differently. It is a measure of their genius how far they stretched the imaginations of their contemporaries and set the agenda for further development in educational thought and practice.

Plato, for example, wrote his *Republic* not, in the first instance, as a treatise on education but, as the original Greek title (*The State*, or *On Justice*) shows, a discussion on statecraft and justice. The issue of education was soon broached, however, because considerations of social policy and justice cannot be addressed without consideration of education: how people govern and submit to being governed depends upon the way they have been educated. So, as will be seen, issues of state and civic participation, and concern regarding government and the quality of social life, continue to preoccupy educational thinkers up to the present day. Balancing this preoccupation with ruling and being ruled there was the contrary question of individual freedom and the quality of the individual moral life.

If anything, the history of educational ideas is an unfolding of the growing development of human freedom both in terms of the individual learner and in terms of civic or political liberty. This is especially pointed in the years leading up to and immediately following the decades of the great revolutions of the eighteenth century which marked the beginnings of democratic government, the recognition of human rights and the spread of individual freedoms.

The concept of teaching and learning is much richer than any particular instance of educational theory or practice. Educational proposals, whether radical or conservative, always promote a political or ideological programme. Education, as Freire reminds us, is not neutral; neither, it may be said, is any particular philosophy of education. The history of educational thought, from Athens in the fifth century BC through to the radical critics of the 1960s, is a history of the attempt to influence the way in which society initiates and socializes its young, the way it forms and controls their beliefs, knowledge, judgements and behaviour. It is also a history of the struggle within society as to who will exercise that control.

The leading educational thinkers of the past were not engaged in a detached, objective evaluation of contending educational ideas. They were attempting to influence the way in which education would be conducted in order to promote the political and social ideals to which they subscribed. Education is future oriented; it is about the way in which the people of the present think the people of the future should live and the kind of society they should live in. It is prescriptive by its very nature. It is not for the sake of detachment or objectivity that churches, states, political parties, radical reformers, revolutionary and cultural interest groups contest the control of education in any society. Their primary interest is not the description of the society as it is, but the definition of the society as it ought to be in the future.

1 Socrates (469/70–399 BC) and the Search for Definition

If there is a patron saint of teaching, albeit a secular one, it must be Socrates, for Socrates embodies the virtues which we have come to expect of teachers: commitment to the pursuit and service of the truth combined with allegiance to the laws and the state. Socrates shows us how these apparently antagonistic, if not sometimes totally contradictory, loyalties can be reconciled. Insofar as they attempt to reconcile this dilemma, all educational innovators are the intellectual descendants of Socrates, for each asks awkward questions of, and poses significant challenges to, the prevailing order while at the same time trying to conserve it, if only by improving it.

Socrates is also revered by philosophers not so much for the content of his teaching, the efficacy of his method, or the manner of his life, but for the manner of his death. He believed that his teaching, his philosophizing, was a divinely inspired gift and a divinely mandated task. For Socrates his teaching was a vocation, an occupation which defined his life and without which his life would be virtually meaningless: his vocation defined who he was.

His life

Little is known with certainty about the life of Socrates. He was born in Athens about 469 BC and he was found guilty by an Athenian court, at the age of 70, on charges of corrupting the young men of Athens and of not believing in the gods of the city. He was condemned to death.

For the most part, our knowledge of Socrates comes from Plato and Aristotle. Plato, who was a contemporary of Socrates, made him the main protagonist in the early and middle dialogues. Aristotle, who was born some 15 years after Socrates' death, would have known of him by hearsay and reputation only. However, we can imagine that a reputation which has persisted over the intervening millennia would have been much more powerful and influential in the century after Socrates' death and in the city where he spent his entire life. Socrates tells us in Plato's *Crito*[1] that apart from periods of military service he left the city only once and never had any curiosity regarding other states or their laws.

Socrates served in the Athenian army and fought in the Peloponnesian War at Potidaea, Amphipolis and Delium. He was not handsome; he is described as looking like a satyr and Aristophanes the playwright describes him as waddling like a duck and rolling his eyes a lot. For all that, he was physically robust: he wore the same clothes whatever the season, went barefoot at all times and was very abstemious in eating and drinking. During his trial he adduced his poverty in his defence as evidence that whatever he had taught to the young men of Athens he had not profited financially as a result. Unlike the Sophists (whom he despised on account of their mercenary motivation as well as for their unprincipled approach to knowledge) he charged no fees. 'If you have heard anyone say that I try to educate people and charge a fee,' he declared at his trial, 'there is no truth in that. I wish that there were because I think that it is a fine thing if a man is qualified to teach.'[2]

A number of singularities mark him out. The first was his claim, generally believed by his contemporaries, that he was the recipient of messages from an otherworldly, or inner, voice which frequently forbade him to do things he was thinking of doing: 'that sign which always forbids, but never bids, me to do anything which I am going to do'.[3] He always followed this inner imperative. He even remarked at his trial that this inner voice had not forbidden his attendance at the hearing that day: consequently he considered the trial to be his destiny. Another remarkable thing was his apparent endorsement as the wisest of men by the Oracle at Apollo's shrine at Delphi, the Delphic Oracle. He described at his trial how a friend of his, Chaerephon, had gone to Delphi and asked the Oracle if any man was wiser than Socrates. The Oracle had replied that no one was wiser.[4]

A third strange characteristic was Socrates' apparent habit of falling into long fits of abstraction: whether some kind of trance, interludes of deep meditation, prolonged periods of concentration or some more pathological condition, we have no way of knowing. All in all, however, Socrates was not like any other.

The judgement of the Delphic Oracle, that there was no one wiser than he, affected Socrates profoundly. (Ironically, the Oracle was a central feature of the superstitious regulation of human affairs which both Socrates and the Sophists opposed. For centuries the advice of the Oracle, as interpreted by the resident presiding priest class, had been sought, and acted upon, by military leaders and politicians.) Socrates' own interpretation of the judgement was that his superior wisdom was simply his realization of his own ignorance!

His procedure for testing the judgement of the Oracle was quite scientific and surprisingly modern: rather than try to confirm the Oracle's judgement by displaying his wisdom, Socrates tried to falsify it. He sought out people who had a reputation for wisdom, supposing that, in conversation with such people, he could find evidence which would refute the Oracle. But he found that those who appeared wise (especially in their own estimation) turned out, on examination, not to be.

The result of this enquiry was that Socrates discovered that his own denial of wisdom was, in fact, wisdom of the highest kind; in attempting to prove the Oracle wrong, Socrates demonstrated it to be correct. 'So I withdrew,' he told his trial,

> and thought to myself 'I am wiser than this man; it is likely that neither of us knows anything worthwhile, but he thinks he knows something when he does not, whereas when I do not know, neither do I think I know; so I am likely to be wiser than he to this small extent: that I do not think I know what I do not know.[5]

As faith in traditional certainties and belief in the moral authority of traditional beliefs declined, Socrates made it his life's work, his vocation, to pursue the truth irrespective of where the search might lead, for the truth was the only possible moral anchor in an uncertain world. His method was relentless and direct, asking questions of any who would listen and engage with him in dialectic, pursuing the truth through the exchange of rational arguments. Socrates forced his contemporaries to reflect, revalue and reconsider their certainties. With scant regard for political power or the status of wealth he demanded of his interlocutors a justification for their most cherished beliefs, or prejudices, regarding their fundamental values about virtue, justice, truth or whatever. He did this in such a way as to leave people in a state of uncertainty and unease about what, until then, they had taken as fixed, certain and unquestionable.

He was married: his wife Xanthippe was reputed to be the most shrewish woman in Athens. At the time of his trial and death he had three sons 'one almost grown up and the other two only children'.[6] One of them was quite young at the time of Socrates' death, apparently. We are told in the *Phaedo* that when his friends arrived to spend the last night in his company, they 'found Socrates just released from chains, and Xanthippe, whom you know, sitting by him, and holding his child in her arms'.[7] What they lived on is a puzzle for Socrates does not appear to have had any occupation other than his philosophizing. 'I have never lived an ordinary quiet life,' he said at his trial.

> I did not care for the things that most people care about – making money, having a comfortable home, high military or civil rank, and all the other activities, political appointments, secret societies, party organizations, which go on in our city.[8]

Socrates and teaching

The experience of testing the Oracle's meaning provided Socrates with three fundamental insights into the process of education.

The first was a recognition that it is possible for the 'teacher' to learn from the pupil just as the pupil may learn from the 'teacher'. Learners have their own knowledge: it may not be the knowledge which the teacher wishes to impart to the learner but it is no less important for all that: it is a poor teacher who will refuse to see the learner's truth.

The second insight was that in order to learn anything we must first of all acknowledge that we do not know it. If one thinks that one knows something then the most fundamental reason for learning and its most powerful motivation – awareness of one's ignorance – is missing. An essential starting point in the process of learning is the realization of one's ignorance.

The third insight identified a basic occupational hazard of teaching: just because a teacher can show that a learner's claim to knowledge is mistaken it does not follow that the teacher is the possessor of the relevant knowledge. Teachers must be continuously open to opportunities to learn and always prepared to acknowledge their own ignorance. Unfortunately, teachers' willingness to acknowledge their own ignorance never became a part of the Socratic pedagogical tradition.

His method

Socrates' method of stimulating learning is well exemplified by his conversation with his friend Meno on the topic of virtue.[9]

It is Meno himself who initiates the discussion. He is a wealthy young man of good family who is considering putting himself under the tutelage of a Sophist. Meno wishes to know whether the Sophists can actually teach virtue or not. He asks Socrates whether virtue can be taught or whether it is acquired by practice. After freely acknowledging his own ignorance in the matter and his inability to provide a satisfactory answer, Socrates elicits a definition (a statement purporting to express the essential nature of something) from Meno. He then begins to undermine Meno's definition by subjecting it to a series of challenging questions. This is the process of *elenchus*: bringing someone from an assertion of knowledge, through questioning, to the perception of contradiction, inconsistency and falsehood. Socratic *elenchus* culminates in the realization of ignorance and a resultant perplexity which is the beginning of wisdom. Meno thought he knew what virtue was but Socrates' questions convinced him otherwise. Meno is now in a fit state to begin the process of learning.

What Socrates seeks in every case is a universal definition, a definition which covers all instances of something, colour, say, or shape. He believes that all things have essential properties which can be discerned by reason, these properties can be summarized in a verbal definition, and such definitions give us true knowledge of reality. Under the influence of Roman/Christian thought, Socrates' dialectical method was eclipsed by the dogmatic theocentrism that centred on matters relating to belief in God as the primary concern of thought of the sixth to the fifteenth centuries AD. The role of rationality and dialectic remained, perhaps, as an aspiration of disaffected intellectuals rather than as a central principle of thought or education. It was not until the Renaissance of the sixteenth century that a sustained effort was made to reintroduce a secular rationality into Western European thought.

Socrates' purpose

Socratic dialectic was not a matter of public entertainment or personal whim. He believed that a universally valid definition of anything – virtue, justice, beauty, truth, honesty, courage – encapsulated the essence of the thing itself. This meant that the sovereign road to wisdom was the discovery of these universal definitions. The dialectic was a process of questioning which tested the legitimacy of proposed definitions and sometimes helped to advance the understanding of the subject at issue. If the proposed definitions were true they would withstand all criticism and prove to be true knowledge. Alternatively, as the initial definition retreated and evolved under Socrates' relentless questioning, less adequate definitions gave way to more adequate definitions or, at the very worst, identified a hitherto unacknowledged ignorance with regard to the matter being discussed.

Socrates' objective was not just enhancing his own personal knowledge or wisdom, much less his reputation as a wise man – he had a very serious social purpose. Ethical living should be the concern not just of the individual but of the society at large: the just society can come about only as a result of the actions of just individuals. In challenging the pretensions to knowledge of his contemporaries he was not just being pedantic; he was convinced that a clear knowledge of the truth is essential for the right control of moral and political life.

'I spend all my time,' he told his judges,

> going about trying to persuade you, young and old, to make your first and chief concern not for your bodies nor for your possessions, but for the highest welfare of your souls, proclaiming as I go, wealth does not bring goodness, but goodness brings wealth and every other blessing, both to the individual and to the state.[10]

He believed that true ideas came in the clear form of definitions which could be discovered by rigorous debate. His purpose was highly practical, not speculative. He differed from the Sophists in this. They regarded technique as all that was necessary for the achievement of virtue. Socrates realized that virtue demanded the truth.

The relationship in education

It is clear from many of the Platonic dialogues which feature Socrates as a central protagonist that Socrates envisaged a specific kind of relationship which should exist between the teacher and the learner. It should be remembered that Socrates (as all of the ancients) was concerned primarily with the later education of the individual, in particular the education of the young men on the threshold of their public service. The pedagogical models adduced by Plato's account of Socrates' life must be applied circumspectly. There is a danger that attempting to teach through the discovery of verbal definitions and constructs would invade educational initiatives which should be based on direct experience. Socrates' moral dialectic is intended for people who have developed an aptitude in language and a capacity for engaging with abstract ideas, conceptualizations. It is utterly inappropriate for children in the earlier stages of their educational experience. The pedagogical relationship envisaged in the Socratic educational scheme then is one of an engagement between equals, a relationship of adults with comparable linguistic, experiential and judgemental competences. It is more appropriate to the education of adults, what would emerge later as university education, than to the education of children.

Ultimately, the Socratic method is a method of critique. It was not for nothing that he described himself at his trial as a 'stinging fly'.

'It is literally true,' he said,

> even if it sounds rather comical, that God has specially appointed me to this city, as though it were a large thoroughbred horse which because of its great size is inclined to be lazy and needs the stimulation of some stinging fly. It seems to me that God has attached me to this city to perform the office of such a fly, and all day long I never cease to settle here, there, and everywhere, rousing, persuading, reproving every one of you.[11]

His death

Socrates' method had a sinister outcome, however. As a result of publicly demonstrating that their claims to wisdom were ill-founded he made many enemies among notable Athenians. Ultimately, these enemies engineered his trial and execution.

Brought to trial, at the age of 70, Socrates was charged with corrupting the young men of Athens and of not believing in the gods of the city. He was found guilty and condemned to die by drinking a draught of hemlock. When the guilty verdict was announced he professed his life's work as trying to 'persuade each one of you not to think more of practical advantages than of his mental and moral well-being'.[12]

The constant search for adequate definitions which dominated Socrates' life should not be dismissed as the preoccupation of an academic, a dreamer or a man of no practical consequence. His method, far from being remote from practical affairs, has profound political consequences. For ultimately the Socratic method is anti-authoritarian. It is a potent weapon against those who claim to have certain knowledge about how human affairs should be ordered and who presume to impose their certainty on the rest of us. This, it should be remembered, was the pattern which had dominated schooling from the beginning. Even in the present day the priority of conventional systems of education is to impose an orthodoxy, whether this be economic, political or religious. The Socratic challenge to orthodoxy has always been seen to be heretical and many, teachers and others, have paid the ultimate price in the name of a Socratic search for truth.

Another positive aspect is that Socrates' notion of learning is a cooperative process of dialogue. If we have no established certainties then we must go forward tentatively, cooperatively and in full awareness of our own fallibility.

Socrates' conversations on the teachability of virtue, in particular, tended to be inconclusive. Perhaps his true convictions regarding whether it could be taught, and how it should be taught, were revealed at the conclusion of his speech at the end of his trial.

When my sons grow up, gentlemen, if you think that they are putting money or anything else before goodness, take your revenge by plaguing them as I have plagued you; and if they fancy themselves for no reason, you must scold them just as I have scolded you, for neglecting the important things and thinking that they are good for something when they are good for nothing. If you do this I shall have had justice at your hands, both I myself and my children.

> Now it is time that we were going, I to die and you to live; but which of us has the happier prospect is unknown to anyone but God.[13]

Despite many offers and opportunities both during his trial and subsequently, Socrates refused to escape the judgement of the court. His reasons are set out in one of Plato's shortest, and in the circumstances, most moving dialogues, *Crito*. Just days before his sentence is due to be carried out Crito tries to persuade Socrates to escape. One argument he uses is to accuse Socrates of abandoning his three sons.

> You are letting your sons down too. You have it in your power to finish their bringing up and education and instead of that you are proposing to go off and desert them ... Either one ought not to have children at all, or one ought to see their education and upbringing through to the end.[14]

Socrates is unmoved by this and other arguments which he dismisses as 'the doctrines of the multitude'. His principal reasons for not attempting to escape have to do with his regard for truth and consistency. By going against the collective wish of the Athenians in sentencing him to death – even though he considers it a faulty judgement – he would undermine the authority of the laws and of the state. And this he could not do for he holds the state in high esteem as the source of all that is good in his life. Although he has spent his life probing deep into the moral frailties of the state and its most prominent citizens it is clear that he is fully committed to the state and its laws. One can be critical and yet be faithful.

> Do you imagine that a city can continue to exist and not be turned upside down, if the legal judgements which are pronounced in it have no force but are nullified and destroyed by private persons?[15]

Once one assents to the authority of the state and accepts the benefits it confers then there can be no reneging on the covenant. So Socrates faces his death unflinchingly and, when the time comes, drinks the draught of hemlock. His last words, as recorded by Plato, were 'Crito, we ought to offer a cock to Asclepius. See to it and don't forget'. This is sometimes interpreted as the final Socratic irony: Asclepius is the god of healing and the offering of the cock is in respect of a cure effected. Socrates' death is the cure for his life.[16]

2 Plato (428–347 BC): Education for the State

Background

Although Plato's dialogues have been written down the method they reveal, the method practised in Plato's Academy, was the method of dialogue, of Socratic dialectic, not the examination of an inert written record. It was the interplay of the debate which yielded truth, the process of discovery operated through discussion. Plato wrote in *The Seventh Letter* that truth is discovered in the course of 'scrutiny and kindly testing by men who proceed by question and answer without ill will'. He even goes so far as to suggest that writing is 'a mean craving for honour' rather than a valid way of discovering or remembering the truth.[1]

So as well as the substantive issues that we find in the dialogues (analyses of justice, virtue, education, and so forth) they primarily illustrate a pedagogical method: the Socratic method of living dialogue.

What is of crucial interest in Plato's discussion of education is not the answers he suggests but his identification of the relevant questions and problems in the first instance. Plato was the first to write about education in a systematic and reflective way. He set the agenda for education provided or controlled by the state. His education programme was firmly located within a broader political programme, not as an optional component, but as an essential ingredient. Public education policy and planning in the Western world have followed Plato's agenda for nearly 2,500 years!

The Polis and the need for security

Plato set out his ideas on the ideal state in *The Republic*, undoubtedly the first European systematic, theoretical exposition of education. If we want to understand the continuity of educational ideas and policies, not only in Europe but in all of those places influenced through European colonization, then *The Republic* is the place to begin.

Plato's recognition of the importance of education in the life of the state was not unique in his time. There was a widespread consciousness throughout the Greek world of the importance of education to political stability and civic welfare. A near contemporary of Plato's, Dioceses the Cynic, is reputed to have declared 'the foundation of every state is the education of its youth'. This was not just theory: the Greek city state of Sparta had already proved the value of a systematic approach to education and training.

Like other Greek city states Sparta had a triple security problem: the need to control a large population of slaves, territorial defence and secure access to Mediterranean ports. It needed stable government and an efficient military capability. It designed an education system to produce a warrior class. The survival of the state, not the needs of individuals, determined the form of the education system.

Plato believed that the only hope for political stability in Athens was a system which would select and train philosophers to be rulers so that the state would be governed according to the highest principles of justice rather than the self-interests of individuals or factions. Everyone would be committed to the common good and priority would be given to collective rather than individual or sectional interests. *The Republic* outlines a plan for education which will bring this about: it is a manifesto for an education system totally controlled by, and subordinate to, state interests.

The educational agenda of *The Republic*

The Republic begins with a discussion on the nature of justice in the life of the state and the individual. In the course of the discussion Plato articulates his vision of the ideal city state (*polis*), a notional city state like the Athens of Plato's time. The aim of the ideal city state, Plato says, is to cater for the happiness of all the citizens of the city. Whereas Socrates had argued for individual virtue as the foundation of the just society, Plato argues for the just state as the prerequisite for individual happiness. The intention of the legislator, Plato reminds us, is not to make 'any one class in the State happy above the rest'. The happiness the legislator seeks is to be in the whole state so that each individual acquires his or her appropriate share of happiness.[2]

The principal instrument in bringing this universal happiness about is education: it is not only the means of *maintaining* political order but is the means for *creating* political order in the first instance. The reform of the city will not be brought about by tinkering with the laws but by radical reform of the education system! All children will be removed from the influence of their parents and taken under the control of the city's Guardians. Here Plato addresses a perennial problem of educational reform, the possible adverse influence of the domestic values of the family, and deals with it ruthlessly! 'All the inhabitants of the city who are more than ten years old' will be sent out of the city, and the Guardians 'will take possession of their children, who will be unaffected by the habits of their parents' and train them in the 'habits and laws' required by the state.[3]

The agenda for education which Plato developed with this end in view addresses the central elements of any educational system. We must decide who will be educated (selection), what they will be taught (curriculum), what are they to become and do (objective), who will teach them (selection of teachers), how will they be taught (method), and with whom they will learn.

Division of labour

The Republic begins with a discussion of the question 'What is justice?' and leads quickly to a discussion of rulers. Just rulers, according to Plato, act for the welfare of their subjects, not for personal gain or profit. But if ruling is not done for personal profit or to earn a salary then no one will wish to do it. Therefore, Plato argues, those who are to rule must be specially selected and trained for the task.

A city comes about because no one is self-sufficient in all the things he or she needs: people gather together in one place in order to exchange specialist goods and services and this is the origin of the city, or *polis*. A city is based on an efficient division of labour so that each participant can specialize at the task for which he is naturally suited by ability and temperament, whether it be farming, a craft, trading, banking, fighting or governing.

Plato describes the city as a complex organization of people drawn together for mutual benefit and support. The city will establish trade and other relations with other cities. There will be conflicts about land, materials and trade opportunities so an army will be required. Like everyone else in this ideal city the members of the army must be specialists, for only specialists will wage war effectively. You do not learn how to wage war simply by taking up arms. 'No tools will make a man a skilled workman or master of defence,' Plato declares, 'nor be of any use to him who has not learned how to handle them, and has never bestowed any attention upon them'.[4] Like every other skill-based occupation, fighting requires knowledge and sufficient practice for one to be proficient. In other words, the *polis* needs a professional standing army: the Guardians.

The Guardians

The Guardians must have a natural aptitude for war but they must also be gentle to those whom they are guarding: as well as being high-spirited, they must also love wisdom. Plato compares them to guard dogs. Whenever a guard dog sees a stranger he is angry, even though no harm has been done to him. But he welcomes those he knows even if he has never been well treated by them. The Guardians must have the temperament of a dog of good pedigree: they must be able to distinguish friend from foe and behave appropriately towards each. How are the Guardians to be selected and prepared for their task?

Plato's system is based first of all on universal access. Education is open to all citizens irrespective of wealth, status or gender. (Slaves, of course, are excluded.) The function of the education at the initial stage is to provide basic literacy and general education and to identify and select out those who will progress to become Guardians. This selection will be based on merit and possession of the necessary qualities of spirit required of the Guardians. Those selected will continue their education and training. As soon as the initial selection of those fitted to be trained as Guardians is made, those not selected will be returned to 'normal life' in the *polis*. They will become the artisans, the tradespeople, the craft-workers, the traders and business people, the farmers, and so forth, in short, the creators of wealth. The Guardians, however, will continue a rigorous training as the military elite.

Plato sees no reason to diverge from the traditional Athenian approach in the initial stages of education: physical training and education in the arts. Education in the arts will come first and will include, in the early stages, telling stories to the small children.

Children must not be allowed to hear any kind of stories composed by just anybody. The stories to be told to the young are of such fundamental importance that they must be strictly controlled. They cannot be allowed to absorb from their stories beliefs which are contrary to those they should hold when they grow up. The state must therefore control the storytellers and select the noblest of their stories while rejecting the others. Nurses and mothers will be required to tell their children only those stories which have been sanctioned by the state to fashion the minds of the young.

This is not just censorship: Plato is unapologetically advocating a positive indoctrination programme. He will forbid stories which show the Gods in a bad light, in which wrong-doing is not appropriately punished, which promote divisiveness, which discourage bravery, moderation or temperance, which heighten the fear of death, encourage excessive levity or show that injustice is profitable. His understanding of child psychology is clear: children cannot tell the difference between what is true and what is not. The truth must be esteemed in the stories since private citizens should not tell lies: for a private citizen to lie to the rulers of the city is like a sick man lying to his physician or an athlete lying to his trainer about his physical condition: it is subversive of the liar's own interests.[5] Moreover, the beliefs that children acquire in childhood are difficult to eradicate and usually remain unchanged into adulthood. Consequently it is of vital importance that the first stories they hear should be well crafted and dispose them to virtue.

The method of teaching the myths and stories must be firmly controlled too so that in all things the future Guardians will be educated in accordance with order and moderation. The simplicity that Plato advocates is not, he is at pains to explain, simplicity in the sense of foolishness, but the simplicity of a good and fine character. The desired qualities can be brought about through exposure to, and practice in, fine speech, excellent music and rhythm, a sense of taste and gracefulness. There is a clear physical as well as an intellectual dimension evident in Plato's early curriculum.

Once the Guardians have been selected they must be continuously watched to ensure they cannot by any means be diverted from their commitment to what is best for the city. True Guardians must be loyal to the city no matter what. They will be subjected to stringent tests at every opportunity. Only those who pass these tests of unswerving commitment to the welfare of the city will be eventually selected. 'We must watch them from their youth upwards, and make them perform actions in which they are most likely to forget or to be deceived, and he who remembers and is not deceived is to be selected, and he who falls in the trial is to be rejected.'[6]

Rulers

Now comes the most necessary step in the development of Plato's ideal city state. The rulers of the city will be the most *guardianly* of the Guardians: those who perform the functions of the Guardians in the highest degree. Recall the reason for setting up the class of Guardians in the first place: they were to be the professional army whose task would be to conquer and secure new land as it was needed by a growing population and who would defend the state and its property against all external and internal enemies. Now it transpires that the best of these professional soldiers will in fact become the rulers of the City: Plato's *polis* is to be an unapologetically militarist state.

Only those who pass the most rigorous tests of commitment to the welfare of the state will become Rulers. Those selected as Rulers will be the true Guardians. Those who do not qualify as Rulers will continue as professional soldiers or 'Auxiliaries' whose duty it is to help the Rulers. The Rulers will rule the city and the Auxiliaries will assist them in a military capacity. Together they will constitute a militarist elite which will hold supreme power.

The realm of the forms

In order to understand Plato's educational programme for those chosen to be Rulers it is necessary to understand his theory of forms.

Plato was fascinated by our ability to make comparative judgements. We can look at two knives, for example, and judge that one knife is better than the other. How can we make such a judgement without having some standard against which the judgement can be made: what is our standard for knife judging, for example? We can examine different geometrical figures (circles, triangles, squares, etc.) and discover the universal properties of each class of shape (e.g. the angles of a triangle always equal two right angles) even though we know that the specific examples we are dealing with are not perfect. How is this possible?

Plato concluded that since all of material reality is imperfect and changeable our standard must derive from somewhere other than the sensible world. For a knife to exist at all we must first of all have the idea of a knife. Insofar as there is an existing knife it must conform to this idea. (This is why Socrates was so determined to arrive at the true *definitions* of things: the definitions described the ideal.) Plato postulated a human soul (the seat of reason) which was independent of the physical body. Before birth the un-incarnated soul inhabits a realm in which all the original ideas of all that exists in the material world are to be found, the Realm of the Forms. But the trauma of birth causes the soul to forget its knowledge of the Forms so that learning becomes a matter of recollection or *un-forgetting*: *anamnesis*. We do not need sense experience in order to know what is true: knowledge is already within us, within the soul, and is discoverable through the use of reason.

The highest of the Forms is the Form of the Good which Plato explains by analogy, the Myth of the Cave, in Book VII of *The Republic*. Just as the sun empowers the eye to perceive the things of the physical world, so the Form of the Good empowers human reason to perceive and understand the things of the spiritual, immaterial world.

The education of the Rulers, then, requires an intensive training in mathematics and philosophy so that they will see beyond the imperfect and mutable physical world to the Realm of Forms and, in particular, come to contemplate and understand the Form of the Good. Only when they have achieved this knowledge are they fitted to be the Philosopher Kings (or Queens) of the new state.

The Myth of the Metals

How will those *not chosen* to be Auxiliaries or Guardians be persuaded that this is a just solution to the problem of the governance of the city? This is another task for the educational system: it will not just provide literacy and intellectual skills but will indoctrinate children in such a way that they will accept the political order unquestioningly. The educational system will not only select for the three categories of citizenship (Rulers, Auxiliaries and ordinary citizens), but it will also persuade everyone that this distribution of social status is fair and equitable. To persuade the population that the division into Rulers, Auxiliaries and ordinary citizens (e.g. farmers, business people, artisans and craftsmen) is just and necessary we find that Plato is not averse to a little indoctrinatory storytelling. This story will relate how, when they were created, some souls were infused with a little gold – these people would eventually become the Rulers; some souls were infused with a little silver – these would become the Auxiliaries; and some souls with a little bronze or iron – these would become the ordinary citizens.

Plato set his face firmly against a hereditary caste system: membership of the gold, silver or bronze category would not be a matter of inheritance but of individual constitution and merit: it was to be a meritocracy but a meritocracy influenced by a deliberate rigorous programme of eugenics. The Rulers will ensure that 'the best of either sex should be united with the best' as often as possible while 'the inferior' should be discouraged from 'uniting' with another inferior. Only the offspring of the union of the best should be reared 'if the flock is to be maintained in first-rate condition'.[7] 'There is nothing,' Plato declares, 'which (the Guardians) should so anxiously guard, or of which they are to be such good guardians, as of the purity of the race'.[8] If the Guardians' own offspring, for example, should transpire to have iron or bronze in their souls there must be no favouritism: each individual must be treated according to his or her nature as revealed through the education process. A child of the Guardian class who reveals a base (bronze) nature must be driven out to join the workers and farmers. But it works both ways: if a child of the workers and farmers is found to have gold or silver in his nature he will be honoured accordingly and brought up to join the Rulers or Auxiliaries.

Neither the Rulers nor the Auxiliaries will have property of any value. All they need they will have at the public expense. They will be persuaded that the possession of material gold or silver is incompatible with the divine gold or silver which permeates their souls.

What Plato wants above all is a permanent arrangement. Once the city is established it must be protected against innovation and change; these are the greatest threats to stability and permanence. The major force in this deeply conservative programme is again education. It is essential that the educational system itself does not change, i.e. become corrupt. This means no innovation; once the form of the education system has been established there must be no modification. The Rulers must ensure that education is not corrupted without their noticing it and be particularly alert against innovations in physical and artistic education.

The soul

The structure of the individual soul mirrors the structure of the ideal state. Just as there are three categories of people in the state (bronze, silver and gold) there are three corresponding parts to the human soul, respectively the appetites, the spirit (which is the source of anger and the motivation for self-defence) and reason. Just as in the state it is the Rulers who rule, so in the individual it is reason which rules the other two parts: the spirit and the appetites are subject to reason as the Auxiliaries and the ordinary citizens are subject to the Rulers. Injustice results from strife among the parts and from meddling in each other's tasks. When the Rulers, Auxiliaries and ordinary citizens perform their appropriate tasks and preserve harmony with the others, we have a just state. When reason, spirit and appetite each performs its appropriate task and preserves harmony with the others we have a just individual.

The place of women

Plato's educational and political system was open to women as well as to men. Despite being physically weaker, and notwithstanding established custom, women would receive the same literary education and be subject to the same physical and military training as men. The only relevant difference is between those with a Guardian nature (gold in their souls) – whether they are men or women – and those who do not have a Guardian nature. Selection is made on the basis of the nature of the individual soul. Consequently, the nature of man and woman is the same as regards the capacity to guard the city. So Plato concluded that 'the same education which makes a man a good guardian will make a woman a good guardian; for their original nature is the same'.[9] Women who have the appropriate nature therefore will be chosen as Guardians along with the men, and they will live together and share the Guardianship.

Children born to the Guardians or Auxiliaries will be taken from their mothers and brought together in a communal nursery where they will be cared for under the general supervision of the Rulers. They will never know who their natural parents are and parents will never know who their individual children are. In this way, the children of the Rulers and Auxiliaries being held in common, there will be no opportunity for parental favouritism. Holding children and property in common will ensure that the Rulers will have no occasion to resort to lawsuits or any other form of dispute and be spared all the dissension which arises out of the possession of wealth, children and families. This means that since the Rulers have no dissensions among themselves there will be no danger of the City disintegrating into competing factions (a perennial political problem in the Athens of Plato).

The city that Plato is proposing is more likely to be brought about in reality if the Rulers are philosophers. The only way in which cities and the human race will thrive is when philosophers rule as kings or kings and rulers become philosophers. In order for the city which Plato has described in *The Republic* to become a reality, political power and philosophy must coalesce and those who wish to pursue political power without the rigorous study of philosophy are forcibly debarred from doing so. So, the Guardians need to be carefully selected, judged and divided into Auxiliaries and Rulers, but the Rulers will have to become philosophers. Or, more correctly, people who are naturally adapted to being both philosophers and rulers will have to be identified and nurtured.

How effective can philosophers be?

To the objection that philosophers would be inept rulers because they are generally useless in practical affairs, Plato replies that this is a misconception based on ignorance. It is as if the ignorant sailor denounced the ship's navigator because he is always looking at the stars and the heavens. Yet it is on the navigator's knowledge of the stars and the heavens, and of the seasons and the winds, that the sailor must depend to bring him safe to shore. In a similar way the city must depend on the man of vision and understanding to guide it. Who better for the task than one who has knowledge of the eternal forms, the ideal paradigms of everything: the Good.

So we see how Plato identified the functions of education to indoctrinate the next generation, to select for economic, social and political roles, to justify economic, social, and political arrangements, to assign life chances, to establish and maintain a militaristic meritocracy, to establish and maintain a stable state. His vision was selective, meritocratic and ruthless.

Whereas Socrates argued that individual morality was a necessary prerequisite to a moral state, Plato argues that a just state is a prerequisite to individual happiness. This is a difference which has dogged education ever since: should we educate for the benefit which accrues to the individual in the first instance, or in the interests of the state (or some other predefined supra-individualist purpose like the economy, the culture, the purity of the race)? Perhaps ultimately this question is irresolvable.

3 Aristotle (384–322 BC): Education for Leisure

His life

Aristotle was not Athenian. He was born in the Greek Macedonian town of Stagira (he is sometimes referred to as the Stagirite) in the fourth century BC. He moved to Athens, the cultural capital of his time, when he was 17 to study at Plato's Academy, Athens' nearest equivalent to the modern university. He prospered in the intellectual atmosphere of the Academy. When Plato died in 347, Aristotle, then in his late 30s, left Athens and settled in the eastern Aegean where a new centre of learning had been established. Aristotle's reputation as a scholar, philosopher and scientist was such that in 343 he was invited (or summoned, probably, in the circumstances, the same thing!) by Philip of Macedonia to be tutor to his son Alexander (who was to enter human history as Alexander the Great). Nothing is known with any certainty about the relationship between Aristotle and Alexander. It appears, however, that Aristotle was kept well informed and supplied with abundant materials for study from Alexander's expeditions and conquests.

When Aristotle returned to Athens, after it had been subdued by Alexander's Macedonians, he established a new institute of learning, at the Lyceum, where he taught and studied until 323. In that year Alexander died and Aristotle, because of his association with the Macedonian conqueror, prudently left Athens in fear of his life. He died a few months later.

The context

Aristotle's educational programme presumes the continuing existence of the Greek city state. By modern standards of political organization the city state was tiny, yet it was economically independent and culturally self-sufficient. For Aristotle the state has a natural priority, being the supreme form of human association.

The state exists by nature because man is by nature a political animal; human beings need human association to flourish. 'It is clear,' he wrote in the *Politics*, 'that the state is both natural and prior to the individual'.[1] By this he did not mean that somehow the state pre-dates the individual citizens historically (which would be absurd) but that we are born into, and die out of, a community: the community transcends the lives of its individual members. The Greek conception of political philosophy embraced the whole of human behaviour, the conduct of the individual as well as the behaviour of the group. For Aristotle (as for Socrates and Plato), individual ethics and politics are inseparable.

Any consideration of political organization must first consider Plato's fundamental question: Who will rule? Aristotle favoured the kind of constitution in which citizens rule by turn. This means that they have two conflicting roles: they must be able to obey when it is their turn to be ruled by their fellows and they must be able to rule in their turn. This apparently paradoxical requirement illustrates the intimate connection for the Greek mind between politics, statecraft and education: how is man to be made morally and intellectually fit to rule and yet to behave appropriately when it is not his turn?

For Aristotle, equality means treating those who are like, alike and those who are different, differently. Nonetheless, he insisted that rulers must be superior to those who are ruled. How is this contradiction to be resolved? Typically, Aristotle's answer is based on empirical observation; nature provides the answer. He observes that nature has divided free men into older and younger. The older are fit to rule, the younger are fit to be ruled. This is the sense in which the same persons rule and are ruled in their turn, but there is also a sense in which they are different because of their age and maturity: the younger are ruled by the older until they, in their turn, become old enough to rule. Education must reflect this developmental difference: those who are to become rulers must first learn to be ruled. Aristotle's objective in his educational programme is unapologetically political. Since all of the citizens of the state (and they are exclusively male) would at some time participate in the rule of the city and at some time have to submit to being ruled, the principal question is what manner of person can submit to being ruled and yet rule justly when his turn comes? What both the ruler and the ruled have in common is that each must be what Aristotle calls the 'best man'. Consequently, he sees it as the primary task of the lawmaker to 'ensure that they both may become *good* men, and to consider what practices will make them so, and what is the aim of the best life'.[2] Aristotle's objective is empirical: we must establish what are the attributes of the good man and work out how these attributes can be promoted.

Leisure

'Leisure' is central to Aristotle's concept of education: his intended audience is an established leisured class. Unlike Plato's, Aristotle's approach is elitist from the start: the rulers of the *polis* will be, without exception, male members of the leisured class. (It is an indication of how imbued our language and culture is by Greek influence that our words 'school', 'scholar', 'scholastic', and so forth all derive from the Greek word *scholé* which means *leisure*.) Aristotle's educational programme was in fact directed at an ascendancy class: people set apart by birth, breeding and wealth to be the leaders of the community or state. His education aims at a three-fold purpose: preparation for a life of cultured leisure, preparation for a life as a citizen of the state and preparation for life as a ruler of the state. Education is a crucial matter of public policy. The central aim of Aristotle's educational programme is to inculcate the virtues needed for the proper employment of leisure in cultural, intellectual and political activities. Remember that this is an economy based on slavery. The *noblesse oblige* of the leisured class was to rule.

Human actions are not all the same: some are necessary and useful, that is, they are means to higher ends. Others are worthwhile in themselves, that is, they have moral worth. So, for example, war is a means to peace, work is a means to leisure, necessary and useful things are necessary and useful because they are the means to what is intrinsically good and noble. We must be able to do the necessary and the useful things because they provide us with the opportunity to do the things which have moral worth. 'These then are the targets at which education should be aimed, whether children's education or that of such later age-groups as require it.'[3]

One consequence of this is that the education of the body and the emotions must come before the education of the intellect on the grounds that the former are inferior to, and ultimately for the sake of, the latter. They are means to a higher end.

Aristotle's political vision appears to be similar to Plato's with regard to the similarity between justice in the individual and in the state. Men, he tells us, have the same ends whether they are acting as individuals or as a community. The best man (the aim of education) and the best constitution (the aim of politics) must have the same definitive purpose.

Education

Education must take account of three realities which circumscribe human development: nature, habit and intellect. Nature is outside the control of the educator: it is a function of geographical location and climate and there is little that can be done to modify its effects. (Aristotle considers it fortunate, however, that in respect of the gifts of nature required for proper government the Greeks are superior to everyone else!) The principal *educational* problem is whether habit or intellect should receive priority in the education of the children. Should education begin with reason or with the formation of desirable habits? Certainly reason and habit must be mutually supportive: each should be subject to correction by the other for it is equally possible to reason incorrectly as to be led astray by one's habits.

Aristotle's educational priorities are based on observation rather than speculation: reason and intelligence are the end towards which human nature tends, but the appetites, that is the unreasoning part of human being, come first and must have priority. This can be seen by the way in which emotion, wilfulness and desire are to be found in children from the earliest age; reasoning and intelligence begin to manifest only as the child grows older. Intellectual virtue, which depends on instruction, requires time and experience to flourish. Moral goodness, on the other hand, results from habit and needs immediate attention.

In general, anything that we have to learn to do we learn to do by doing it. Learning the virtues is like learning to exercise any skill or craft: they are both learned through practice. 'We become just,' Aristotle tells us, 'by performing just acts, temperate by performing temperate ones, brave by performing brave ones.'[4] This is why the matter of habit formation from the earliest age is so important:

the habits we form at the earliest age determine the kind of person we will become. So it is important that good habits are developed in the early years as a foundation for the development of intellectual excellence in later years.

Education must begin with the care of the body. Infants should be adequately nourished and allowed freedom to move their limbs. 'To prevent the still soft limbs from becoming bent,' Aristotle tells us, 'some nations still make use of mechanical devices which keep the children's bodies straight.'[5] (Presumably the 'mechanical devices' to which he refers include practices like swaddling clothes which were still so widespread in eighteenth-century Europe that Rousseau felt constrained to denounce the practice.) This was done in the belief that too early use of the limbs would lead to deformation. Aristotle, on the contrary, believed that it is good for infants to exercise all the physical movements that they are capable of.

Up to the age of 5 children should not be taught anything but should be allowed to play and grow. Aristotle's views on what is now called 'early childhood education' are remarkably liberal. From birth to 5 it is not a good idea to try to teach infants anything, or to make them engage in activities that would interfere with their growth. They need plenty of physical exercise, particularly through play.

He advocates a moderate approach to the care of infants and young children: they should not be mollycoddled but neither should they be subjected to the full rigour of an athletic training. Throughout his writing on education, Aristotle is at pains to emphasize that there should be no excess in the education of the young aristocrat. In the case of physical fitness, for example, the aim is not to generate the physical fitness needed by an athlete but that needed by the citizen for health and the production of offspring. At the other extreme too much coddling and unfamiliarity with hard work is equally undesirable. What is needed is something in between: a physical condition which is capable of hard work but not equal to excessive toil. Rather than the specialized strength of the athlete, education should aim at a general bodily strength appropriate to the various activities typical of free citizens. This idea of 'moderation' is a recurrent idea in all of Aristotle's writing. We should avoid extremes and aim always for the middle course, the mean between the extremes.

Although vigorous exercise can be undertaken after puberty, physical and intellectual activity must always be kept separate for he considers that each naturally works in the opposite direction from the other: physical effort interferes with the mind, mental effort interferes with the body.

Censorship

Like Plato, Aristotle acknowledges the need for censorship and care in the selection of stories for the young. The stories to which they are exposed in childhood will influence their development and thus must be chosen with care. Those who have responsibility for the welfare of young children must pay careful attention to the kinds of stories which will be told. Everything that children hear should be preparation for their future occupations as cultured men and as citizens of the state.

Aristotle had his worries, and strong views, about the contemporary equivalent of television. He would forbid 'debased paintings' or unedifying stories for children: nothing that represents 'unseemly actions' should come within the experience of the child. Younger persons should not attend comedies nor recitals of corrupting verse until they have reached an appropriate age ('the age at which they come to recline at banquets with others and share in the drinking');[6] by this time their education will have rendered them completely unsusceptible to the ill effects of such entertainments. 'We must keep all that is of inferior quality unfamiliar to the young,' Aristotle concluded, 'particularly things with an ingredient of wickedness or hostility.'[7]

Neither should children be contaminated by the company they keep – especially the company of slaves – and they should not be exposed to unseemly conversations. Aristotle prescribes severe punishments for anyone corrupting the children in their conversation – not quite as severe as the millstone solution advocated some centuries later but certainly in the same spirit: any young person guilty of corrupting children would be punished 'by measures of dishonour and a whipping'; while older corruptors would be punished 'by measures of dishonour not normally visited on free men, precisely because his conduct has been that of a slave'.[8]

Formal education: public or private?

The formal educational system proposed by Aristotle is surprisingly modern in structure. (Or is it that modern educational structures are surprisingly archaic?) After their fifth year children should spend two years observing the lessons that they will soon have to learn themselves. After that education is divided into two phases, from 7 to puberty, and from puberty to 21. This corresponds, for Aristotle, to three seven-year periods, 0–7, 7–14 and 14–21, which reflect natural divisions, 'for all skill and education aim at filling the gaps that nature leaves'.[9] Aristotle here appeals to a belief regarding human development which was evidently common at the time and which still leaves an impression on contemporary education systems, based as they are on notions of age-related infancy, childhood and adolescence.

Should responsibility for the education of the young be a matter of public policy or private provision? Aristotle is unequivocal about this question. Let us remember that the education he is concerned with is not just for idle leisure, but for the optimal use of that leisure, for, among other things, the governance of the *polis*. Rather than each parent looking after the private formation of his own children it is the responsibility of the lawgiver, the state, to arrange for the education of the young. Education must be the same for all, not dependent on the arbitrary choices of individual parents; it should be a public responsibility since there is only one aim for the state. 'In matters that belong to the public, training for them must be the public's concern.'[10] The citizen is not just an unattached, free-floating ('unencumbered', in the contemporary liberal terminology) individual. No one, in Aristotle's words, 'belongs just to himself', all citizens belong to the state, 'for each is a *part* of the state; and the responsibility for each part naturally has regard to the responsibility for the whole'.[11]

The state

Aristotle's state embraces the entire social, political and economic organization of the populace. Contemporary notions of 'community' may be closer to the Aristotelian conception than 'state'. Mainly as a result of modern liberal theory, 'state' has come to be seen in opposition to the individual, a menacing entity which threatens the freedom of the individual and which must be held in check. 'Community', on the other hand, denotes smaller, more intimate and more necessary forms of association where virtue is conceived in terms of civic function as well as of individual character. This may explain why Aristotle sees the state as a natural phenomenon (it 'belongs to the class of objects which exist by nature'[12]) and man as, by nature, a political animal. Anyone who can live without a state (i.e. without a human community) is either subhuman or superhuman: 'for the real difference between man and the other animals is that humans alone have perception of good and evil, just and unjust, etc. It is the sharing of a common view in *these* matters that makes a household and a state.'[13]

Just as Aristotle's conception of the state is different from ours, so too is his use of the word 'statesman'. For Aristotle 'statesman' simply meant a citizen who was active in running the affairs of his political community.

Curriculum

There are certain essentials which Aristotle generally agreed should be included in the curriculum for those between 7 and 14: reading and writing, physical training, music and drawing. But children must not learn useful tasks or skills which will turn them into 'mechanics': such skills will have a deleterious effect on the body and will debase the mind. Remember that these are the children of an ascendancy class who will never have to earn a living: their vocation is to be free men. Only certain pursuits are worthy of free men, and even in these cases educators must be on guard that they are not pursued too assiduously: 'Too great a concentration on them, too much mastering of detail – this is liable to lead to the same damaging effects' as an excessive engagement in physical training.[14] Expertise in any activity will damage the body and debase the mind.

Education of the young is neither trivial nor an optional form of entertainment. Aristotle is clear about the distinction between the playful and the serious: education is not a matter of amusement. 'Learning brings pain, and while children are learning they are not playing.'[15] There's no gain without pain and Aristotle advocates play only as an appropriate respite from work: he who toils needs rest, and play is a way of resting, while work is inseparable from toil and strain. Educators must therefore admit play, but keep it to its proper uses and occasions: it is a cure; the relevant movement of the soul is a relaxation, and, because we enjoy it, rest.[16]

Play should not be confused with leisure. Leisure is altogether different. Leisure for Aristotle is spending time in civilized cultural pursuits. Music, for example, will be included in the curriculum, not because it is necessary or useful as reading, writing, drawing or gymnastics are useful, but because it is intrinsically desirable as contributing to the life of leisure: 'There is a form of education which we must provide for our sons, not as being useful or essential but as elevated and worthy of free men'.[17]

Of course reading and writing, drawing or gymnastics can also contribute to the life of leisure because they have applications which transcend the purely utilitarian. Reading and writing, for instance, are frequently the means to learning other subjects; drawing enhances the appreciation of physical beauty. Constantly demanding a practical justification of a subject of study, to be constantly asking 'What is the use of it?', is 'unbecoming to those of broad vision and unworthy of free men'.[18]

Music

Aristotle devotes a great deal of effort to developing the role of 'music' in the education of the young. What is generally translated into the English word 'music' had a much wider application in the original Greek. It was 'the skill presided over by the Muses' and could be broadened to mean the arts in general, sometimes even including painting and sculpture. For Aristotle, music in this broad sense is a stimulus to virtue or human excellence. Music can help in the formation of character just as gymnastics can help in the formation of the body.

In any case should music, or the arts generally, be included in the education of the young? Including the arts has advantages: they provide amusement which is relaxation, a cure for the wear and tear brought about by work; they are civilized pursuits which promote social intercourse. But the crucial question is whether they promote the development of the character and the soul. Aristotle believed that they do: music in the narrow sense, for example, has the power in both melody and rhythm to cause emotion and to influence character. 'Music,' he writes, 'has indeed the power to induce a certain character of soul' and so the young must be educated in it.[19] *The harmony of music has an affinity to the harmony of the soul.*

Should children be taught to engage in performance (in any of the arts) or should it be sufficient if they are able to listen or observe with a trained sensibility, with developed taste and judgement? Musical education must include performance because it is difficult, if not impossible, for someone who has never played or participated to develop the ability to judge others' performance adequately. In addition, learning to play an instrument will provide children with a desirable occupation.

But will performance turn them into performers, mere mechanics, inferior to the free men they should become, ill-fitted for the role of citizen and soldier? A highly skilled musical performance is not appropriate for the free man of Aristotle's state for performers are considered to be mechanics, not gentlefolk. For this reason children will not be encouraged to acquire the level of skill needed by the professional performer. They will learn to perform, but not very well, for excellence in performance is the role of a hireling, not of a free man.

According to Aristotle, music in the general sense confers three benefits: it promotes the education of character, it brings about catharsis (the purging of emotions, mainly pity, fear and excitement) and it enhances relaxation. So for the education of the 7–14-year-old forms of artistic expression which are primarily ethical in character should be chosen.

Although Aristotle intended that only the males of the relevant class would participate in the political life of the state he did not exclude women from the benefits of education. This was not a personal entitlement but due to the crucial role which women must play in the formation of the citizens and rulers of the future. Since the child is not fully developed, his virtue is not a purely individual matter; it is relative to his state of development and to those who are acting as his mentors. If the well-being of the *polis* depends on the well-being of its children then children *and* women (the primary carers) must be educated. 'And it must make a difference; for women make up half the adult free population, and from children come those who will participate in the constitution.'[20]

If Aristotle ever got round to describing the content of such an education in detail the account has not survived so that his treatment of curriculum is scant. In general, his major contribution is to the relationship between education and the state: the need for an education which will support the cohesion and unity of the community and prepare its citizens for their dual role as subjects and rulers.

4 Jesus (5/4 BC–27/8 AD?): Education for the Common Man

Background

It is the beginning of the first millennium of the modern era. A young Jewish preacher faces a crowd of his compatriots in Judea, a Roman possession in the Middle East. He knows these people. They are simple, unlettered folk: small farmers and farm labourers, artisans, fishermen, and so on. But they are the inheritors of an ancient ethical tradition. They need only to be reminded of it and of its significance. They have heard that this man can work wonders but they are there to listen – for they belong to an oral culture: word of mouth is their principal, if not their only, means of communication and their chief means of storing and moving information. They learn and remember through stories, through striking and memorable images, analogies and allegories, metaphors and similes, riddles and aphorisms.

The circumstances of the birth of Jesus and of his early infancy are well rehearsed annually at Christmas. The story is so well-known that it is unnecessary to repeat it here. He was born into the family of a carpenter and he spent his early years in a village called Nazareth in Judea at the very beginning of the first millennium.

He was first and foremost a Palestinian Jew. This simple reality often comes as a surprise even to some of his most ardent followers, many of whom seem to believe that he was in fact the first Aryan West European, if not the first American, as witness the pictures of the pink-cheeked, blue-eyed child with the curly golden locks which adorns homes, schools, places of worship and children's bibles.

Jesus' message

Little is known of Jesus' life, education or activities from the time of his birth to the time he began his public teaching. One significant gospel account of his childhood, however, is reported by the evangelist Luke and concerns the occasion, in Jesus' twelfth year, when his parents took him to Jerusalem for the Passover. After the first day of the return journey his parents discovered that he was not with the travelling group as they had supposed, and they returned to Jerusalem to search for him. They found him 'after three days', Luke tells us, 'in the temple, sitting in the midst of the doctors, both hearing them and asking them questions. And all that heard him were astonished at his understanding and answers'. It is interesting that on the cusp of adolescence and adulthood we see him in an educational situation engaging in dialogue with learned teachers. It is tempting to think that this is intended by the evangelist as a portent of Jesus' future career as a teacher as well as his rootedness in tradition.

The content of Jesus' teaching was not original. The core messages – the virtue of charity and the importance of loving God and one's neighbour – were not new to the people who heard him teach. In ancient Judaism charity – loving God and one's neighbour – was a central duty for each believer. *Deuteronomy* enjoins love of God and love of neighbour: 'Always be open-handed with your brother, and with anyone in your country who is in need and poor'. Isaiah also urges the faithful to attend to the less fortunate, the oppressed, the hungry, the homeless and the naked as part of their religious obligations.

Jesus was but one in a long line of teachers of an ancient ethical tradition. It was a tradition in which teaching was crucial. The Psalmist writes, 'Teach me Thy way, O Lord, and lead me in a plain path ... Teach me Thy way, O Lord; I will walk in thy truth ... Teach me good judgement and knowledge ...'

Jesus wrote nothing. Although the tradition to which he belonged was a scriptural tradition the context within which he taught was essentially an oral tradition. There were foundational written texts but these were sacred books: available to the people only at second hand as read and interpreted by a priest class, rabbis or scribes. What marks Jesus as a teacher, therefore, is not the content but the methods he used to communicate his message in a way that was striking, understandable and, above all, memorable. As any teacher will tell you there is little point in teaching a lesson which no one will remember.

Memory

In preliterate societies information was spread by word of mouth. For oral transmission the risk of distortion and of forgetting must be minimized. So the message must be uttered in a form which is direct, comprehensible and, above all, easy to remember. Jesus understood that memory was of fundamental importance. His contemporaries were capable of what would seem to us prodigious feats of memory: they had to be for they had no other way of storing information which was relevant and important.

Jesus and the teachers of his time faced a number of problems of method. Their audience, for the most part, comprised illiterate, unsophisticated people whose wisdom was embodied in myths, proverbs, anecdotes, legends and stories. These were what they understood best. A second problem was that there were no mass media of any kind so the message had to be presented in a way that commanded attention, was immediately comprehensible and essentially memorable. An underlying concern of all teachers of the time would have been with the mnemonics of their presentations: the capacity of the message to be memorized and retransmitted with the minimum of distortion.

Jesus' methods

One method available to Jesus was direct preaching. We see this at its best in the famous Sermon on the Mount and in the Beatitudes he enunciated on that occasion: Blessed are the poor in spirit ... Blessed are they that mourn ... Blessed are the meek ..., etc.

The repetition of the declaration 'Blessed are ...' has a compelling, almost hypnotic, effect. The similar structure of each of the declarations aids the memory: it is like a poem or a song. The images invoke familiar experiences: poverty, hunger, thirst, mourning, and so on. The contrasts are striking: poverty/possession, mourning/comfort, meekness/power, hunger/repletion. The language is simple and the syntax is uncomplicated: this is not a learned argument but a set of memorable reassurances for ordinary people. It is not difficult to imagine someone in an oral society going home and repeating the entire message verbatim.

In general, Jesus' teaching is replete with memorable images and metaphors. Some examples: The salt of the earth: 'but if the salt have lost his savour, wherewith shall it be salted?'; the light of the world. 'A city that is set on a hill cannot be hid. Neither do men light a candle, and put it under a bushel, but on a candle stick; and it giveth light unto all that are in the house'.

Today, 2,000 years later, these are still compelling images: they are simple and direct. Even in sophisticated times they invoke ideas which are basic and elemental. Once heard they are unlikely to be forgotten: we may forget where or when we heard the phrase 'the salt of the earth' or about 'hiding one's light under a bushel' but we will not forget that we have heard them or how they relate to our own fundamental human experience.

The record of Jesus' teaching is brimful of such proverbial sayings. Many of them have entered vernaculars the world over, their meanings and significance virtually unchanged since they were first uttered: 'Do not let your right hand know what your left hand is doing', 'Sufficient unto the day is the evil thereof', 'Neither cast ye your pearls before swine, lest they trample them under their feet', 'By their fruits you will know them'. Whether these sayings were originally composed by Jesus or whether they were already part of the vernacular of his time is irrelevant. Composed or chosen they encapsulate his message in a striking and memorable form.

> Behold the birds of the air, they do not sow, neither do they reap, nor gather into barns; yet your heavenly Father feedeth them. Are ye not much better than they? ... And why take ye thought for clothing? Consider the lilies of the field, how they grow; they toil not, neither do they spin. And yet I say unto you that even Solomon in all his glory was not arrayed like one of these.

Jesus also favoured the use of exaggeration for dramatic effect; again in order to make the message not only clear and under-standable but also to make it memorable. Who could forget or fail to understand the seriousness of the judgement of those guilty of corrupting the young: 'it is better for him that a millstone were hanged about his neck, and he were cast into the sea'. Or, in a similar vein, 'If thy hand offend thee, ... if thy foot offend thee, if thine eye offend thee, cut it off, pluck it out, for ... it is better ... to enter into life maimed' than to go into hell whole.

There is no avoiding this kind of message couched in memorable metaphors. Whether you believe it or not you can neither ignore nor forget such a message: it combines the power of exaggeration and simplicity with an almost ritualistic or liturgical repetition. It is a simple direct message for an unsophisticated audience, uncluttered by theological qualifications or philosophical hedging.

Jesus did not scruple to clothe his message in the language of self-interest – which most people understand better than anything else. Again note the use of the familiar and the homely:

> Lay not up for yourselves treasures upon earth, where moth and rust doth corrupt, and where thieves break through and steal; but lay up for yourselves treasures in heaven where neither moth nor rust doth corrupt, and where thieves do not break through and steal ...

Moths, rust and thieves have not lost their capacity to make us feel insecure even to this day. In this example also note how the use of negatives ('lay not ... neither ... do not') reinforce the message: direct your concern to the next life and you can transcend all of the risks of this one.

Jesus frequently uses familiar occupations to appeal to the lived experience of his listeners in order to make the message more immediate. He was a master of the striking contrast:

> false prophets, which come to you in sheep's clothing, but inwardly they are ravening wolves ...

> do men gather grapes of thorns, or figs of thistles? ...

> By their fruits ye shall know them.

His listeners saw themselves, their friends, neighbours and families in these images of shepherding, farming, gardening and viniculture. This kind of familiarity is an inescapable requirement for any moral philosophy which is to have practical application for ordinary people. The examples Jesus used were not complex, remote, strange or alien; they required no glosses or subtexts; they required no 'experts' to interpret them. Quite the contrary: they were not only familiar but almost intimate. He could not have come closer to his listeners' shared experience.

> Take heed, watch and pray: for you know not when the time is come. It is like a man taking a long journey, who left his house and gave authority to his servants, and to every man his own task, and

commanded the doorkeeper to stay awake. So you stay awake, for
you know not when the master of the house will come, at evening, or
at midnight, or at the cockcrowing, or in the morning: lest coming
suddenly he find you sleeping. And what I say to you I say to all:
Be watchful!

Parables

Parables have been defined as 'earthly stories with heavenly
meanings'. More prosaically, a parable is a simple story used to
illustrate a moral or spiritual lesson. Jesus was a great parablist:
he was a gifted story-spinner and teller. People like nothing better
than a good story, a yarn; they remember stories and, more
importantly, they want to pass them on. When we hear a good joke
or piece of juicy gossip we immediately want to tell it to someone
else. So stories are an incomparable means for spreading a message
because stories, good stories, in a sense replicate themselves. And
this is of vital importance to the teacher in the oral community: the
'word' must take legs, it must spread itself beyond the original
limited audience of listeners.

Jesus' parables are memorable: who can forget the parable of
the prodigal son who dissipated his inheritance in glorious
dissolution and then came back for more – much to the chagrin
and resentment of his elder, more domesticated brother; or of the
unjust steward who insured his future by fiddling all his master's
debts just before he got the sack; or of the good Samaritan who
assisted the unknown stranger. Not only are these stories memorable and retellable, they are so because they are familiar. We know
the people in the stories; we *are* the people in the stories.

Notable too is that in some of Jesus' stories the central characters
are not morally admirable (the prodigal son, the unjust steward):
there is an ambiguity about the moral context. Jesus was not a
moralizer, he was not in the business of teaching an inflexible and
restricting moral code. He wanted to engage the listener in the
moral ambiguity of the stories so that *they begin to think* morally.
(Some of his aphorisms – 'But many that are first shall be last and
the last first' – as well as the specifics of the parables resist any
definitive literal analysis. Indeed many of the sayings and proverbs
of Jesus are more like Zen *koans* insofar as they invite prolonged
meditation rather than intellectual or literal analysis.)

The story of the good Samaritan, for example, came as Jesus' response to a question from a lawyer who asked: 'And who is my neighbour?' A typical lawyerly question; it is almost Socratic in its appeal for a sufficient definition. But instead of giving a legalistic, definitional answer, or engaging in a Socratic dialectic, Jesus tells a story. A man in need is ignored in turn by the priest and the Levite, people who might have been expected to have a professional obligation to help him. In the event he is helped by the Samaritan who might have been expected, because of a traditional enmity, to have left the needy one to his fate.

Jesus asks the obvious question: 'Which now of these three, thinkest thou, was neighbour unto him that fell among the thieves?'

The lawyer was discomfited; the answer was obvious, but he was unable to bring himself even to speak the name of the despised Samaritan: 'He that showed mercy on him,' he said. Not alone had he had his question answered but he was now confronted with his own prejudice. He has learned that neighbourliness is not a matter of legalistic, or even verbal, definition, it is a matter of contextualized moral perception and action; it is not a system of rules or legalisms, it is a way of responding to the world. Such a realization is the epitome of heuristic teaching.

The absence of a specific moral code (apart from the traditional injunctions regarding love of God and one's neighbour) is a significant feature of Jesus' teaching. He does not advocate slavish compliance with rules, but thoughtful moral engagement with the situations he describes.

The shorter parables are little gems – models of the economics of the best storytelling:

> What man of you having an hundred sheep if he lose one of them would not leave the ninety and nine in the wilderness and go after that which is lost until he find it? And when he hath found it he layeth it on his shoulders rejoicing. And when he cometh home he calleth together his friends and neighbours saying unto them: 'Rejoice with me for I have found my sheep which was lost'.

In fewer than 75 words the story is told, the listener is challenged to interpret its meaning – and all in the subjunctive mood at that! The subjunctive is an important part of the technique: it draws the listener in ('What man of you ... if?') by imposing an immediacy and demanding an imaginative involvement which is inescapable.

This story is about me or you, or somebody very like me or you. Or what about this one – 55 words, again in the subjunctive mood, and again imposing an irresistible involvement:

> What woman having ten pieces of silver if she lose one piece would not light a candle and sweep the house and seek diligently till she find it? And when she have found it she calleth her friends and her neighbours together saying 'Rejoice with me for I have found the piece which was lost'.

Miracles

And then, of course, there were the miracles and wonders which were central to the teaching of the message. The miracles were never introduced gratuitously: they were sparingly used to superb pedagogical effect – to focus attention, to emphasize a connection, to underscore a point.

Take, for example, the cure of the paralytic:

> And behold they brought to him a man sick of the palsy, lying on a bed; and Jesus seeing their faith said unto the sick of the palsy; Son be of good cheer; thy sins be forgiven thee.

> And behold certain of the scribes said within themselves 'This man blasphemeth'.

> And Jesus knowing their thoughts said, 'Wherefore think ye evil in your hearts? For whether is easier to say, 'Thy sins be forgiven thee', or to say 'Arise and walk'?

> But that ye may know that the son of man hath power on earth to forgive sins (then saith he to the sick of the palsy) 'Arise, take up thy bed and go unto thine house'.

> And he arose and departed to his house.

> But when the multitudes saw it, they marvelled, and glorified God, which had given such power unto men.

It is difficult to ignore a man who can do a trick like that – or to be indifferent to, much less forget, what he says.

His end

But it was in such incidents that the seeds of Jesus' destruction were set. The scribes and the Pharisees did not take kindly to being made to look foolish before the unwashed masses in Judea of the first century, any more than the powerful of Athens had enjoyed the experience of being made to look foolish by Socrates centuries earlier. And just as Socrates had challenged the pedagogical (as well as moral) authority of the professional class of teachers, the Sophists, so Jesus challenged the orthodox guardians of the tradition, the scribes and the Pharisees, both in his interpretation and his method of presentation. Among other things his enemies tried entrapment:

> And they asked him 'Is it lawful to pay tribute to Caesar or not?' But Jesus perceived their wickedness and said 'Why do you tempt me, you hypocrites? Show me the tribute money'. And they brought unto him a penny. And he said unto them, 'Whose is this image and super-scription?' They said to him, 'Caesar's'. Then he said to them 'Render to Caesar the things that are Caesar's and unto God the things that are God's'.

Like Socrates, Jesus was a master of the leading question: when in disagreement with his listeners he did not denounce, argue or attempt to intimidate with appeals to authority: he simply asked a question. In an attempt to trick him they brought forward a man with a withered hand and asked Jesus whether it was lawful to heal on the Sabbath day. Jesus' response was, again, in the form of a hypothetical story:

> What man shall there be among you that shall have one sheep, and if it fall into a pit on the Sabbath day, will he not lay hold on it and lift it out?
>
> How much then is a man better than a sheep? Wherefore is it lawful to do well on the Sabbath days.

He then restored the hand of the afflicted one, just to show that he could!

'Then the Pharisees went out', we are told, 'and held a council against him, how they might destroy him.'

He rephrases issues in terms of the economic self-interest of his hearers; he flings out a rhetorical question; he launches an un-answerable riposte: 'How much then is a man better than a sheep?' Indeed. What could they answer? The crowd must have hugely enjoyed seeing the pompous Pharisees caught in a trap of their own setting; but the Pharisees' desire for revenge was in proportion to their embarrassment.

Where Socrates had attempted to define an ethic based on reason, Jesus attempts to reinterpret an ethic based on an ancient authority. They shared the circumstances, if not the manner of their deaths: Jesus was condemned, as was Socrates, because he made the status quo uncomfortable. He undermined the conventional wisdom and the control of the powerful over knowledge. It is not the mighty but the lowly who are the true inheritors of the tradition.

> Verily, I say unto you, except ye be converted and become as little children, ye shall not enter into the kingdom of heaven. Whosoever therefore shall humble himself as this little child the same is greatest in the kingdom of heaven.

Jesus' teaching must be engaged with. It is not dialectical, as Socrates' was, but it is participatory: Jesus does not give answers, he asks questions and provides direction, a general guide to the personalized moral life. He used stories, proverbs, figures, analogies and metaphors to illustrate and enliven the essential moral or ethical message he had inherited. The message was not new. What was new was the pedagogy, the way in which the message was interpreted and communicated. The injunctions of *Deuteronomy* were bald imperatives; the lawyer whose question prompted the story of the good Samaritan knew them well. Jesus explained to people who knew these injunctions what they meant in ordinary terms and for ordinary lives. The images he selected were images with immediacy and relevance to his hearers: fishermen, shepherds, farmers and artisans. They knew effortlessly and with certainty what he meant when he spoke about a sower going out to sow his seed, about vineyards and viniculture, about the hazards of travelling, about building houses on inadequate foundations, etc. Jesus' use of metaphors and analogies, both simple and complex, made sure that his listeners engaged with the moral messages, understood them, identified with them and remembered them. What more could any teacher hope for?

5 Marcus Fabius Quintilian (35–<100 AD): The Education of the Orator

Context

With Marcus Fabius Quintilian we are still in the pagan, pre-Christian world which, apart from the shift of power from the Hellenic states to Rome, and the imperial expansion of the latter, has changed little since the time of Socrates and Plato.

Quintilian was born in Spain about 35 AD and died sometime before the end of the first century. He became the leading practitioner and teacher of oratory and rhetoric in the Roman dominions. During the reign of the Emperor Vespasian (69–79) he was appointed as Professor of Rhetoric at Rome, i.e. he received a state salary. His appointment continued under Titus (79–81) and Domitian (81–96). Latterly he became tutor to the imperial family.

Quintilian's principal legacy to the civilized world is a manual for the education and training of orators which he wrote in the last years of his life. It is the *Institutio Oratoria* – the *Institutes of the Orator*. In it Quintilian addresses the very practical issue of identifying the characteristics of the ideal orator (or as we might consider in the present day, the ideal statesman or politician). He also prescribes the education necessary to achieve such an ideal. At first sight his aim appears to be firmly in the tradition of the Greek Sophists who sold instruction in civic virtue (including public oratory as a significant element). But, as we shall see, Quintilian added a particularly Socratic priority to the Sophist curriculum.

Rhetoric and philosophy

Today the concept of rhetoric has become devalued; 'empty rhetoric' or 'mere rhetoric' is often intended to denote expressions which lack moral conviction or practical import. But in Quintilian's time rhetoric was the central concern of the higher education of the ruling classes and an essential element – and perhaps the most important element – in the formation of citizens for public service. Only one who was properly skilled in rhetoric, i.e. who was an able orator, was considered qualified to serve the Empire in administration, in the law courts or in commanding legions. The successful orator was the man who could change opinion (and hence bring about changes in policy) by entertaining, informing and persuading his listeners.

By Quintilian's time the philosophical tradition, the pursuit of knowledge and truth, had become corrupted from the high ideals of the Greek golden age. Quintilian comments that while many of the philosophers of old taught honourable things and lived and acted accordingly, the name of philosopher in his own time some-times cloaked vices. These pseudo-philosophers, he claimed, did not pursue wisdom but through the 'assumption of a stern and austere mien accompanied by the wearing of a garb differing from that of their fellow men' attempted to conceal their moral depravity.[1] Quintilian also castigated them because they had excluded them-selves from the realities of public life. They were without practical experience of the matters on which they presumed to lecture others.

Given such low and dismissive opinions of the practical relev-ance of the contemporary philosophers we might have expected that Quintilian would lean more to the tradition of the Sophists, the tradition of the orators, the tradition of political technique. However, he did not abandon the philosophical tradition entirely. He realized that the orator needed not only to learn the skills of oratory but also to concern himself with truth and virtue. The ideal orator must be a man of integrity, a good man, and not one who just pretends to be such. So, therefore, the excellent orator is required not only to be a consummate speaker: 'we demand of him not merely the possession of exceptional gifts of speech, but of all the excellences of character as well.'[2] Quintilian goes even further: not only should the orator be a good man, but 'no man can be an orator *unless* he is a good man'.[3] Virtue is not an optional extra.

The principles which inform a life of moral integrity should not be left to philosophers alone. The citizen who is prepared to play his part in the management of the state, who can 'guide a state by his counsels, give it a firm basis by his legislation, and purge its vices by his decisions as a judge',[4] must be an orator. The orator therefore must be the real sage: expert in the science and practice of oratory and exemplary with regard to his morals.

However, Quintilian's ideal of moral integrity did not include moral or philosophical critique of the status quo; this was for the eminently pragmatic reason that such criticism carried a high cost in Imperial Rome in the first century: usually the life of the critic at the hands of despotic Emperors.

Education

The *Institutes of the Orator* was addressed to a class of people whose sons were destined for careers in public service, in the law courts, in civil administration or in the upper echelons of the Imperial army. Quintilian's concern is the education of individuals from the earliest possible age for a career in public life. He recognized, as few had done before him, the vital importance of early educational experience to the life and interests of the adult the child would become. Nothing is irrelevant to his future career as an orator: that is, no part of the child's life and early experience was extraneous to his preparation for his career. Although in the wider scheme of things elementary education might be of less importance than other considerations, nonetheless if it is neglected it precludes the possibility of progress. Therefore Quintilian advocates that the process of formation begins in infancy.

It is this determination to take charge of the entire education of the future functionaries of the Empire that makes Quintilian's programme of continuing interest.

Are orators born or made? Both. The aspiring orator requires certain natural endowments, since precepts and skills are no good unless they complement natural endowments. 'The student who is devoid of talent will derive no more profit from this work than barren soil from a treatise on agriculture.'[5] The natural endowments required include a clear, articulate and audible voice, strong lungs, good health and a sound constitution, as well as physical grace. Any of these can be improved by study and application but if they are not present to a sufficient degree then no amount of effort can compensate for the deficiency.

There are three distinct stages in the education of the orator. These stages correspond closely to the traditional divisions in education which prevail to the present day and which re-echo the seven-year stages of growth endorsed by Aristotle: from birth to 7 we have the infant school, from 7 to 14, the secondary or grammar school, from 14 to adulthood, an advanced specialist education.

Up to 7 years of age the child is to be educated at home. For the future orator this home education must be very carefully super-vised. In the first place the parents themselves must be cultured people. In addition, the child's nurse should 'be of good character' and 'she should speak correctly as well'.[6] The boy's *paedagogus* (the slave who supervises him and takes him to and from school) should be well educated, or at least be aware of his educational limitations! The future orator's companions should also serve as good models for linguistic and moral behaviour. Above all, his tutors must be competent.

Curriculum

What should children under the age of 7 be taught? With commendable psychological insight Quintilian realized that chil-dren's memories are particularly receptive and effective at this age. Advantage should be taken of this while taking care that they are not given negative attitudes to learning. The learning of the young child should always be enjoyable, akin to a diversion or game rather than to a task. Parents and teachers should be careful that the boy 'does not come to hate' his studies, and for this reason 'even when the years of infancy are left behind his studies must be made an amusement'.[7] In addition, praise, success and appropriate rewards should be common. In general, Quintilian's approach to education is consistently humane: his regard for learning is never allowed to diminish his respect for the individual learner and his understanding of the nature of boyhood.

Up to the age of 7 children should be taught the rudiments of reading, writing and arithmetic and their speech training should begin with rhymes which contain difficult words and combinations of sounds. His approach to the teaching of writing anticipates many more modern innovations: the child should, for example, be given ivory letters to play with. Handling, examining and naming them will be a pleasure and be more beneficial than simply learning the names and order of the letters. He approves of any approach that may 'delight the very young' and so promote learning.

His attitude to learning reading is enlightened too. He advises against putting undue pressure on children although he considers it acceptable that they be taught reading as early as possible. Quintilian realized that reading is retarded by undue haste: it causes reluctance and hesitation on the part of pupils who attempt too much and then lose confidence. Reading should be confident, first of all, and allowed to be slow until such time as practice leads to correctness and speed together. He appears to favour a phonic approach: 'as regards syllables, no short cut is possible: they must all be learnt ... once learnt, let him begin to construct words with them and sentences with the words.'[8]

Concerning the learning of a language the choice for the young Roman pupil of the first century was between Latin and Greek. Latin was, of course, the vernacular and was acquired by the children as their mother tongue. Greek, however, was still a living language and was often the preferred language of the educated and cultured classes, much as French was in nineteenth-century Europe. So Quintilian advocates the teaching of Greek first because the child will already know Latin. But he insists that the formal study of Latin should follow shortly so that an exclusive emphasis on the formal teaching of Greek would not contaminate the pupil's competence in Latin. 'The result will be,' Quintilian hopes, 'that, as soon as we begin to give equal attention to both languages, neither will prove a hindrance to the other.'[9]

Public or private?

When it comes to the more formal education, Quintilian addresses one of the perennial questions of education policy which we have already seen in Plato and Aristotle: whether the education of the children at this age be public or private. In the context of first-century Rome (as in the context of the Athens of Aristotle) this is not a choice between public and private *schools* but a choice between private education under a tutor at home or education in a common school.

Quintilian's preference is based on pedagogical rather than political or ideological considerations. He favours public or common education for a number of reasons. First of all it promotes social development. Secondly, teaching a class of pupils is more stimulating for a teacher than teaching one pupil only; having a class of pupils, an audience, gives his teaching energy and spirit. However, parents should avoid schools where he is likely to be neglected because of classes being *too* large. It is a sign of a good teacher that he will not undertake to teach more pupils than he can teach properly. Quintilian is well aware that there is an optimum size for a class. Beyond this optimum size any pedagogical stimulation is outweighed by the danger of individual pupils' being neglected. A third benefit of public over private education is the benefit to the pupil of being taught in the company of others. This allows him opportunities for developing friendships and for engaging with appropriate role models among his peers. Younger children especially will find that imitation of fellow pupils is easier and more pleasant than attempts to imitate the Master.

There are many benefits to the boy himself: he will have the stimulus and excitement of the company of his peers, he will have a standard of comparison by which to judge his own ability, he will make enduring friendships, he will develop the capacity to empathize with others, 'that instinct which we call common feeling', he will learn what is taught to others as well as to himself, he will see merits praised and faults corrected and he will learn the incentive of competition. Because his specific purpose is the education of the orator who will spend his career in public performance 'in the utmost publicity and in the broad daylight of public life'[10] Quintilian identifies one crucial reality about public or common schooling which is often forgotten even in these enlightened times: that the pupil performing in a classroom is performing before an audience; answering the most trivial question is a public performance in the full gaze of the child's peers. This is a decided benefit of public education for the future orator, whose career will involve addressing various assemblies in the glare of public life, for he will be accustomed to such performance from his earliest years.

The selected teacher must be able to recognize the limitations imposed by his pupils' immaturity. He must be, Quintilian says, 'a sensible man with a good knowledge of teaching and must be prepared to stoop to his pupil's level', just as an understanding adult will adapt his pace when walking with a small child. Teaching must be related to the age (or what we would now call the developmental stage) of the learner, so the master must avoid overburdening the intellects of his pupils. He should not 'burden his pupils ... with tasks to which their strength is unequal, but curb his energies and refrain from talking over the heads of his audience'.[11]

Work, play and control

Quintilian's attitude to play is very positive. He considers that a balance between play and work is essential to the well-being of the learner for a number of reasons. The love of play is a sign of an alert and lively mind and pupils who have been re-invigorated by play bring renewed energy and interest to their studies. But he advises moderation: too little opportunity for play may induce a dislike of study, while too much may foster a propensity for idleness.

Quintilian is quite unambivalent in his attitudes to means of class control or individual discipline: corporal punishment ('flogging') should be avoided not only because it is an offence to the dignity of the pupil and ultimately ineffective ('if a boy is so insensible to instruction that reproof is useless, he will, like the worst type of slave, merely become hardened to blows'[12]), but also, and more importantly, because the failures it is intended to address are in fact failures of the tutor not of the learner. If the master is negligent in his responsibility to constantly monitor the pupil's study and progress there is little point in punishing the pupil.

This form of punishment does not promote the moral training of the learner; in the long run it is counter-productive. For if corporal punishment is the only way of correcting the child's behaviour what happens when he grows up and has no longer any fear of being whipped?

The grammar school

The second stage of the child's education, from 7 to 14, is the grammar school. In Quintilian's time (and for a long time afterwards) the word 'grammar' meant a great deal more than simply the rules which determine the relations between words. Grammar was the art or science of letters or literary studies and embraced the study of literature as well as the study of linguistic accuracy and correctness; in the intellectual climate of the time 'grammar' had much the same status as science does today. Quintilian considered 'grammar' to have two components: the art of speaking correctly and the interpretation of the poets.

Quintilian's grammar school would promote a knowledge and appreciation of literature as well as a knowledge of correct speaking. Nonetheless, we should not lose sight of the reality that, although there was literacy, Quintilian's culture was predominantly oral. It depended far more on word of mouth for the transmission of information and opinion than on the written word. For this reason, although the written word does not have the ascendancy which it came to have in later centuries, reading is basically considered as a performance, the recreation of speech. This is seen in Quintilian's advice regarding reading aloud. The Master must give instruction regarding breathing, tempo, sense, volume, and so forth. Above all, Quintilian insists on 'but one golden rule: to do all these things, he must *understand* what he reads':[13] a heartfelt plea for what is nowadays called 'reading for meaning'.

Quintilian's concern is not solely with what is useful (grammar and oratory) but also with what is morally desirable. He wishes his pupils to be motivated by praise, by a sense of glory and by a competitive spirit. Noble sentiments should provide the learner's motivation so that he will be moved by his sense of honour: he will behave well, not to avoid punishment but because reproach is shameful. Consequently, the authors whom the student will study in the grammar school are selected for their moral character as much as for their literary content: the boys 'must learn not merely what is eloquent,' he insists, 'it is even more important that they should study what is morally excellent'.[14] In this regard he appears to echo the concern of both Plato and Aristotle with the moral content of the literary material (stories and poetic texts) to which the learner is exposed. He realizes that children are affected in the long term by the sense of what is heard and read. The mind of the child is impressionable so it is important that his studies are based not only on excellent literary models but on excellent moral exemplars.

As a practical preparation for the training in rhetoric, Quintilian proposes that the student should learn to relate Aesop's fables (yes, they *are* that old) in an elegant style.

Regarding the relationship between the written and the spoken word, Quintilian anticipated the more recent views of the great George Bernard Shaw. Like Shaw, Quintilian argued that since the purpose of writing is to preserve speech, every word should be written as it is pronounced so as to preserve the connection between speech and sight!

Music is essential in Quintilian's curriculum for music benefits the future orator in two ways: it contributes to the melodiousness of the voice and to the grace of the body so that speech and gesture combine harmoniously. Dancing should be taught, for a while at least, so that the student will acquire physical grace. The acquisition of physical grace is the purpose of physical training as well as of dance.

Mathematics must be taught: arithmetic and plane geometry are necessary for practical purposes in arguing cases of commerce or land ownership in the courts. In addition the student will learn order from geometry: the logical relation between principles and conclusions is as crucial in rhetoric as it is in mathematics.

In sum, then, the cycle of studies in Quintilian's grammar school comprises grammar (including literature), composition, music and a little dancing, mathematics, elocution and physical training. This cycle of studies was not arrived at as a result of an *a priori* educational theory: on the contrary, it derives from Quintilian's knowledge of the practical outcomes that people want. He has lived the life he teaches.

In determining *how* the subjects will be taught – whether concurrently (all together) or consecutively (one at a time) – Quintilian opted in favour of having the subjects studied concurrently. Those who advocate the serial approach, i.e. the study of one subject at a time, underestimate the power of the human mind. To be restricted to one subject only for prolonged periods of time would be intolerable – it would lead to boredom and fatigue. The variety, on the other hand, of addressing several subjects in the course of a day would mirror the human mind ('so swift and nimble and versatile'[15]) which rarely restricts itself to one thing but embraces a multiplicity of interests at the same time. There is another, pedagogically important, psychological point to be taken into account: a change of occupation in itself refreshes and restores the mind. It is difficult to concentrate for long on a single task: so, for example, reading provides a welcome change from writing and the monotony of reading is itself relieved by changes in the subjects being studied.

And so Quintilian endorses the basic structure of the school curriculum and timetable which has persisted to this day: a multiplicity of subjects which are taught concurrently, in relatively short time periods, allowing for regular change and variety of experience.

The master of rhetoric

The third stage in the education of the orator is the equivalent of present-day university education. Now the student, his mind trained by the grammar school, begins to furnish his mind with the best that has been thought and written, he undertakes courses in composition and declamation and takes lectures on the formal theory of rhetoric. All of this will be supplemented by private study. There was no specific teaching of philosophy apart from whatever works of the Greek philosophers the student might be required to study as part of his general reading. Although it is a vocational programme, a special emphasis throughout was on the moral character of the student.

And what of the master of rhetoric himself? What is the profile of the ideal teacher? Quintilian identifies a number of characteristics which would, even today, attract widespread endorsement. The good teacher must adopt the benevolent disposition of a parent, since he is acting *in loco parentis*. Not alone must he be without moral fault but he must not tolerate moral faults in his students. He should be severe but not harsh, amiable but not indulgent: severity will generate hatred and excessive amiability will generate contempt. He should advocate what is honourable and good, and admonish rather than punish the shortcomings of his students. He should not be quick to anger but neither should he ignore faults. His manner of teaching should be unaffected, consistent and firm. He should be prepared to answer his pupils' questions and encourage those who are not inclined to ask questions. He should be sparing in his praise but such praise should be genuine. He should avoid sarcasm and abuse.[16]

Even today there is nothing in this description with which we could quarrel: it shows a keen insight into the psychology of the learner, a sound grasp of the personal and intellectual characteristics required of the good teacher, and a clear recognition of the ethical imperatives of teaching.

Quintilian's views were very influential during the Renaissance and the *Institutes of Oratory* was for centuries regarded as the standard and authoritative work on education. This helps to explain how many of its particulars are so familiar to us today. In many respects – the doctrine of *in loco parentis*, the structure and organization of the academic secondary school, the structure – if not the specific content – of the secondary school curriculum, the psychological insights, the value of the individual personality of the learner and the emphasis on the centrality of character formation, the moral value to the community of liberal, humanistic education – we are the inheritors, through the Renaissance, of the grammar school of Marcus Fabius Quintilian.

6 Aurelius Augustine (354–430): Education for the Inner Life

His life

Aurelius Augustine, son of a minor Roman official, was born in 354 AD in the North African town of Tagaste (now Souk-Ahras, Algeria). Augustine received a good education and initially followed a career in teaching. His teaching experience was considerable: he taught grammar at Tagaste and rhetoric at Carthage and Rome. He was appointed Professor of Rhetoric at Milan – a post he held until his conversion to Christianity at the age of 32. (Christianity was no longer an outlaw religion in the Roman Empire, having been granted recognition by the Emperor Constantine early in the fourth century.)

The story of Augustine's spiritual development is told in his *Confessions*. Despite what he assures us was a rather dissolute lifestyle in his youth, he experienced deep moral turmoil and constantly sought a spiritual home which would satisfy his keen and enquiring intelligence. In his 20s he was attracted to Manichaeism, which taught that the world is the creation of two opposing forces (good and evil, spirit and matter, light and darkness) and that each human being is a product of the intermixing of two substances: spirit (soul, good, light) and matter (body, evil, darkness). The purpose of life is the ascendancy of the soul through knowledge of the transcendent world of the spirit. Augustine abandoned Manichaeism because its principal advocates were unable to provide a sufficiently rigorous explanation for their beliefs.

Although he longed for conversion he was unwilling to accept the moral changes in his life that it would entail. His struggle with himself came to a dramatic end one evening in a Milan garden. He heard a child's voice calling 'take up and read'. He opened the Letters of St Paul that he had left nearby and read in the letter to the Romans the words ' ... put ye on the Lord Jesus Christ, and make not provision for the flesh, in concupiscence'.[1] This was his moment of epiphany.

His conversion was irrevocable. He abandoned his secular life and soon returned to North Africa where he devoted himself to the promotion of the Christian Church. He exchanged, as it were, a teaching career for a teaching vocation.

By 395 Augustine had been appointed bishop of Hippo Regius (the modern Annaba on the Algerian coast) and the remainder of his life was spent in the service of the Christian Church in this diocese.

Augustine's world view[2]

Augustine's picture of the universe is Platonic. There is a realm of unchanging reality behind the unreliable world of change and decay. Human experience is divided between the physical order which is the object of sense experience and the spiritual order which is the object of the intellect. This immaterial world of ideas or forms is stable and permanent, not subject to corruption or change. Although this world of ideas or forms is immaterial, beyond the reach of sense experience, it is accessible to human understanding, it is intelligible. We access it by turning away from the realm of the senses and 'looking' inward to the realm of reason: the route to the higher is through the inner.

The Platonic Forms became for Augustine the ideas in the mind of God upon which the creation of the material world was based: the Divine blueprints, as it were, for creation.

Because the world of everyday experience is constantly changing it is unsatisfactory as a source of knowledge. The insights it offers must be referred to standards found in the intelligible world; the intelligible realm is our only source of reliable knowledge.

So there are two worlds, the material and the spiritual: we access the first through sense perception, the second through intellectual understanding. The world which is accessible to the senses, the physical world, is made in the image of the intelligible world. It is the second, the intelligible world, which is our source of truth. The sensible world, the world of everyday experience, can generate no knowledge but only opinion; the intelligible world is our guarantee of truth.

The human soul, or mind, operates on both the sensible and the intelligible levels. On the sensible level it undertakes action through the body with regard to temporal and material things. On the level of the intelligible its function is to know the truth through the contemplation of eternal things. The eternal truths are present to contemplation by the eye of the mind just as physical things are accessible to the senses of the body.

So there are two kinds of things that people must know: things that relate to physical existence and well-being and things that relate to their spiritual well-being. The first is knowledge, the second is wisdom.

Human and divine

Human beings have access to the eternal ideas in the divine mind because the human mind is created in its image: the human mind sees not through physical eyes but 'it sees by means of intelligence'.[3] The more the rational human soul approaches God in love, the more it benefits from an intelligible light and 'sees', that is understands, what is lit up by that light. In this way Augustine joined Plato's philosophy of knowledge of the perfect forms with the Christian idea of the influence of a personal God.

The material world is not evil in itself: it is morally problematic because it distracts us from the true pursuit of happiness. The fault is with our perception and our will: our will tends to pursue transitory goods such as wealth, power and pleasure: we see our self-interest in terms of material interest. Moral evil is not a thing, therefore, but a wilful attachment to these lower (material) things to the exclusion of the higher (spiritual) things.

Authority and reason; faith and understanding

At the time of his conversion Augustine acknowledged two roads to learning, authority and reason. He embraced the authority of Jesus Christ as revealed in the New Testament but he did not abandon the quest of reason that had dominated his intellectual life: truth must be grasped not just by faith but also by understanding: authority and reason provide two complementary pathways to truth.

Authority comes before reason, however, and faith comes before understanding. This does not diminish the role of reason in the development of human knowledge. It simply asserts a psychological priority: unless we believe in something, however minimal our belief, we will not pursue it. 'Unless you believe,' Augustine tells us, quoting the prophet Isaiah, 'you shall not understand'.[4] It is only those things in which we have some belief which will beckon us on to fuller investigation of their complete significance. Reason should not be downplayed in the matter of religious faith: reason comes from God and it is reason that makes us superior to all other material creatures.

Augustine illustrates the relationship between thought and belief with the familiar experience of the child who initially accepts his beliefs about the world from his parents and teachers and acts confidently on this basis. As he grows older, however, he will want to understand the reasons behind his beliefs. In day-to-day matters adults also act in accordance with their beliefs. They take these beliefs on trust since there is never sufficient time to pursue rational explanations of all matters.

When Augustine writes that, 'There are some things which we do not believe unless we understand them, and there are other things which we do not understand unless we believe them',[5] he is referring to the difference between scientific knowledge (which we do not believe unless we understand) and the knowledge of spiritual reality (which we do not understand unless we believe).

Like the Greeks, Augustine considers reason to be distinctively human. It is the ability to engage in deductive reasoning and to recognize the force of logical necessity. Reason is the means by which the human soul engages with immaterial realities (logical necessity or mathematical truths, for example). Reason gives us access to truths that are absolutely reliable.

Human being

Human being is a union of two elements: a body which is material and transient, and a soul which is spiritual and immortal. The close union of these two elements explains our contrary tendencies and divided loyalties. The relationship of the body and the soul is not a relationship of equals. The soul is superior to the body, gives it life and is responsible for directing its behaviour. It is, in the modern phrase, the 'ghost in the machine'. The soul is not divisible or made up of parts, nor is it subject to change and decay as the body is. Yet the soul and the body are not two distinct things, together they comprise the totality of being human. '(S)piritual man and carnal man are not two things but one. Both are one and the same thing, namely man living according to the principle of his nature.'[6]

Each component is guided by an appropriate form of perception (sense and intellect). Acts of perception are not gratuitous or involuntary: just as we will not see clearly unless we *look* so we will not understand clearly unless we *attend*. Seeing and understanding both require active participation on our part. This is especially important in relation to education. Far from being a matter of the passive reception of instruction by a teacher, learning is an active process demanding effort and attention, will and memory as well as intellect.

The activity of human intelligence requires the Divine Light. For mental activity, thought, is really a kind of mental vision. The illumination which makes this vision possible comes direct from God. Augustine's doctrine of illumination holds that the human mind is illuminated by God so that it can perceive, or 'see', intelligible realities. (As when we acknowledge understanding by saying, 'I see'.) This is not a matter of divine revelation: wisdom does not come unbidden or without sustained effort. But it cannot come at all without that inner light which makes the intelligible 'visible' to human reason.

Our knowledge of the intelligible realm is not simply a matter of faith. Our grasp of the principle of non-contradiction, for example, is not just an unfounded belief, neither is it a proposition based on empirical evidence. Augustinian illumination explains how such a necessary and universal truth can have the kind of necessity that understanding, as opposed to belief, requires.

Like Plato before him, Augustine compares the mind's relation to intelligible objects with the relation of the eye to visible objects. In the latter case the eye can only perceive the visible object if there is sufficient light to do so; if there is no light there is no vision. Analogously, unless the intelligible object (e.g. logical necessity, a mathematical truth, or an intuitive truth such as the principle of contradiction) is somehow illuminated by an independent source, it will not be preceptible to the understanding.

Education

The principal task of education is to reconcile man's contrary natures (the physical and the spiritual) and to draw out the latent possibilities of each person so that he or she more fully realizes the divine within. It is through the *inner* life of the individual that wisdom must be pursued.

> Descend into yourself; go to the secret chamber of your mind. If you stray from your own self, how can you draw near to God? For it was not in the body but in the mind that man was made in the likeness of God. In his own likeness let us seek God; in his own image recognize the Creator.[7]

The soul does not grow in the sense of taking up more physical space (since it takes up no physical space at all) but in the sense that it becomes capable of doing and knowing more: it grows in understanding.

The soul is capable of three equal capacities: will, memory and intellect, these three 'are one mind and one essence'. Will, memory and intellect together constitute the concept of 'character' that was to become so central to Western education. 'The merit of a boy's character,' Augustine believed, 'depends on the tenacity and facility of his memory, the penetration of his intellect and the strength of his will'.[8] This gives the template for education: these are the capacities which the educator must address.

Teaching and language

The dialogue *De Magistro* (*Concerning the Teacher*) is Augustine's only work specifically concerned with teaching. It was probably written as a tribute to his son Adeodatus who had died at the age of 17 shortly after Augustine's return to North Africa.

The Teacher argues that it is a mistake to believe that teachers can communicate knowledge to their students through the medium of language. Through a detailed examination of the nature of language Augustine comes to the conclusion that words do not communicate knowledge directly. If we know something already then the word – the verbal symbol for the thing – merely reminds us of what we already know. If we do not know something already then the word cannot teach it to us since the word is only a conventional name for the thing, a sign, not the thing itself, and it is completely unlike the thing which it signifies. There is a distinct difference between signs and realities. 'We do not learn anything by means of the signs called words,' Augustine insists. 'For we learn the meaning of the word only after the reality itself which is signified has been recognized.'[9]

We do not learn what a head is, for example, by hearing the word 'head' repeatedly. On the contrary we learn the meaning of the *sound* 'head' only from its constant conjunction with the recognizable object. Teachers sometimes behave as if knowing the word is the same as knowing the words – what we might today call verbalism. The converse is the case: the meaning of the word is clear to us only when we already know the thing to which the word refers. The young child learning language hears words only as sounds until he has experience of the thing the word represents or signifies. Augustine remarks that we must learn to connect the sound with the thing, but the latter must be known to us already. We do not, for example, learn what a dog is by repeatedly hearing the word 'dog'. We learn the meaning of the word by associating it with the object in the environment (a dog) with which we are already familiar. Before this association is made the word is merely a sound. We learn that 'dog' is a sign when we learn what it is a sign of. So learning proceeds from experience to language.

Augustine argues in *The Teacher* that the efficacy of language ultimately depends upon direct knowledge of the world that the language refers to. We can learn from teachers if we can relate what they tell us to our prior experience: learning from others is a matter of being reminded of our prior experience and may include having our attention directed to aspects of this experience which we may not have noticed before. The true function of language, on this account, is not to insert ideas into our minds but to evoke those which are already there.

Augustine provides a telling example of the precedence of the experiential method of learning over the verbal method of teaching. We can give a detailed verbal account of the process of walking. We can provide clear descriptions regarding the movement of the feet, ankles, knees, etc. in proper sequence. Despite the accuracy of such an account it is of no value to someone learning to walk in normal circumstances. In fact Augustine's point is that the significance of the verbal account can be meaningful only to someone who knows how to walk already. The sign is 'learned from the thing cognized rather than the thing being learned from a given sign'.[10] We do not learn reality through words, we learn words through reality.

Another example adduced by Augustine is the case of the child learning his mother-tongue. This is not accomplished, in the first instance, by mastering the rules of grammar. It is accomplished in the normal course of events without systematic instruction at all. The child learns how to talk from listening to those who can already do so and imitating them, by having the desire to say something. The direct method puts verbal theory in a secondary place and emphasizes the priority of the learner's active engagement with whatever is to be learned whether this is a matter of outer, sense experience or inner, intellectual experience.

All teachers can do then is to remind learners of things they have already learnt for themselves, stimulate them to learn new things, or provide them with opportunities for relevant experience. Augustine is not dismissing teachers, he is rather redefining their role in a way which is more consistent with learning as an *activity*. The teacher's words simply direct the attention of the learner either to the object or experience which the teacher is providing or to the learner's previous experience stored in the memory.

The discussion in *The Teacher* concludes that the real teacher is not the external teacher who occupies a space in the classroom but the internal divine teacher who inhabits our minds. The teacher in the classroom *stimulates* the learner but the act of learning occurs only when we consult and attend to the internal teacher: 'it is the truth that presides within over the mind itself; though it may have been words that prompted us to make such consultation'.[11] This is why Augustine frequently refers to teaching as *reminding*. If we know what a word means 'we recall rather than learn' what it signifies; 'if we do not know, we do not even recall, though perhaps we receive the impulse to inquire'.[12]

Teachers and learners

This redefinition of the teacher's role appears to be a major demotion of the human teacher. Augustine even goes so far as to say that there are really no human teachers at all: 'we should not call anyone on earth a teacher'.[13] The reason we normally speak in terms of teachers 'causing' learning is that there is often no evident lapse of time between the instructive activity of the teacher and the learning. (This is an example of the logical fallacy of *post hoc, ergo propter hoc* 'after this, therefore because of this' – the mistaken belief that just because one thing follows another it is caused by it.)

Just because the learning follows the teaching temporally it does not mean that the teaching caused the learning.

We should not conclude from this, however, that there is no role for the teacher, or that the task is futile. Augustine simply means that the assumption that teaching works on the basis of the direct transference of ideas through the medium of language is mistaken: the one that people think they have learned from 'was only a prompter'.[14]

Teaching and learning are not two separate activities but two aspects of the same activity. The teacher/pupil relationship is one of mutual engagement: each is simultaneously teaching and learning from the other. So the teacher does not occupy the central, dominating role in the classroom nor does the pupil occupy the inferior passive role.

As well as having a deep understanding of the subject matter to be learned (and the experiences necessary to promote it), the teacher must approach the learner sympathetically. Motivated by love of what he teaches, and of his pupils, it is his principal task to generate interest and enthusiasm. Showing a keen insight into the psychology of learning, Augustine had written in his *Confessions* that 'a free curiosity has more force in our learning than a frightful enforcement'.[15] The teacher must begin with what the learner already knows: 'Unless we have some slight knowledge of a subject in our minds, we cannot be kindled with any enthusiasm to learn it.'[16] Learning cannot be forced: pupils can be influenced but not compelled to learn. It follows from what Augustine has said about language that what is to be learned must be adapted to the interests and experience of the pupils and be presented at an appropriate level of difficulty: 'those subjects are studied more eagerly when people do not despair of being able to grasp them', Augustine insists.[17] When a person has no hope of being able to learn what is required, no matter how important he may perceive it to be, 'he either loves the subject in a lukewarm manner or does not love it at all'.[18]

Augustine realizes that learners differ in their individual capacities, interests and circumstances. The teacher must adapt his teaching to the individual circumstances and needs of his learners. The teacher should also realize that just as he affects his students so the students, by the very fact that they are all together, affect one another in various ways.

The moral influence of the teacher is crucial to the formation of the character (the combination of will, memory and intellect) of the learner. Teachers must act consistently in accordance with the principles they are attempting to promote. It is possible for the wicked man to teach those who wish to learn but his effect would be much greater if he lived by his teaching. Learners 'no longer listen attentively to a man who does not listen to himself and, in despising the instructor, they learn to despise the word that is taught'.[19]

In general then, Augustine advocated a teacher/learner relationship in which the learner is an active participant, and in which the teacher acknowledges the priority of the learner and takes account of the specific capacities and circumstances of the individual learner. In short, he advocates a learner-centred system of education.

Conclusion

Augustine's main influence has been on the development of Catholic education in the first instance. His educational ideas were formed at the same time as he was developing the philosophy which would dominate Catholic thinking for the better part of two millennia. He is an important link between the classical and Christian worlds. Among his lasting contributions to educational thought and practice were his downgrading of the importance of a predominantly linguistic pedagogy and the placement of the learner rather than the teacher at the centre of the teaching/ learning process. This was a change that took the Western world many centuries to accommodate and it is only with the growth of child- or learner-centred education in the nineteenth century that we find a lasting reaction against verbalism and teacher-dominated pedagogies. Augustine realized that learning is not the mere accumulation of facts but the achievement of understanding, an enlightenment. It is not rote learning which is the aim of teaching, but motivating the learner to engage with experience so that he or she achieves insight into the true nature of the experience.

7 John Amos Comenius (1592–1670): Education as a Human Right

His life

John Amos Comenius (Jan Kamensky), the first great educational visionary of modern times, spent his life planning for the renewal of human life through education. He realized, as no one had since Plato, the political power of education and its potential for social reconstruction.

Comenius was born in 1592, in Moravia, nowadays the eastern province of the Czech Republic, into a small evangelical sect called the Moravian Brethren. The Brethren combined simplicity of faith and earnest personal piety with an emphasis on fraternal relations and community solidarity, values which inspired Comenius' throughout his life.

His early schooling was minimal. He was 16 before he entered on the study of Latin at Prerov, an experience which left an indelible impression on him. He wrote of the deficiencies of the schools of the time in blood-curdling terms: they were 'terrors for boys and shambles for their intellects', where lessons were 'stuffed and flogged' into students.[1]

He was particularly critical of the teaching of Latin. At the time Latin was the sovereign key to universal understanding and to social and geographical mobility. As it was taught it was a disaster. Comenius complained that even the most menial of workers in a foreign environment will learn the rudiments of the vernacular two or three times quicker than the children in school learn Latin through instruction.[2]

He graduated from the University of Herborn, in Germany, in 1612 with his interest in educational reform already sharpened by the progressive ideas he had encountered there.

Teaching reform

Soon after graduation Comenius was appointed rector of the school at Prerov where he himself had formed such a poor opinion of the teaching methods. Here he undertook the first of his educational reforms. He simplified the Latin Grammar and wrote an elementary introduction to Latin for his pupils. In 1618 he was ordained, made Minister of the Moravian Brethren church at Fulneck in Moravia, and took charge of a new school.

His first significant work was the *Janua Linguarum Reserata* (*The Gate of Tongues Unlocked*), an introduction to the study of Latin. It was hugely successful as a primer throughout Europe and established Comenius' reputation as an educational reformer. The *Janua* became the foundation of Comenius' most celebrated book, the *Orbis Pictus* published in 1657. This is an abridged version of the *Janua* with the addition of pictures illustrating the words and phrases being taught. It was the first illustrated school text.

Until the end of his life, he demonstrated a faith in the reformative power of education. 'There is no more certain way under the sun,' he wrote, 'for the raising of sunken humanity than the proper education of the young'.[3]

The years he spent at Fulneck were to be the last tranquil period that Comenius would ever spend in his native land. As a result of the European-wide disruption of the Thirty Years' War Comenius was forced into a fugitive and nomadic existence which would last his lifetime.

Education

Education in Europe in the sixteenth and seventeenth centuries was disorganized, sporadic and elitist: opportunities were available only on the basis of privilege. With Comenius we enter the modern era. He wrote about education in what we would now recognize as the language of human rights: should be universal education and appropriate for all children in society. A corollary of this principle is that education must be accessible: schools must be provided in 'every well-ordered habitation of man',[4] presided over by teachers specially selected and trained for their task.

His proposals have a particularly modern tone: education as a human right shared by all: 'all who have been born to man's estate have been born with the same end in view, namely that they may be men, that is to say, rational creatures'.[5] Even those of apparently dull intellects require as much education as they are capable of benefiting from: 'The slower and weaker the disposition of any man, the more he needs assistance.'[6] No one's intellect is so weak that it cannot be improved.

He adduces four reasons in support of the universal right to education: (a) the goal of life (redemption) is the same for all; (b) human nature is the same in all; (c) differences of ability are usually due to deficiencies which can be rectified; (d) that all embark on education as equals does not require that they finish so.[7]

Girls, since they 'are endowed with equal sharpness of mind and capacity for knowledge' will of course be included. Historically they have often attained the highest positions 'since they have often been called by God himself to rule over nations, (and) to give sound advice to kings and princes'. They are capable of advanced study, and 'of prophesying and of inveighing against priests and bishops'.[8] Unfortunately Comenius immediately qualified the principle in respect of women arguing that 'their tendency to curiosity shall be developed' only insofar as it is appropriate 'to those things which it becomes a woman to know and to do'!][9]

The schools he envisaged would be common schools, not divided on grounds of gender, ability, class or wealth and free from the brutality, excessive verbalism, and hopelessly confused and ineffective methodologies which characterized contemporary educational institutions. Is it possible to reform education? Comenius promises that his system will ensure that the 'young shall be educated in all subjects which can make them wise, virtuous and pious. This education shall be completed before maturity is reached. It will be conducted 'without blows, rigour or compulsion' in as gentle, pleasant and natural a manner as possible. Nonetheless it will be thorough, leading to genuine understanding.

Comenius' proposals for universal schooling are strikingly similar to what prevails universally today: nursery school up to the age of 6; from 6 to 12, primary or vernacular school (where instruction is given in the mother tongue of the children); secondary or Latin school from 12 to 18; and finally university education based on merit and achievement.

Comenius attempted to develop what might be called 'idiot-proof' teaching methods: methods which would minimize the possibility of failure due to the individual shortcomings of teachers. Once proper methods were developed it would be possible to teach pupils in great numbers. 'As soon as we have succeeded in finding the proper method,' Comenius promises, 'it will be no harder to teach school boys in any number desired than with the help of the printing press to cover a thousand sheets daily with the neatest writing'.[10]

The Great Didactic

The Great Didactic is Comenius' masterwork on educational reform. The intention behind his great scheme was to set out 'the whole art of teaching all things to all men' in such a way that it would be certain, pleasant, enjoyable and thorough, 'in a manner as to lead to true knowledge, to gentle morals, and to the deepest piety'. The method would be based on first principles, on 'the unalterable nature of the matter itself'.[11] His intention was, in principle, empirical and psychological: 'to follow the lead of nature in all things, to observe how the faculties develop one after the other, and to base our method on this principle of succession'.[12]

The full title of this monumental effort both summarizes *The Great Didactic* and sets out Comenius' educational programme:

> *The Great Didactic: setting forth the whole art of teaching all things to all men or a certain inducement to found such schools in all the parishes, towns, and villages of every Christian Kingdom, that the entire youth of both sexes, none being excepted, shall quickly, pleasantly, and thoroughly become learned in the sciences, pure in morals, trained to piety, and in this manner instructed in all things necessary for the present and for the future life, in which, with respect to everything that is suggested, its fundamental principles are set forth from the essential nature of the matter, its truth is proved by examples from the several mechanical arts, its order is clearly set forth in years, months, days and hours, and, finally, an easy and sure method is shown, by which it can be pleasantly brought into existence.*

Comenius was in no doubt that what he was presenting to the public was of great moment.

In former times, Comenius declared, the art of teaching and learning was unsystematic and haphazard, as a result learning was a difficult, wearisome business. Only exceptional people could benefit from the education available. By placing the art of teaching on a proper foundation *The Great Didactic* will transform the world of education and benefit all: parents, teachers, students (who will now be able to learn 'without difficulty, tedium, complaints or blows') and schools. For states it will produce desirable citizens, for the Church it will provide a reliable supply of learned pastors and appreciative congregations.[13]

Educational opportunity

The aims set out in *The Great Didactic* derive from Comenius' beliefs regarding the nature of human being and the ultimate purpose of human life. Man has 'a threefold life, the vegetative, the animal, and the intellectual or spiritual'.[14] Correspondingly 'his life and his abiding-place is threefold: the mother's womb, the earth, and the heaven'. He passes from the first to the second by birth, 'and from the second into the third by death and resurrection'. The life in the womb is preparatory to the life on earth, which is preparatory to the third which 'exists for itself and is without end'.[15]

Similarly, the aims of education are threefold and comprise knowledge, virtue and piety. The capacity for knowledge, virtue and piety already 'naturally implanted in us' must be nurtured by education, by action and by prayer respectively.[16]

Education formation

Is it possible, however, to imbue the young with knowledge, virtue and piety as Comenius supposes? The 'seeds of knowledge, virtue, and piety' are innate in all human beings so that all that is necessary to bring them to fruition is 'a gentle impulse and prudent guidance'.[17] What is true of nature in general is true of human nature in particular.

Progress depends on proper nurturing: it is only through a proper education that people can become fully human. This is a decidedly modern insight: the need for what we now call 'socialization'. Man is a 'teachable animal': no one can really be a man unless he has been 'trained in those elements which constitute a man'.[18]

He illustrates this conviction with the story of the Wolf Boy of Hassia:

About the year 1540 in a village called Hassia, situated in the middle of a forest, a boy of three years old was lost, through the carelessness of his parents. ... Some years afterwards the country people saw a strange animal running about with the wolves, of a different shape, four-footed, but with a man's face. Rumour of this spread through the district, and the Governor asked the peasants to try and catch it alive and bring it to him. This they did. ... The Prince had the Wolf Boy educated and kept him continually in men's society. Under this influence his savage habits grew gentler by degrees; he began to raise himself up on his hind legs and walk like a biped, and at last to speak intelligently and behave like a man.[19]

Whether Comenius himself believed this story his use of it illustrates his belief not only in the power of education to *form* the individual but also to *reform* the individual.

The programme
Throughout *The Great Didactic* the continuity between human nature and nature in general is stressed and horticultural metaphors are frequently used to illustrate the educational. For instance, 'it is evident that the circumstances of men and of trees are similar' but there is a clear difference between nature in the raw, as it were, and cultivated nature. A wild tree will only produce sweet fruit under the care of a skilled gardener. Similarly, while a man will grow of his own accord 'into a human semblance' he cannot develop into a 'rational, wise, virtuous and pious creature' unless these virtues are 'first engrafted in him' when he is young by skilful educators.[20]

The curriculum must be as broad as possible ('universal') because no one in his later life should encounter anything so unfamiliar that he cannot make proper judgement upon it and engage with it appropriately.

Comenius follows the Augustinian tripartite division of the capacities of the soul into intellect, will and memory: through the appropriate use of these capacities we pursue the three aims of education: knowledge, virtue and piety. The three should be inseparable: knowledge is of no benefit without virtue and piety while the learning of a man who is without virtue is 'as a jewel of gold in a swine's snout ...'.[21]

Schools
The Great Didactic is eminently methodical. Each educational principle is associated with a natural process and a familiar human

activity. A general principle of nature ('nature prepares the material before she gives it form') is illustrated by a natural process (the bird prepares the nest before it lays its eggs) and repeated in a familiar human pursuit (a builder prepares his materials before he begins his work). The existing system is then shown to be deficient in applying the principle (teachers do not have the requisite materials in preparation; and they prefer classifications and abstract rules to objects and experiences). Finally, under the heading *Rectification*, he shows how educational practice can be brought to conform to natural procedures if the significant deficiencies in schools are addressed systematically.

Empiricism

Despite his deep and abiding faith and his insistence that the ultimate aim of education was salvation, Comenius is at root an empiricist: all human knowledge is ultimately derived from sense experience, there is no innate knowledge. In this he diverges from Plato and Augustine and follows the tradition of Aristotle as mediated through Thomas Aquinas. '*Nihil in intellectu*,' Aquinas wrote, '*quod prius non fuerit in sensu*': there is nothing in the intellect which was not first in the senses. (This was to become the fundamental principle of the British Empiricists, notably John Locke, in the eighteenth century.) Comenius reminds us that Aristotle had 'compared the mind of man to a blank tablet ... on which all things could be engraved' and urges on us the comparison of the brain ('the workshop of thought') to wax which has the capacity to retain the impression of any sensation so that it is then accessible to the memory.[22] The 'intellect takes the material of all its thoughts from the senses', and performs the 'operations of thought' by acting on the 'images of things that are brought before it'.[23] So he anticipates classical empiricism which is characterized by developing universal concepts from repeated sensory experience of various particular things in the material world.

Classrooms

Five measures are necessary 'in order to effect a thorough improvement in schools':[24] books and teaching materials should be held in readiness; the understanding of things should come before the understanding of words; language should be learned through use, not through the study of grammar; knowledge of things should precede knowledge of their combinations; and examples should come before rules.

Comenius' universe is ruled by order: Nature is orderly because Nature has an overall design and purpose which comes from the Creator. Insofar as human affairs are *dis*-orderly it is because they are contrary to the way the world should be managed. So one thing that is necessary to initiate radical educational reform is order, particularly as the basis of curriculum and teaching methodology: the art of teaching requires the skilful arrangement of time, subjects and method. Comenius was particularly fond of the printing press analogy for teaching, yet at first sight it appears to be contrary to his principal reliance on analogies with nature. Is education like cultivation or is it like a mechanical process? Both; it is a mechanical form of cultivation whereby natural processes are maximized by the application of mechanical methods. This is clearly seen in his blueprint for classroom organization.

The organization of education

For centuries, teachers had used a haphazard diversity of methods across a diversity of subjects using diverse texts. Instructional efforts were directed at individuals rather than at classes of scholars. But just as the sun shines on everything indiscriminately and yet to the benefit of all, so each class of scholars should be addressed by one teacher, using one textbook, utilizing the same method of instruction for all in sequential, graduated steps. Using such an approach Comenius is confident that it is 'possible for one teacher to teach several hundred scholars at once'!

This remarkable feat will require appropriate organization. The scholars will be subdivided into groups of ten under the supervision of a senior or advanced pupil. This leader will assist the students in his (or her) division, hear their lessons and inspect their written work. This frees the teacher to concentrate on general didactic instruction and on the general supervision of the conduct and progress of the class as a whole.

Comenius suggests how the teacher will optimize the effect of his teaching by following certain 'rules': being entertaining, exciting interest, remaining visible, using visual aids, repetition, questioning, praising the attentive and correcting errors. He should also, from time to time, randomly test the scholars.[25]

The education system

Comenius proposes four levels of education corresponding to four six-year periods as follows: the Mother School (0–6), the Vernacular School (6–12), the Latin School (12–18) and the University (18–24).

Age	0–6	6–12	12–18	18–24
Description	Infancy	Childhood	Boyhood	Youth
Location	Every home	Every hamlet and village	Every city	Every kingdom and province
Title	Mother School	Vernacular School	Latin School or Gymnasium	University (and travel)

The various levels of schooling are not intended to deal with different subjects but 'graduating the instruction to the age of the pupil and the knowledge he already possesses'.[26] In particular, the Mother School should be primarily concerned with the external senses, the Vernacular School with imagination and memory, the Latin School with understanding and judgement and the University with 'subjects that have special relation to the will'.[27]

The Mother School is the child's home where the infant will receive the first education in all of the important areas of study. Comenius refers to these in rather academicist terms (metaphysics, physics, optics, etc.) but in reality he is merely identifying the kinds of things a child will learn in a well-ordered home: a first education of the senses, observation, memory, language, numeracy, reasoning, music, morals, manners, hygiene, piety, and so forth. He expects nothing that a well-regulated family/household could not provide by way of pre-school preparation for the child. He adds a distinctly modern aid: he wrote a handbook for mothers and a picture book for infants with pictures of the 'most important objects'.[28] *The School of Infancy*, the guide for mothers, identified the kinds of educational experiences they could provide as preparation for the formal curriculum. So, for example, the child would make a beginning in the study of physics by handling things, of optics by learning the names of colours, astronomy by becoming familiar with the phases of the moon and the night sky, etc.

His advice was clear, consistent and insightful. He advocated pre-natal care of the expectant mother. Afterwards she must nurse the child herself and later provide plain and simple food for his physical nourishment, picture books for his intellectual nourishment, and a prayerful environment for his spiritual growth.

The Vernacular School would provide formal elementary education. Each of six standards would have its own classroom and its appropriate class book. The curriculum would include reading, writing, arithmetic, singing, religion, morality, history, cosmography, mechanical arts as well as 'as much economics and politics as is necessary ... to understand what they see daily at home and in the state'.[29] Above all the instruction of the children at this stage should 'ever be combined with amusement'.[30]

The duration of the Latin School or secondary programme would be six years. The curriculum appears daunting, if not downright infeasible. Students should learn four languages as well as the seven liberal arts which had been the common staple of European education since the fourth century.[31] In addition, Comenius would require a knowledge of physics, geography, chronology, history, morality and theology! It is not the aim of the Latin School programme to instil a 'perfect knowledge' of all of the subjects, however, but a knowledge sufficient to benefit from 'any more advanced instruction that the scholars may receive in the future'.[32]

Complete training in any of the sciences or disciplines should be reserved for the University. Entry should be selective, based on academic attainment in a public examination at the conclusion of Latin School. Selected candidates should also be 'diligent and of good moral character'.[33] Those who do not win a place at University 'had better turn their attention to more suitable occupations, such as agriculture, mechanics, or trade'.[34] Students 'of quite exceptional talent' should be encouraged to pursue all of the branches of learning so that there will always be 'some men whose knowledge is encyclopaedic'.[35] In the interests of fairness, the university examinations should be overseen by external examiners appointed by the State or the King.

His end

Comenius was a practical and insightful writer on education and many of his ideas can be found in the practices and structures of practically all modern education systems. Yet his work was virtually ignored after his death and was rediscovered only late in the nineteenth century when the development of universal education had already made significant progress. He was clearly more successful as a prophet than as a reformer. He died in Amsterdam on 4 November 1670.

Comenius was probably the first great internationalist educator: he had a profound faith in the socially (re)formative power of education and in its promise for national and international progress. His writing reveals a prophetic anticipation of many of the issues which would assume importance with the advent of universal education in the nineteenth and twentieth centuries: developmental theories of learning, the danger of excessive verbalism and the notion of learning readiness. His deeply Christian inspiration joined his belief in education to his belief in the possibility of universal peace and harmony. His use of natural metaphors for human growth and learning anticipated the romantic stress on nature. Crucially, he recognized the fundamental role of the family and early childhood experience in determining the subsequent educational success of the child.

But above all he was the first to plan seriously for a universal scheme of education which would recognize the right of everyone, irrespective of gender, class, creed, economic status or culture, to an education which would afford them the opportunity for full personal growth.

Comenius' grand plan for universal education depended upon a number of things that European society of the seventeenth century could not provide: a supply of trained teachers, sufficient schools in each town and village, a means whereby the children of the poor would be enabled to attend, a proper supply of class books and appropriate and effective pedagogical methods.

8   John Locke (1632–1704): Education for the English Gentleman

John Locke was one of the leading philosophers of the seventeenth century. His *Essay Concerning Human Understanding* and his *Two Treatises on Government* were epoch-making books. The former initiated a revolution in our understanding of the workings of the human mind, the latter of the ways in which human society ought to be organized and conducted. The *Two Treatises on Government* had a profound effect on the development of political thinking which led to the American and French revolutions.

His life

Locke attended Westminster School in London before entering Christ Church College, Oxford in 1652. He had little patience with the traditional liberal curriculum and applied his mind to studies of his own choosing, particularly experimental science and medicine. He graduated in 1656 and he was appointed tutor in Christ Church in 1660.

In the summer of 1666 Locke became acquainted with Lord Ashley, later the Earl of Shaftesbury. He joined Ashley's household as family physician. Even at this stage of his career Locke had established a reputation as a scholar and man of learning for by 1668 he had become a Fellow of the Royal Society.   •

Locke spent from 1675 to 1679 in France for health reasons and returned to an England deeply divided on the question of Royal succession. Ashley supported the exclusion of Catholics from the succession, an unpopular and dangerous position since the reigning monarch, James I, was a Catholic. Ashley fled to Holland. Locke prudently followed his patron.

Locke remained in Holland until 1689 when James II had been replaced by the Protestant William of Orange. His *Two Treatises of Government* (1690) were published shortly afterwards. These attempt to demonstrate first that there is no Divine, or absolute, right for Monarchs, and second that Government is a trust to secure the public good. The ruler's authority is conditional and is forfeit if the ruler fails to govern for the good of the subjects. Also published at this time was his *Essay Concerning Human Understanding*. This seminal philosophical work laid the foundations for British Empiricism and provided a contemporary version of the doctrine of the *tabula rasa*. According to this theory the human mind is initially devoid of ideas but is receptive to, and formed by, experience.

Parents and children

Before writing his principal work on education, *Some Thoughts Concerning Education*, in 1693 Locke had written about the family and parental responsibilities in a political context. Seventeenth-century analogies between divine, regal and paternal authority had been used to bolster the notion that kings were above the law and held absolute power over their subjects – the so-called 'Divine Right of Kings'. In his *First Treatise* Locke had argued that any analogy between kings and fathers was illicit. The authority of fathers, he argued, was not unlimited since it extended only until the child was capable of taking adult responsibility.

In the *Second Treatise* Locke tried to give a detailed account of the authority parents actually have over their children.

He rejected the view that the mother's relationship with the child was inferior to the father's. The reality of familial relationships is not the absolute authority of a father but the shared authority of both parents: it is a matter of *parental* rather than *paternal* power since if 'we consult Reason or Revelation, we shall find (the mother) hath an equal title'.[1]

The authority of parents is not absolute but related to the child's need for restraint and education. It is a temporary authority strictly circumscribed by the child's ability to take rational control of his own freedom. Freedom is contingent on reason, and until such time as reason is sufficiently developed God has made it the business of parents to 'govern the Minority of their children'. In other words, it is the business of parents to take care of their children until the latter have developed sufficiently to take care of themselves.

This obligation is neither permanent nor discretionary: parents do not have a choice whether to care for their children or not. Although temporary, the care and education of children, Locke asserts, 'is a charge so incumbent on parents for their children's good, that nothing can absolve them from taking care of it'.[2]

The principle of equality set out in the *Second Treatise* (in a state of nature all men are born free and equal) cannot be extended to children since children 'are not born in their full state of equality, though they are born *to* it'.[3] In other words, childhood is a developmental process which requires parents to assume *temporary* 'rule and jurisdiction' over the child.

Childhood is an imperfect state: the child has the *capacity* for knowledge and reason but these capacities have not yet been developed. Childhood ends when children arrive at the state of knowledge and reason required to exercise control over their own affairs when, that is, they acquire reason or knowledge sufficient to understanding the rule of nature or the civil law by reference to which they can govern themselves.

The conventional time for the transfer of responsibility is the age of majority, which in Locke's time was 21. Until then the law allows children to have no will of their own: they are subject to the will and understanding of their parents. As an exception to the general rule of freedom children join the company of Lunatics, Idiots and Madmen.[4]

Thoughts concerning education

Compared to his philosophical and political works, Locke's *Some Thoughts Concerning Education* (1693) is relatively lightweight. His experience of teaching was not extensive: he was not a teacher either by experience or inclination. He had spent four years as lecturer in Greek at Christ Church, Oxford. As well as family physician Shaftesbury had used him as tutor and educational advisor to his son and, later, grandson.

Some Thoughts Concerning Education was written when Locke was in exile in Holland. Letters to his friend Edward Clarke had included advice on the rearing of Clarke's son. Locke justified its publication on the grounds that it may assist those 'that dare venture to consult their own reason in the education of their children rather than wholly rely upon old custom'.[5]

It is every man's duty to do all that he can to advance the welfare of his country and, Locke tells us: 'The well educating of their children is so much the duty and concern of parents, and the welfare and prosperity of the nation so much depends on it, that I would have every one lay it seriously to heart.'[6] His conviction, deeply rooted in the social hierarchy of his time and place, is that if the 'sons of Gentlemen' are properly educated society in general will flourish: 'For if those of that rank are by their education once set right, they will quickly bring all the rest into order.'[7]

Although *Some Thoughts Concerning Education* was focused primarily on the education of a boy, Locke anticipates the objection that he neglects girls:

> (T)he principal aim of my discourse is how a young gentleman should be brought up from his infancy, which in all things will not so perfectly suit the education of daughters though where the difference of sex requires different treatment, 'twill be no hard matter to distinguish.[8]

Locke appears to be ambivalent regarding the power of education to shape the individual. On the one hand he declares that, 'the difference to be found in the manners and abilities of men is owing more to their education than to anything else'.[9] Yet elsewhere he appears to qualify this view substantially. He acknowledges that it is the nature of the individual – what we might now call his genetic makeup – which is decisive: 'God,' he tells us, 'has stamp'd certain characters on men's minds which, like their shapes, may be a little mended, but can hardly be totally alter'd and transform'd into the contrary'.[10]

Strangely, as the promoter of the image of the newborn mind as a *tabula rasa*, Locke considers that children manifest individual differences even prior to the influence of experience. He refers to 'the natural make of (the boy's) mind' and declares that 'there are not more differences in men's faces, and the outward lineaments of their bodies, than there are in the makes and tempers of their minds'.[11] So the 'tabula' is, apparently, not entirely 'rasa' at all!

Locke's approach to education is vocational, i.e. utilitarian and pragmatic. The education of a young gentleman should reflect the station in life for which he was destined. In order that the education be appropriate it should first be determined what course of life the boy is destined for so that he will learn what will be of most frequent use to him in his life's career. The education is vocational in a very narrow sense: Locke's concern was with the education of members of a particular class – those who will be landowners, politicians, clerics, administrators or officers, in short, English gentlemen.

It is surprising that such a well-connected intellectual as Locke appears to have been ignorant of, or at least indifferent to, the work of Comenius whose *The Great Didactic* and pansophist proposals were widely known among the newly emerging scientific community. On the contrary, Locke's recommendations for Working Schools[12] do not reflect any great regard or concern for the rights of the children of the poor: the recommendations include indentured slavery until the age of 23!

Virtue

Locke himself had not been very happy at Westminster school and argued that the education of a young gentleman should be undertaken at home, 'in his father's sight under a good governor' rather than in a public school.[13] Virtue, 'the great and main end of education',[14] is the key; everything else is secondary. Not the least important of Locke's reasons for favouring education at home rather than at boarding school is that the virtuous formation of the boy is more likely under the supervision of his father, in his own home, rather than in the company of unformed youngsters like himself. Locke's opinion of the companions that the boy would be likely to meet in a boarding school is low. Indeed his opinion of the moral climate of his time is dire: 'the early corruption of youth is now become so general a complaint'.[15] If a young gentleman is sent away to school, Locke asked, how is he to be protected from 'the contagion of rudeness and vice, which is every where so in fashion?' Since 'virtue is harder to be got than a knowledge of the world; and if lost in a young man, is seldom recover'd' it is better to protect his innocence until he has developed sufficient self-confidence to face the world with assurance. 'Sheepishness and ignorance of the world, the faults imputed to a private education, are neither the necessary consequences of being bred at home, nor if they were, are they incurable evils. Vice is the more stubborn ...'[16] However the home-based alternative is not without risk since it throws the child into contact with 'the folly and perverseness' as well as 'the ill examples' which they will meet 'amongst the meaner servants'![17]

Virtue should be 'the great and main end of education' so tutors should place it at the centre of their instruction. The desired result is not just that the young man should know about virtue but that he should develop 'a true relish of it, and (place) his strength, his glory and his pleasure in it'.[18]

How this is to be done is a central concern of *Some Thoughts Concerning Education*.

Physical health

The boy's physical well-being is the first concern of the *Some Thoughts Concerning Education*. The very first sentence declares the interdependence of physical and mental flourishing: 'A sound mind in a sound body is a short but full description of a happy state in this world. He that hath these two, has little more to wish for; and he that wants either of them, will be but little the better for anything else.'[19]

Locke's method of cultivating this 'sound body' is partly based on his observation that the children of the poor become physically hardened through exposure to the elements. (His interest in empirical science might have prompted him to comment on the relative mortality rates of the poor at the time.[20]) His recipe for a healthy boyhood is almost ascetic: 'plenty of open air, exercise and sleep' together with a plain diet which will include neither wine nor other 'strong drink'. Boys should be given little or no physic (medicine); their clothing should be 'not too warm' or too tight. To the modern sensibility one recommendation is strange if not bizarre: his head and feet should be kept cold, and, in particular, his feet should be accustomed to cold water and 'exposed to wet'.[21] His shoes should be 'so thin, that they might leak and let in water, whenever he comes near it'. To be doubly sure of this 'have his shoes made so as to leak water'![22]

Reason

Reason does not play a very significant part in his proposals: for Locke is fundamentally committed to a rather authoritarian relationship between fathers and sons, a relationship which relies on the greater power of the former to command the submission of the latter in an attitude of 'respect and reverence'.[23]

At some points Locke appears to consider a gradualist, developmental approach to reason: 'age and reason as they grow up loosen (the bonds of the parental subjection) till at length they drop quite off, and leave a man at his own free disposal'.[24] He advocates reasoning with children in a manner 'suited to the child's capacity and apprehension'. Arguing with a child as one would with an adult serves only to confuse, not instruct. What he *is* advocating is that the treatment of children should be reasonable so that they understand that adult intervention is 'useful and necessary for them; and that it is not out of *caprichio*, passion or fancy' that the adult commands or forbids.[25]

In the last analysis, however, Locke is more concerned that the child should behave properly than that he should necessarily understand the reasons for his behaviour: 'what he is to receive from education,' he warns, 'what is to sway and influence his life, must be ... habits woven into the very principles of his nature'.[26]

In general, Locke's attitude is well summed up when he writes: '(Children) should be brought to deny their appetites; and their minds, as well as bodies, be made vigorous, easy, and strong, by the custom of having their inclinations in subjection, and their bodies exercised with hardships: but all this, without giving them any mark or apprehension of ill-will towards them'.[27]

Book learning and method

Book learning comes a close second to virtue in Locke's educational priorities. The main concern of the son of a gentleman will be service to his country. So together with moral and political knowledge he will require a knowledge of law and history.

The secret of successful teaching is orderly method. This is not just a call for methodical pedagogy but the need for the pupil to acquire method in his life and learning: his tutor 'should take pains to ... accustom him to order, and teach him method in all the applications of his thoughts'.[28]

In general Locke's approach is open and humane but his admonitions tend to be rather short on detail. It is as if he knew what was needful but did not quite know the practical requirements as to how it might be accomplished. He declares approvingly:

He that hath found a way how to keep up a child's spirit easy, active and free, and yet at the same time to restrain him from many things he has a mind to, and to draw him to things that are uneasy to him; he, I say, that knows how to reconcile these seeming contradictions, has, in my opinion, got the true secret of education.[29]

Indeed. This is as useful as advising athletes to cross the finishing line before everyone else. It is one thing to know what needs to be done, quite another to discover and practise the means of doing it. Locke realizes, for example, that children are more likely to learn what is enjoyable and so he endorses a playful approach to learning: 'anything children should be taught,' he tells us, 'might be made as much a recreation to their play as their play is to their learning'.[30] But *how* are we to make entertaining the drudgery of much of learning?

Effectiveness in teaching and learning depends on the capacity of the learner to stick to the task. Tutors should try to make all the child's tasks as 'grateful and agreeable as possible' or at the very least avoid associating them with what is disagreeable. To this end Locke advocates close observation of the child and his 'changes of temper'. 'Favourable seasons of aptitude and inclination' should be noted and used to the advantage of their learning. What is to be learned must be represented to the scholar in positive terms. A tutor who has taken the trouble to know his pupil's mind will be able to 'fill his head with suitable ideas, such as may make him in love with the present business'.[31]

Locke recognizes that the best efforts of the tutor will be limited both by the native capacities of the individual child as well as by the general tendencies of children. His advice is to accentuate the positive:

> In many cases all that we can do, or should aim at, is to make the best of what nature has given, to prevent the vices and faults to which such a constitution is most inclined, and give it all the advantages it is capable of. Everyone's natural genius should be carried as far as it could ...[32]

This recognition of the limitations imposed by the capacity of the individual learner is an important part of Locke's approach. One of the significant advantages of promoting a private rather than a public education is the need it imposes on the teacher to take account of the ability and interests of the individual pupil.

Whatever the specific pedagogical methods, however, the pupil should realize that his tutor acts out of love and only in pursuit of the good for the child.

Discipline

Locke does not evince any principled objection to beating children although he frequently expresses respect for the humanity of the child. While his attitudes to discipline and punishment are enlightened they are based on utility rather than humaneness. His main objection is that any form of physical punishment will be counterproductive. 'Beating,' he writes, 'and all other sorts of slavish and corporal punishments, are not the discipline fit to be used in the education of those we would have wise, good, and ingenuous men'. Such discipline should be used 'only in great occasions, and cases of extremity'[33] when all other forms of encouragement and inducement have been tried and have failed.

Like others before him he sees this kind of punishment as a sign of the failure of the tutor to motivate or inspire the learner. As 'the most unfit of any (form of chastisement) ... (it) naturally breeds an aversion to that which 'tis the tutor's business to create a liking to'.[34]

His ideas on corporal punishment were not entirely consistent, however. It appears that his recipe for the education of the young gentleman in question, Master Clarke, was not entirely successful. In one of his letters to Clarke Senior he suggests that the boy might be sent to Westminster (Locke's old school) 'or some other very severe school, where if he were whipped soundly while you are looking out another fit tutor for him, he would perhaps be more pliant and willing to learn at home afterwards'.[35] This advice is not recorded in *Some Thoughts Concerning Education*.

Curriculum

Reading and writing are central in the curriculum of the young gentleman. Locke cautions against too much pressure to accomplish literacy: what is pleasantly experienced is more likely to appeal and more likely to be learned. It is more important that reading be learned properly than that it be learned by a particular age: 'cheat him into (learning to read) if you can,' he advises, 'but make it not a business. 'Tis better it be a year later before he can read than that he should get an aversion to learning'.[36]

Although not opposed to the learning of foreign languages Locke stresses that the child's first, native language should have priority. It is his own language that he should 'critically study and labour to get a facility, clearness and elegancy to express himself in'.[37] While the young gentleman will also receive instruction in French and Latin, these studies should not interfere with his learning of English for English is the language which he will use constantly in all of his affairs.

When French and Latin *are* studied they are to be studied not for the sake of scholarship but for their utility. They should be taught by the direct method, not through the study of grammar. The class of men he is writing about (the gentry) will use foreign languages for the purpose of communication, for which purpose 'the original way of learning a language by conversation ... is to be preferred as the most expedite, proper and natural'.[38] This enlightened view challenged the orthodoxy of teaching language at the time by means of grammatical rules and the study of texts. It is only relatively recently that the educational establishment has adopted Locke's views in this matter with any conviction.

Practical accomplishments

Despite the fact that he is legislating for the education of a man of property, Locke advises that the boy should be taught at least one manual trade. Locke favoured gardening, husbandry and 'working in wood as a carpenter, joiner or turner'. Such occupations are desirable 'fit and healthy recreations for a man of study or business'.[39] Even if the parents 'frighted with the disgraceful names of mechanick and trade' are reluctant to allow their son to engage in manual activities one thing relating to trade 'they will think absolutely necessary': the ability to keep accounts. As a man of property the pupil will need to be able to deal with merchants' accounts, and should not think 'it is a skill that belongs not to them, because it has received its name from, and has been chiefly practised by men of traffic'.[40]

Conclusion

The most surprising thing about Locke's views on education is that the *Thoughts* reflects little of the empiricist theory of knowledge developed in such detail in the *Essay Concerning Human*

Understanding. We are given no insight regarding how alternative forms of instruction, experience or learning activities might affect the formation of the mind. Indeed, the *Thoughts* could have been written by a man who has never read the *Essay*! In general, the efficacy of instruction is judged on the utility of the learning. Nonetheless the *Thoughts* does reveal an intuitive grasp of psychology and the long-term effects of various experiences on the development of the young.

Locke's reputation rests almost entirely on his philosophical work which undoubtedly sets him among the first rank of philosophical thinkers. In comparison, the *Thoughts* is relatively slight and lightweight. Although it contains some humane insights into the problems of educating boys it does not seriously challenge the educational practices of the time or develop what had gone before, especially the pioneering work of Locke's contemporary, Comenius. If Locke had written nothing else the *Thoughts* would probably not be remembered today except as, perhaps, a footnote to the history of educational ideas. But because the *Thoughts* was written by the author of the *Essay* and of the *Two Treatises* it has been taken seriously, perhaps more seriously than it deserves.

9   Jean-Jacques Rousseau (1712–1778): The Education of Nature

The man who invented childhood as we understand it today was himself effectively abandoned as a child; he abandoned his own five children in turn to a foundling hospital; he didn't marry their mother until he had lived with her for 40 years; he had a preference for masochistic sexual experiences; he suffered all his life from a bladder complaint which made him irascible and quarrelsome; he became a convert to Catholicism because of a woman's influence only to recant later in life; and he was irredeemably paranoid. Jean-Jacques Rousseau was not the kind of individual to endear himself to advocates of family sanctity. But he set in motion a movement which immeasurably improved the condition of children and the quality of their lives and education for centuries.

His life

Born in the Republic of Geneva in 1712, Rousseau's mother died shortly after his birth and he was brought up by his father. His early childhood was happy. 'No royal child,' he wrote, 'could be more scrupulously cared for than I was in my early years ... always treated as a beloved son.'[1] When he was eight however, he was sent to board with a tutor 'to learn Latin and all that sorry nonsense that goes by the name of education'.[2]

At 16 Rousseau deserted Geneva to seek his fortune. At Savoy in France he came under the influence of his first benefactress, Baronne de Warens. She provided him with a home and employment. More significantly she encouraged him in his efforts to educate himself in letters, philosophy and music.

From 1742 in Paris he became acquainted with leading figures of Parisian scientific and cultural life, including Denis Diderot who commissioned him to provide entries on music for the French *Encyclopédie*. In 1750 Rousseau's *A Discourse on the Sciences and the Arts* won a prize from the Academy of Dijon. The essay foreshadowed his principal philosophical preoccupations: human history as a story of degeneration from a prior state of innocence. His opera, *Le Devin du Village* (*The Village Soothsayer*, 1752) won acclaim from the fashionable and, more importantly, from the French Court.

During his early years in Paris Rousseau met Thérèse Lavasseur who became his life-long companion, the mother of his five children and eventually his wife. It is conventionally charged against Rousseau that, despite his expressed concern for the reality of childhood, he had five children with Thérèse and that, contrary to her wishes, he abandoned all of them to foundling hospitals to be looked after at public expense. He made no effort to conceal the matter but whether his justification and self-exculpation in the *Confessions* are persuasive is a matter of opinion.[3]

In 1755 Rousseau left Paris and moved to nearby Montmorency. Here, in a remarkable burst of creative genius, he produced the works by which he is best known: a novel, *Julie or The New Heloise* (1761) which proved to be his most popular and commercially successful work, *The Social Contract* (1762) his most influential political work and *Émile* (1762) probably the most influential European book on education since Plato's *The Republic*. As a result of widespread outrage at the unorthodox religious ideas presented in Book IV of *Émile* (the 'Profession of Faith of the Savoyard Vicar'),[4] Rousseau fled France and until 1770 he lived as a semi-fugitive. Eventually he returned to France under pardon and died there on July 2, 1778.

Society and nature

Émile describes the upbringing of a boy from infancy to adulthood and proposes well developed theoretical principles of education and nurturing. Rousseau had clearly read Locke's *Some Thoughts Concerning Education* and in a sense *Émile* is a response to Locke's book: it contains several direct references to Locke, not all of them negative.

In his theory of the social contract Rousseau had tried to balance the natural freedom of the individual with the need for the constraints of social organization. The contract involves a trade-off of natural liberty for civil liberty and the exchange of the rule of might (in the state of nature) for the rule of law (in society). This is why *Émile* begins with the declaration: 'Everything is good as it leaves the hands of the Author of things; everything degenerates in the hands of man.' Man ruthlessly subordinates nature to his will. 'He mutilates his dog, his horse, and his slave,' Rousseau writes, 'he turns everything upside down; he disfigures everything; he loves deformity, monsters.' Man wishes everything natural, including human nature, to be 'fashioned in keeping with his fancy like a tree in his garden'.[5] It is society, not nature, which is the source of corruption in the world.

Everything is good in its natural state and children, contrary to the doctrine of original sin, are born naturally good. As a creature of nature, the child should live in accordance with his nature rather than strive against it. So the purpose of education is not to ameliorate the perceived ill-effects of original sin (defective under-standing, egotistical wilfulness and an inclination to evil) but to enable the child to live his life to the fullest. For Rousseau it is a fundamental axiom 'that the first movements of nature are always right'.[6]

Émile

Émile addresses the problem of how to reconcile the conflicting aims of education: the natural development of the child (spon-taneity, imagination, initiative) with preparation for life in society (submission, conformity, obedience). This conflict translates into a choice between 'making a man or a citizen': in Rousseau's view we cannot make both simultaneously. The aims are in conflict for they refer to two opposing forms of education: the individual (natural) and the social (civic) respectively. Rousseau opts for the former as having priority: the development of the natural man is the theme of *Émile*.

Émile is a novel which contains a treatise on education: it has been said that it is enough of a treatise to spoil it as a novel and enough of a novel to spoil it as a treatise. It is easy to confuse the purely romantic or literary aspects of the story with the educational aspects. For example, it is often objected that the proposal to assign one tutor to one pupil is naïve and impractical; and so it would

TOURO COLLEGE LIBRARY

be if it were a serious proposal; but it is not. It is simply a literary device which allows for the elaboration of the educational ideas. Indeed, Rousseau cautions us not to take his prescriptions too uncritically.

Education

Rousseau distinguishes three kinds of education, the education of nature, of things and of men. The growth of our organs and faculties is the education of nature; what we learn from our experience of our physical surroundings is the education of things; the use we learn to make of this growth and experience is the education of men, human culture.

A small infant playing with wooden blocks manifests all three. The child is developing willy-nilly and learning to control her body, balance, hand–eye coordination, and so forth. This is the education of nature. At the same time she is learning the properties of the blocks, their texture, qualities, effects, relations with other objects, etc. This is the education of things. While we can, to some extent, direct her play with the blocks, we cannot change the nature of the blocks: things are what they are and she must learn to accommodate to them. Each side of each block has a picture, number or letter printed on it. As the child plays she is becoming familiar with conventional forms of pictorial and symbolic representation. This is the beginning of the education of man, the initiation into human culture.

For Rousseau nature is quite beyond human control since we cannot intervene in the natural development of the individual without disfiguring or deforming. The education of things is only partly within our control since we can only partially control the characteristics of the world our children inhabit. We can, for instance, protect them from dangerous objects or substances but we cannot rid the world of such. Sooner or later the individual will have to come to terms with them.

One corollary of engaging with the world of physical objects is that the consequences of our actions are felt immediately. This is not a moral consequence, it is a natural consequence: if we fall into water we get wet. This gives rise to the *discipline of natural consequences*. Rousseau insists that Émile should never be subject to moral sanctions but simply left to suffer the natural consequences of his own actions.

The only education which we can control is the education of man, the initiation of the child into human culture. But even here, he warns, 'our power is largely illusory, for who can hope to direct every word and action of all those who surround a child?' The central priority of the educator is to harmonize the three forms of education as far as possible: this means necessarily following the imperatives of the one that is most beyond our control, the education of nature.[7]

Rights

Émile's education must begin with the understanding of his rights, not his duties. The first feelings of the child are centred on himself. All of his initial instincts are directed towards his self-preservation and his well-being. In modern terms he is egocentric. It follows that his first notion of justice springs from what he believes himself entitled to from others. One of the errors of 'ordinary education' is the attempt to direct children's attention to their duties, stressing obedience and submission. This is the opposite of what is required. What children understand and what interests them are their own rights. Duties to others will follow.[8]

Infancy

In the first book of *Émile* (on the treatment of infants) Rousseau addresses himself directly to mothers, 'this first education belongs incontestably to women'. He is highly critical of the contemporary practice of swaddling rather than allowing babies the natural movement of their limbs. The fundamental natural human impulse is to activity, both physical and mental. Rousseau also condemned the practice of sending infants out to wet-nurses with whom they could have no natural bond of affection: the separation deprived them of the invaluable moral formation which bonding with their mothers provides.

Given the psychological knowledge of the time, Rousseau's insights are remarkable. He points out the importance of stimulation of the senses, the power of habit, the need to avoid phobias and irrational fears, the need for unimpeded movement, and the significance of crying as the child's first communication. His comments comprise a fund of sound advice to mothers based on good sense and close observation.

His most trenchant criticism is reserved for fathers, and, given his own history as a father, it is worth quoting at length:

> A father, when he engenders and feeds children, does with that only a third of his task. He owes to his species men; he owes to society sociable men; he owes to the state citizens. Every man who can pay this triple debt and does not do so is culpable, and more culpable perhaps when he pays it halfway. He who cannot fulfil the duties of a father has no right to become one.[9]

Is there a note of regret here? A trace of self-accusation?

In any case the practical reality is that for many reasons fathers must entrust the education of their children to another, ideally a friend but, more realistically, someone especially prepared for the task, a professional tutor.

Childhood

In the second book of *Émile* Rousseau settles to the task of Émile's education now that he is no longer an infant animal (in that his responses are instinctive and unreflective) but a human boy.

Rousseau's main approach is one of non-interference, what might even look to modern eyes like indifference. 'Far from being attentive to protecting Émile from injury, I would be most distressed if he were never hurt and grew up without knowing pain. To suffer is the first thing he ought to learn and the thing he will most need to know.'[10] This apparently unfeeling view is qualified later when he advises against either severity or indulgence. A balance must be struck between a negligence which threatens well-being and a concern which suffocates the child's opportunity to engage meaningfully with the world, a necessary submission to the education of things a necessary preparation for the travail of life. Over-protecting children prepares 'great miseries for them: you make them delicate, sensitive' and removes them from the real world to which they must return one day.[11]

During his boyhood Émile must be considered a child. In *Julie or the New Heloise* Julie had reflected over her first child as follows:

> The first time that I held my eldest son in my arms, I reflected that childhood is almost a quarter of a long life and that one rarely attains the other three-quarters; and that it is a cruel caution that makes this first part unhappy to ensure happiness in the rest which will never come, perhaps.[12]

This is as good a summary of Rousseau's attitude to childhood as one could find: life is uncertain, so the child should be permitted to enjoy as fully as possible whatever allowance of life and freedom he has.

Rousseau repeats this sentiment in *Émile*: childhood is not simply a preparation for adulthood, it is a state of being with an intrinsic value. We should deprecate any education which suppresses the child's natural inclinations in the present for a future which he may not live to see. It is 'false wisdom' to subordinate the immediacy of the child's life in the present to an uncertain future. On the contrary we should celebrate childhood:

> Love childhood; promote its games, its pleasures, its amiable instincts … Why fill with bitterness and sorrow those early years passing so quickly? … The man must be considered in the man and the child in the child.[13]

Happiness, freedom, needs and books

Happiness is the aim of education. Negatively defined, unhappiness is the excess of desire over power: we are unhappy when we want more than we can get. We are happy when we desire only what we can have. The man who 'wants only what he can do and does what he pleases' is truly free. This Rousseau calls his 'fundamental maxim'. 'It need only be applied to childhood,' he concludes, 'for all the rules of education flow from it'.[14] The education of the child should proceed from the needs of the child, from the child's natural propensity or inclination, the prerequisites of normal development, and not from anything else. If education follows the needs of the child, if the focus is on what is within the child's capacity to attain, there will be no need for compulsion.

Rousseau anticipated many of the discoveries of twentieth-century developmental psychology. He recognized that the sensations, perceptions and emotions of children are not the same as those of adults: childhood has its own ways of seeing, thinking and feeling. It is foolish to try to impose adult ways on children because they are simply not capable of thinking, seeing or feeling in an adult way.

The function of reason is to control strength. Since a child has little strength he has little need for reason: reason is 'the bridle of strength, and the child does not need this bridle'.[15] So Rousseau dismisses the notion that one should reason with children in childhood. Reason is the product, not the means, of education; it is the 'masterpiece of a good education'. To attempt to raise a child by reason 'is to begin with the end, to want to make the product the instrument'.[16] If children could appreciate reason they would not need to be educated at all!

Rousseau does not mean that Émile does not possess powers of reasoning or will never, in his childhood, be required to use such powers. Obviously, any time he makes deductions, constructs chains of cause and effect, or relates behaviour to its consequences, Émile will have to exercise his capacity to reason and it will improve with exercise. What Rousseau wishes to avoid is the reasonableness which Locke advocated when directing the behaviour of children. We should never, Rousseau advises, explain ourselves to children or justify our decisions to them (withholding or granting permission for instance). The child should come to regard the decisions of the adult as as inflexible as the natural order, for what the child understands at this stage – the stage of boyhood – *is* the force of nature. Adults should, like nature, be firm, consistent and totally impervious to argument or pleading in their dealings with children.

> What you grant him, grant at his first word, without solicitations, without prayers – above all without conditions. Grant with pleasure, refuse only with repugnance. But let all your refusals be irrevocable ... Let 'No', once pronounced, be a wall of bronze against which the child will have to exhaust his strength at most five or six times in order to abandon any further attempts to overturn it.[17]

The adult should be loving, but consistently strict and unyielding.

Pedagogy

Rousseau's principal pedagogical innovation was the virtual abandonment of formal, verbal instruction. Boyhood is not the time for instructive discourses, it is the time when the child learns from experience and observation: 'Do not give your pupil any kind of verbal lessons; he ought to receive them only from experience.'[18] Émile learns about the world because he engages meaningfully and intelligently with the world. The priority is engagement with the world of things. Rousseau's view is empiricist: 'everything that enters into the human understanding comes there through the senses,' he writes, 'man's first reason is a reason of the senses ... our first masters of philosophy are our feet, our hands, our eyes.' Intellectual reason follows.[19]

Virtue too becomes known through experience. We must not attempt to impose concepts such as truth, honesty, piety, etc. Virtue is taught by example, never by precept; education regarding the moral world, like education regarding the physical world, is not a matter of learning verbal formulae: example is the key. Preaching and moralizing are pointless, if not actually counter-productive. Rousseau advises teachers to: 'leave off pretences. Be virtuous and good. Let your examples be graven in your pupils' memories until they can enter their hearts.'[20]

If verbal instruction is to be downgraded then its principal medium, the book, must also lose its pre-eminence in the education of the young. Rousseau makes no apology for this demotion: 'To substitute books for all that (experience) is not to teach us to reason. It is to teach us to use the reason of others ... to believe much and never to know anything.'[21] Books will have little part to play in Émile's boyhood: 'At twelve he will hardly know what a book is.' Rousseau denounces reading instruction as 'the plague of childhood' and books as 'the instruments of children's greatest misery'.[22] He does not deny that the young Émile must learn to read, but his reading should be based on need, not on the conventional belief that it is a necessary prerequisite to education.

The best method of teaching reading is not the clutter of paraphernalia which has turned children's nurseries into printing shops, rather it is the 'desire to learn', motivation. Once the child has acquired the desire to learn to read 'any method will be good for him'.[23] Émile's reading at this stage will be based on simple messages which concern himself (invitations and the like). Books will play no part.

At the age of 12 Émile has attained the limit of boyhood. From now on he is growing towards adulthood. Rousseau's description of Émile (the ideal child) at this stage is rhapsodic. By now he is rich in experience, understands nature, thinks and judges clearly, talks only of what he understands and is proficient in practical activities. He is indifferent to habit, routine, custom, rules and authority. He follows his own preferences and submits only to necessity. He does not distinguish between work and play. 'His games are his business, and he is aware of no difference.'[24] He 'has come to the maturity of childhood. He has lived a child's life. He has not purchased his perfection at the expense of his happiness.'[25]

Pre-adolescence

The third stage of development, 'the third stage of childhood', is the period from 12 to 15. Rousseau continues to call it childhood: for 'this age approaches adolescence without yet being that of puberty'.[26] This is the time for labour, instruction and study, but it is not directed towards any narrow vocational objective. Rousseau's aim is broad but simple, 'living is the job I want to teach him'.[27]

Now moral education begins. Up to now the stress has been on necessity, Émile had to learn to accommodate himself to the material world. Now he must begin to understand the cultural world and to learn what is useful and how to survive. 'We shall soon,' Rousseau promises, 'get to what is suitable and good.'[28]

This is the age of curiosity; Émile's curiosity is met, not by didactic lessons, but by appropriate problems. Rousseau is the earliest advocate of the so-called heuristic method, learning by discovery. This is not a haphazard or arbitrary process; it requires Émile's exposure to the right experience and a motivating question. The problems that he addresses should be proportionate to his capacity which should be known to his tutor. 'Put the questions within his reach and leave them to him to resolve.' Émile should know what he knows because he has discovered it for himself: he should 'not learn science but discover it'.[29] He will not be taught the sciences but he should acquire a taste for them, and 'methods for learning them when this taste is better developed'. This is 'a fundamental principle of every good education'.[30]

The study of the sciences is aided by equipment made by Émile himself. This underscores learning manual crafts in a natural way, hand-in-hand with the development of scientific curiosity and thought.

Books

Again at this stage Rousseau is unequivocal in his attitude to books and to book learning: 'I hate books,' he declares in the shortest, and most surprising, sentence in *Émile*. 'They only teach one to talk about what one does not know'. But there is one exception, a book which 'provides the most felicitous treatise on natural education'. The first book Émile will read will 'for a long time ... compose his whole library'.[31] The book which Rousseau endorses with such enthusiasm is *Robinson Crusoe*, a manual of independence, survival and self-sufficiency.

Although Rousseau goes on to delineate Émile's education up to his marriage, his historic contribution has been to the way we treat, rear and educate our children up to the end of childhood. He was the first to take childhood seriously, and in many ways civilization is still in the process of catching up with his vision of the child – in school, in society and in the home.

Although he is associated with the pre-revolutionary sentiment in France and its associated egalitarian principles, Rousseau's reflections on education do not contain any proposals for universality. The universalist dream of Comenius has disappeared. Unlike Comenius, Rousseau, like Locke, was concerned only with the education of a particular class, the gentry. Rousseau is quite unequivocal about this. 'The poor man,' he declares, 'does not need to be educated. His station gives him a compulsory education. He could have no other.'[32] While the poor man learns what he needs to know through the exigencies of his life the rich man learns nothing of value either to himself or to his society without the kind of education that Rousseau proposes. Rousseau's position in this regard is evident in the *Considerations on the Government of Poland* where he makes it clear that the only 'poor' which concern him are 'the poorer nobility', the 'children of poor gentlemen'.[33] The truly poor must await other champions.

10 Jean Heinrich Pestalozzi (1746–1827): The Education of the People

In the film *The Third Man* the cynical Harry Lime referred contemptuously to Switzerland: 'In Switzerland,' he said, 'they had brotherly love, five hundred years of democracy and peace, and what did they produce? The cuckoo clock!'

The narrator, Holly Martens, might have replied that they also produced two of the most influential educational thinkers in European history: Jean-Jacques Rousseau and Jean Heinrich Pestalozzi. As well as being a compatriot, Pestalozzi is Rousseau's true educational successor: he spent his entire adult life trying to implement the educational principles set out in *Émile*, not for the sons of gentlemen but for the truly poor.

Background

Pestalozzi came of a Protestant family of Italian origin. Despite his father's early death he appears to have had a happy childhood. His mother had a deep and lasting influence on his thinking in relation to child rearing and education.

In his early life Pestalozzi was a political activist and was, for a short time in 1767, imprisoned for his political activities. This experience helped form the idea of an indissoluble relationship between education and political life. In the eighteenth century, despite the rhetoric of Swiss democracy, ordinary people living outside of the major cities were little more than serfs. The only education available to them was primitive and unenlightened. Pestalozzi believed that education was the key to fitting the individual for his place in society and for an active role as a member of a democratic political community.

The birth of his only child (significantly christened 'Jean-Jacques') provided him with his first experience of the theory and practice of education. He attempted unsuccessfully to implement the doctrines of Rousseau in Jean-Jacques' education. He was unable to reconcile freedom and restraint, the innate desires of the individual with the need for social cohesion and conformity. (Jean-Jacques' moral and physical debility may well have been constitutional rather than induced by a misguided application of Rousseauist principles. He was delicate in health all of his life as well as being epileptic. He died at the age of 31.)

His son's development reinforced Pestalozzi's Rousseauist belief that learning begins with experience and observation and that words come later: words are learned through things, not vice versa. He also accepted that the child's life, at least in its early stages, should be happy and free from undue restraint and punishment. Attempting to force the pace of experience or learning can only do harm to the natural progression in the development of the child.

Education

Experience had led Pestalozzi to the conviction that instruction is nothing more than aiding the process of human development. This can only be accomplished, however, when we understand the 'eternal laws by which the human mind is raised from physical impressions on the senses to clear ideas'.[1] The secret of effective instruction is to ensure that what is being taught harmonizes with the powers of the child at any given time. This requires an organized sequence of instruction which is adapted to the development of the child's capacities. This continues Rousseau's formal break with the pedagogical tradition of following the logic of the subject matter and replacing it with the psychology of the learner.

Pestalozzi felt that Rousseau had taken the liberty of the child too far for the child's good. The development of the child's self-control should be a priority from the first through engagement in tasks of appropriate difficulty. Liberty and submission need not be mutually contradictory: indeed liberty can be beneficial only within constraints. 'Liberty is a good thing, and obedience is equally so. We should re-unite what Rousseau has separated.'[2]

The Neuhof Experiment

Pestalozzi was, first and foremost, a practitioner. His first public educational enterprise occurred in 1774 when he and his wife Anna took poor children into their home at Neuhof. They intended to give the children the rudiments of an education, the experience of a secure family life, and the basis of a vocational skill: spinning, weaving and farming methods for boys, household skills for girls. The enterprise was initially successful: at its peak it catered for about 50 boys and girls between the ages of 6 and 18.

The intention was that the small community would be economically self-sufficient and, at the same time, provide the children with the opportunity to pursue their own full human development. The produce of the enterprise would pay for the children's education and training, while the children would retain their natural autonomy by subscribing to their education and training with the produce of their own labour.

It soon became apparent that there was an irreconcilable tension between the requirement of profitability (social participation and economic independence) and the purely educational objectives (personal development and autonomy) of the scheme. Pestalozzi had tried to meet the demands of simultaneously making a man and making a citizen by giving his pupils social freedom, through the mastery of a trade, and striving to promote their individual self-fulfilment. Another factor contributing to the failure of the Neuhof initiative was Pestalozzi's incorrigible ineptitude in practical business affairs. He seriously over-reached his capacity to manage the business and allowed his enthusiasm to over-rule practical caution. One added practical difficulty was that frequently, as soon as children became proficient and profitable producers, parents or other relatives took them away, depriving the initiative of the profit that it needed to remain viable.

When the experiment came to an end in 1779 it had ruined the Pestalozzis financially and undermined their health irretrievably: only the generosity of friends saved the roof over their heads. However the experience was not a total loss. It enabled Pestalozzi to develop his educational ideas and provided the experiential background for his first educational work *Leonard and Gertrude: A Book for the People* (1780). The book was a huge success nationally and internationally.

Leonard and Gertrude

Like *Émile*, *Leonard and Gertrude* is a work of narrative fiction. It describes how the example of one family can regenerate a community. In the fictitious village of Bonnal the home of Leonard, the village mason, becomes the model educational institution. Gertrude, the mother, becomes the ideal educator. The basic message is that the best education is a continuation and a development of a good working-class home. The individual and the group are indissolubly bound and one cannot prosper at the expense of the other. The life of the family is the life of the wider community in microcosm: the educative work of the family must be continued in the wider society supported by appropriate social legislation to bring about social cohesion, reform and improvement.

The mother is the model educator because she responds naturally to the child's needs. From the moment she begins to interact with the infant she is, in effect, teaching. Through her the child learns to perceive the world as ordered, comprehensible and predictable. By following her instincts as a mother she develops the experience and knowledge of the child in a way which is unforced and enjoyable. Her intention is to keep the child interested and occupied, not to be deliberately didactic.

Gertrude does not set up any impossible ideal; she simply acts as a natural mother. The conversational and emotional commonplaces are emphasized so that their true educational significance is highlighted. She does not instruct, present lessons, or conduct tests. But in the hundreds of everyday interactions with her child – washing hands, combing hair, feeding, comforting – interactions accompanied by her conversational commentary, she engages the child with the activity. The good mother imposes order and meaning on the world of the child's experience. This is the natural way of teaching and learning: the world is revealed to the child, he is trained in the use of his senses and the development of his powers of attention and observation.

> Gertrude never adopted the tone of instructor toward her children; she did not say to them: 'Child, this is your head, your nose, your hand, your finger'; or 'Where is your eye? your ear?' but instead she would say: 'Come here child, I will wash your little hands', 'I will comb your hair', or 'I will cut your fingernails'. Her verbal instruction seemed to vanish in the spirit of her real activity, in which it always had its source.[3]

The success of *Leonard and Gertrude* made Pestalozzi a major figure in European education. He received correspondence from all over the continent: in France he was declared a 'Citizen of the

French Republic'. This recognition in France gave him his next practical opportunity to engage in education.

Stanz, Burgdorf and Yverdun

In 1798 the French army passed through Switzerland to attack Austria, destroying the town of Stanz en route. Pestalozzi was given the task of making material and educational provision for children who had been rendered homeless by the French action.

Despite difficulties Pestalozzi succeeded, single-handedly, in transforming the children's lives. There were lessons in the morning and work in the fields or in the house in the afternoons with more lessons in the evening. The children soon became more open, contented and cooperative. Within a year Pestalozzi could write that the children:

> soon felt that there existed in them forces which they did not know ... they acquired a general sentiment of order and beauty ... They willed, they had power, they persevered, they succeeded, and they were happy.[4]

Independent observers were impressed not just by how much the children had learned in such a short time, but also by their health and cheerful demeanour. They acknowledged that these results originated in Pestalozzi's personality as well as his method of combining the practical activities of the children with their more formal educational activities.

The following year retreating French forces brought an end to the experiment when the building was commandeered for use as a military hospital. Moral: never trust the military!

Pestalozzi's next educational enterprise was in Burgdorf. Despite his considerable reputation he was initially appointed only as an assistant teacher (the principal teacher was the local cobbler!) but he was soon given complete control of the infant school. His results were phenomenal and he was given the mastership of the second boys' school in the town. His confidence in his pedagogical ability and in the psychological insights set out in *Leonard and Gertrude* grew. In 1799, with financial help from friends, he opened a new school and teacher training institute in Burgdorf.

Here his systematic investigations of teaching began as he tried to compose a theoretical handbook for student teachers. The result was his great theoretical work on education *How Gertrude Teaches Her Children*, which was written in the form of letters addressed to a friend. *Gertrude* is not another story about Gertrude but an account of Pestalozzi's own educational experiences, experiments and theories. 'I sought for laws,' he wrote, 'to which the development of the human mind must, by its very nature, be subject.' He presumed that they would follow the pattern of physical nature, and he hoped they would provide a 'clue to a universal psychological method of instruction'.[5]

Pestalozzi needed a method of instruction which could be successful independently of the excellence of the individual teacher. He was convinced that universal education could not be practicable until teachers (at least at the elementary stages) became, as it were, merely the instruments of method. They must be trained to apply 'mechanical formulas of instruction' based on 'eternal laws, according to which the human mind rises from mere sense-impressions to clear ideas'.[6] In other words, the success of the educational programme should not depend on the innate skill of the individual pedagogue but on the efficacy of the method. In effect, Pestalozzi believed that universal education could only succeed with a supply of adequately trained teachers rather than relying on individual enthusiasm, or on a sufficiency of 'born' or 'gifted' teachers. His work at Burgdorf was spectacularly successful and, as the reputation of the schools and the teacher training centre spread, a continuous succession of visitors (many of them notable) bore testimony to the effectiveness of Pestalozzi's methods.

Following political developments in Switzerland the schools and the teacher training institute were moved to Yverdun on the southern shore of Lake Neuchâtel. This was to be the scene of Pestalozzi's educational efforts for the next 20 years and became the Mecca for educationalists from all over Europe. Unfortunately, the establishment became too big for Pestalozzi's scant administrative abilities and he found himself increasingly at odds with younger and more ambitious colleagues. Eventually the school was closed in 1825 when Pestalozzi was 80 years old.

Anschauung

Pestalozzi's methodology attempted to reproduce the natural process of turning sense experience into understanding while respecting the psychological development of the learner. Central to his methodology is the notion of 'Anschauung', the basis of all knowledge and experience.

The German word 'Anschauung' has no direct equivalent in English. Its nearest equivalent would be something like the 'intuitive immediate awareness of objects or situations'. Pestalozzi himself wrote that, 'Anschauung is the immediate and direct impression produced by the world on our inner and outer senses – the impressions of the moral world on our moral sense and of the physical universe on our bodily senses'.[7] Pestalozzi distinguishes three aspects of Anschauung: number, form and name: these categories encompass all human experience of the sensible world.

Knowledge begins in experience not in words. Sense-experience will be perceived in three ways: in terms of the number of the objects presented, the shape and features of the object and the name of the object. We first of all distinguish in our sense-experience between the one and the many, this is number; we next note the similarities or dissimilarities of shape or features in a group of objects, this is form. Number and form are 'the special elementary properties of all things'.[8] Finally we fix the object in our memory by means of language, we give it a name, or learn its name.

Imagine the response of an individual, who has never seen an orange before, when presented with a tray of oranges. The first thing she will perceive is that there is more than one of the item. She will next attend to the colour, shape, texture, smell, weight, and so on. Only then might she ask 'What is it?' meaning 'what is its name?' It is primarily by the name that she will remember the experience of the object and represent it to others.

These then should be the powers to be developed in the child through education. 'Number, form and language are together the elementary means of instruction,' Pestalozzi declared. The external properties of an object, its number and qualities, are 'brought home to my consciousness through language. It must then be an immutable law of the Art (of instruction) to start from and work within this threefold principle'.[9]

Children must be taught to look at objects individually, to perceive the form, size and proportions of each, and to acquire, as soon as possible *afterwards*, the words and names associated with the object and its qualities. So the fundamental instruction of the child will be concerned with counting, measuring and speaking.

These competences 'lie at the basis of all accurate knowledge of objects of sense,' he declares. 'We should cultivate them with the psychological Art, endeavour to strengthen and make them strong and bring them, as a means of development and culture, to the highest pitch of simplicity, consistency and harmony.'[10]

Pestalozzi did not mean that children's experience should be limited only to what was accessible to direct, first-hand experience, however. What is not immediately present to sense-experience can be presented attractively in 'observation books'; pictures compiled in a systematic order allowing for the development of the child's vocabulary in association with the pictures: think of ABC books as a contemporary example.

Drawing, an essential element in Pestalozzi's educational plan, should be introduced as early as possible as a means of encouraging children to attend to number, form and proportion. It should be introduced in graduated exercises. Since 'Nature herself has subordinated (the art of writing) to that of drawing', drawing should have precedence because it facilitates the formation of letters, 'and saves the great waste of time spent in making crooked (and incorrect) forms again and again'.[11]

The child should engage with reality through the actual objects themselves or, lacking the objects, pictures or other non-verbal representations. In arithmetic, for example, the child will learn counting and the rules of number through manipulating real objects or at least selections of dots representing real objects. In this way 'we lay the foundation of the whole of the science of arithmetic'.[12] It is not the numbers which are important in the first instance but the quantities and relationships that the numbers represent. It is the practical experience that the child should always encounter first.

This is an example of *Anschauung*: the apprehension of the reality *before* its symbolic representation in words or numbers.

Anschauung requires, then, that there must be an analysis of the object of experience in terms of number, form and name. Only then does a knowledge of words become meaningful and useful. The child must first have knowledge of the associated reality either directly, through empirical experience of the object itself, or through seeing pictorial representations of it. The method is a natural method: 'Like nature with the savage, I always put the picture before the eye, and then sought for a word for the picture.'[13]

Reading

The child must be a proficient talker before he can be taught to read. It is clear from Pestalozzi's insistence on the priority of number, form and name that the emphasis initially must be on the child's powers of observation and of speech. These must be significantly developed before he is required to learn to read or to spell. 'The child must be brought to a high degree of knowledge, both of things seen and words,' he warns, 'before it is reasonable to teach him to spell or read.'[14]

Pestalozzi was dismissive of what he called 'Socratising' education, that is attempting to teach through verbal definitions and constructs rather than through direct experience of things.[15] He did not deny that such an approach had a certain value but reminded a colleague that 'Socrates was surrounded by young men who had a background in the knowledge of words and things,' but that a Socratic approach is 'utterly worthless for teachers and children in the public schools' where no such prior knowledge can be taken for granted.[16]

The civic and moral dimension

The civic dimension to Pestalozzi's work is critically important. His earliest inspiration was the relationship between education and political or communal life. Knowledge must, above all, be practical, that is, applicable in a meaningful way to the life of the individual, in harmony with our inmost nature.

> Perhaps the most fearful gift that a fiendish spirit has made to this age is knowledge without power of doing and insight without that power of exertion or of overcoming ... Knowing and doing are so closely connected that if one ceases the other ceases with it.[17]

Although he did not advocate direct state intervention in education this does not mean that governments are absolved from responsibility in the matter. Pestalozzi appeals for what we might now call 'empowerment'. Governments can never act towards individuals with the same sensitivity and compassion as people themselves can. It is particularly important that each citizen should be facilitated 'in those matters in which he could accomplish and contribute anything himself to forward the public good'. Public policy should spare no effort to cultivate 'intelligence, disposition, and abilities' so that each can contribute to the public welfare.[18]

Hand, head and heart

Pestalozzi agrees with Rousseau that the child is born good and that his earliest moral education comes from his relationship with his mother. The child is born to virtue: virtue is to be preserved, not created. The inner, spiritual nature of the individual is vital to the development of moral character through which a man becomes 'independent, free and contented'. He is less than enthusiastic about the role of Nature in this regard, however. For Pestalozzi, Nature is blind and primitive and cannot lead to a moral outcome for physical nature 'is in her very nature blind; her ways are the ways of darkness and death'. Therefore moral education must be separated from 'blind sensuous Nature' and entrusted to the 'moral and spiritual being and its divine, eternal, inner light and truth'.[19]

The true agent of the child's moral formation is the mother. It is she who provides the primary emotional foundations on which the moral life is built: feelings of love, of confidence, of gratitude and of obedience. Pestalozzi's account of the genesis of the moral life anticipates much modern psychoanalysis. Human development begins in the desire for the satisfaction of physical needs. In the relationship with the mother the physical needs are satisfied and love is born. When fear intrudes into the life of the infant child it is again the reassurance provided by the maternal presence that begets confidence and gratitude.[20]

Pestalozzi stressed that the three main divisions of education – the physical, the intellectual and the religious/moral – should be harmonized: 'The education of all three sides of our nature proceeds on common lines in equal measure, as is necessary if the unity of our nature and the equilibrium of our powers are to be recognized from the outset.'[21]

The powers of man, the physical, the intellectual and the religious/moral should be cultivated in such a way that no one of them will predominate over the others. Nonetheless, the true standard of any activity is ultimately to be judged by its contribution to spiritual growth.

Conclusion

Pestalozzi sought a practical scheme of education suitable for all: the ultimate end of such an education is a preparation for independence, fitness for life. He was committed to an educational programme of universal application and in particular one which would prove suitable for the education of the poor. ('The poor man's child needs a greater refinement in the methods of instruction than the rich man's child.'[22]) He realized that if the child is a part of nature then it is necessary to understand the nature of the child as a developing entity. With such an understanding it should be possible to devise a general method of instruction based on psychological principles. Pestalozzi's educational vision was always rooted in the realities of life; he could contain within his conception both the sublime and the pragmatic:

> O blooming youth, our hope and pride! You are like a garden in all its glory. But mind you that the world is fed by the fruits of the field, not by the flowers of the garden. Get ready then, for the day when, without adornment, you must attend to the real business of your life![23]

When Pestalozzi died in 1827 he left no educational system. But he left the germ of the science and discipline of educational psychology which would have an immeasurable effect over the following centuries. His real influence was on visionary educators who came later.

11 Friedrich Froebel (1782–1852): The Garden of Education

If we acknowledge Jean-Jacques Rousseau as the liberator of childhood we must hail Friedrich Wilhelm August Froebel as the originator, prophet and principal advocate of the kindergarten – the garden of children – a radically new concept of early childhood education.

Background

Born in Thuringia in 1782, Froebel's mother died when he was 9 months old and he was reared by his father, a Lutheran Pastor 'of the old orthodox school of theology', and a step-mother. His early childhood in his father's home was far from happy.

Matters improved when, at the age of 10, he went to live with his maternal uncle in Switzerland. Here he received a little formal schooling but more importantly, he experienced a secure and affectionate family life for the first time. He was, by his own account, an introspective child: 'it was my habit to analyse and question, and my conclusions were quite clear and positive even if they were not put into words.'[1]

At the age of 15 Froebel was apprenticed to a forester. The experience was of little lasting interest but it allowed him to develop an interest in mathematics and botany. At 17 he visited the University of Jena where his brother was a student. He found the university atmosphere congenial and stayed to attend classes. That he was influenced by the various strands of German Idealism which prevailed at the time can be seen in the idealistic convictions of his later writing. In *The Education of Man*, for example, he wrote about 'an eternal law (that) pervades and rules all things'. This law is 'expressed in the external world of Nature, in the inner world of mind and spirit, and in life where these two are unified'.[2] In short he had discovered a perspective which was both subjective and objective and which made possible the perception of 'unity in diversity' which was to be such a central theme in his educational work.

He was obliged to give up his university studies due, it appears, to financial difficulties: before he left Jena he spent nine weeks in the university prison for non-payment of debts!

Educational career

In 1805 he acquired a post as a drawing master in Frankfurt. This experience, together with a short visit to Pestalozzi's educational community at Yverdun, enkindled a life-long interest in education and schooling. As a result, when he was appointed tutor to the sons of Caroline von Holzhausen, he took the boys to Yverdun and spent the next two years there as Pestalozzi's general assistant. The experience allowed him to develop and refine his own educational ideas. He expressed dissatisfaction with Pestalozzi's methods describing them as 'too crudely empirical' and at the same time 'not scientific enough' because they 'failed to recognize or value science in its divine nature'.[3] In addition, he felt that 'there was no organic connection' between the subjects in the Pestalozzian curriculum.[4]

Even at this early stage the profound spiritual philosophy concerning the unity of the Universe which characterizes Froebel's educational theory is evident. 'There is a universal pattern of development,' he wrote in his autobiographical letter to the philosopher Krause. Each level in development has its own 'point of culmination' which allows for renewal of its knowledge of the 'unity of being' before it proceeds to the next level of growth. He concludes, 'I regard the simple pattern of development from the analytical to the synthetical, such as I find in pure thought, as the course of development of all being'.[5] Thus he sees human life not as static but as dynamic, a 'constant and progressive process of becoming'.[6]

In 1816, following a period of military service in the war against France and terms of study at the Universities of Göttingen and Berlin (where he studied crystallography) Froebel opened his first school at Griesheim. He gave it the grandiose title of *The Universal German Educational Institute*. His first pupils were his five nephews though the enrolment grew when he moved the school to Keilhau the following year and he was joined in the enterprise by friends. He married in 1818. His educational experiences at Keilhau prompted him to write *The Education of Man* which was published in 1826. Although it covers the education of children only up to 10 years, this book served to establish for Froebel an international reputation as an innovative and progressive educational thinker.

In 1831 he left Keilhau and went to Switzerland where he opened another school in Lucerne leaving the Keilhau school under the management of colleagues. While in Switzerland he was invited to lecture to teachers at Burgdorf and it was here that he and his wife undertook the establishment of an orphanage and school for the canton of Berne.

The idea of the kindergarten

It was only when Froebel established another school – a school for psychological education, as he described it – at Blankenburg in Thuringia that he began to perfect the methods and materials for the adequate education of the young child. He was now 55 years old and this was the school which, in 1840, was to become the first true kindergarten. The story goes that Froebel was searching about for a name for his school. One day, travelling from Keilhau (which was the location of his first school) to Blankenburg he came on the view of the valley of the River Rinne stretching out before him like a great garden. 'I have found it!' he exclaimed. 'Kindergarten the name shall be.'[7] The name, garden of children, conveys vividly the impression of a place where small children grow in accordance with the laws of Nature.

Educational ideas

Froebel's educational theories rest on a highly developed and complex philosophy which he continued to elaborate throughout his life. They were based on the mystical and spiritual insights of a rather unsystematic pantheism rather than on well-founded philosophical or psychological theories.

There are two distinct realms in human experience: the realm of nature and the realm of the spirit, or reason. Nature and reason are the twin polarities of the world: both are expressions of the divine, the Absolute. Without mind or spirit matter (nature) is inert and lifeless; it remains formless, it is mere chaos. Spirit manifests itself in order. It is only through the infusion of the spiritual into the material that the cosmos originated and continues to exist.

In this universe of matter and spirit humankind is the living unity of nature and reason: the union of the material with the spiritual. Individual human destiny is for each to achieve full consciousness of his or her own essential nature: this is the meaning of 'becoming' mentioned above. This 'becoming' is achieved by learning to see the meaning and purpose of all human activities and by expressing human nature in accordance with fixed cosmic laws. 'The individual is trying to achieve conscious understanding of himself and of life in its basic unity and immense diversity,' Froebel wrote, 'and ... to act from his own choice and in conformity with the harmony that obtains throughout the universe.'[8]

Development

In all of Froebel's educational writing *Darstellung* is a central concept. It is usually translated as 'creative self-expression' or 'self-active behaviour'. It does not mean self-indulgence or unstructured expressionism. It refers to the innate urge of the human organism, of any organism, to push out to greater life. Impulses well up in the child: these impulses need to find expression in a manner which promotes both the child's personal development and his or her adjustment to social or communal realities. Such self-active behaviour is purposive and progressive: it leads to the world beyond the immediate experience of the individual and at the same time enables the individual to go even further.

Through this self-active behaviour the human being develops or unfolds in accordance with a set pattern which is already contained within the individual. 'All the child is ever to be and become,' he wrote, 'lies, however slightly indicated, in the child, and can be attained only through development from within outward.' In some sense, analogous to bud and leaf, or to acorn and oak, each individual's future development and formation is 'contained in the beginning of its existence'.[9]

This reference to 'the development and formation of the whole future life' was not a reference to any kind of individual pre-destination. It referred to the *general* pattern of human development: a sequence of stages, each one evolving into the next in a fixed and unchangeable order. This feature of Froebel's thought pre-figures the theories of developmental psychologists of the twentieth century. As a natural phenomenon each human being is like the seed of a plant or a flower: it already contains the blueprint of what it is to become: its growth is the unfolding of what is already there.

The optimal growth of the plant or flower requires the optimal conditions for growth. The function of the adult – parent or teacher – who intervenes in the growth of the child is to assist this process of unfolding and growth. It is usual, since the nineteenth century, to express this intervention with horticultural metaphors: the wise gardener facilitates the natural unfolding and growth of the human seedling by providing the right environmental conditions. Hence the name kindergarten. But Froebel warns that it is easy to confuse assistance with interference: a vine must be pruned, 'however good the intention, the vine may be entirely ruined in the process ... unless the gardener pays attention to the plant's natural growth'. There should be no disruption of the smooth unfolding of the individual over the years of growth; the child's development should proceed as a continuous unbroken process. The child's progress should be overseen and continuously protected by the adult. Sudden discontinuities and fragmentation of the child's experience should be avoided because they distract attention, both the child's and the adult's, from 'the living connection, the inner living essence' and are 'therefore highly pernicious, and even destructive in their influence'.[10]

Religion

Froebel's commitment to nature went much deeper than illustrative metaphors and catchy names, however: he was totally convinced of the necessity to rear the child in harmony with nature, inner psychological nature as well as the outer nature of the material cosmos. What he meant by Nature was not just the botanical world of trees and plants but the whole of reality, physical, spiritual and social. Man is essentially and innately spiritual. 'I saw this,' Froebel confided in his 'Letter to the Women in Keilhau', 'expressed through the concept of God as creator ... I saw it expressed in the life and work of Jesus and in the workings of the Holy Spirit.'[11]

The Education of Man begins by asserting that an eternal law 'pervades and rules all things'. This eternal law is manifested in the external world and in the inner world of mind and spirit. Nature and spirit are unified in human life. This universal order, the order of the cosmos experienced by human understanding, is the manifestation of a living unity which is 'all-pervading, self-cognisant and everlasting'.[12] This is Froebel's pantheism: God is not outside of reality, He is immanent, sustaining the universe from within. The reality of God is accessible through faith and reason, Froebel maintained; He can be known emotionally or rationally.

Everything that exists has the purpose of realizing its unique purpose. This is especially so in the case of human beings who, because they are both perceptive and rational, have a special responsibility to realize their essential nature. Man 'is meant to reveal the divine element within him by allowing it to become freely effective in his life'.[13] This provides the 'single aim' of education: 'it should cultivate man's original divine nature and so it should depict in and through human life that which is infinite and eternal'.[14]

The relationship between Nature and God is analogous to the relationship between a work of art and the artist. The work of art possesses no material part of the artist and yet it is vivified by his spirit: it is the spirit of the artist that is communicated to others by the work of art. Similarly, although the material universe is not God, 'it is in Nature that God's spirit lives and works; it's here that it is expressed, communicated and developed'.[15] The unity in the diversity of nature is precisely this principle of the Divine.

The entire kindergarten system rests mainly on the view of human activity and play as the imitation of Nature as a creative and dynamic force expressing the Divine immanence into the world.

Kindergarten and school

One of Froebel's principal contributions to our understanding of childhood is his emphasis on play as the pre-eminent activity of early childhood and the 'highest level' of child development. In play children spontaneously express the inner thoughts and feelings that they can express in no other way since they do not have the linguistic or representational skills to do so. 'Play,' he declares, 'is the purest creation of the child's mind' and so it 'promotes enjoyment, satisfaction, serenity, and constitutes the source of all that can benefit the child'.[16]

Contrary to the preconceptions of most adults, child's play is not a purposeless, formless activity. It is not trivial: 'it is serious and deeply significant'.[17] We can acquire some sense of children's future personality through watching them in their freely chosen play. For the child's play to be beneficial, however, it must be directed and controlled, for without such guidance it is likely to degenerate into aimless triviality: 'play must not be left to chance'. Not alone must the educator guide the play but 'he must also often teach this sort of play in the first instance'.[18]

Froebel would direct the child's play by providing the child with materials which structure and direct the play appropriately. In the kindergarten children are encouraged ('guided') to engage in play so that they 'reach the aim desired by nature', that is achieve their maximal development. Froebel justifies this apparently contradictory intervention in the play of children which he considers 'freely chosen' by invoking a 'general law of development' which obtains in both the natural and in the spiritual world (which are both, it will be remembered, manifestations of the Divine immanence). 'Without law aiding guidance there is no free development.'[19]

Froebel maintains a clear distinction between the kindergarten for the small children and the school for the older children. The former does not displace the latter: they are equally important at their own appropriate time. The experience of the kindergarten is an essential preparation for the experience of the school. If the developmental imperatives of the individual's early childhood have not been met then the efforts of the school will be frustrated: the child must first be himself before he can turn his interest to the world.

The transition from the kindergarten to the school, from child-centred education to curriculum-centred learning, marks the transition from childhood to boyhood. The demands of the wider world replace the self-absorption of the child. The 'free' play which was so much a feature of the kindergarten is supplanted in the school by a preoccupation with study and work. School requires the child to begin the process of coming to terms with the nature of the external world and engaging with the 'significance of external things'.[20] In the earlier stage of the kindergarten the child makes the internal external through play; in the later stage of the school she makes the external internal through study. School is primarily concerned with objects in their particularity and in their universality: instruction predominates. The pupil is confronted with the external world (including his own self, for he is part of that world) as something separate and distinct. Instruction shows how individual entities are interconnected and establishes general intellectual concepts.

The emphasis of the kindergarten is on the process of development, the emphasis of the school is on the quality of the outcome of the pupil's learning. The school makes the transition from experience to cognition, from self-growth and development to the consideration of properties and relations, from sensuous and direct intuition to abstract thought. Play is the characteristic activity of the kindergarten, study (work) is the characteristic activity of the school: interest shifts from the process of learning to its product, from internal criteria to external criteria.

Work

Both play and work, however, are activities whereby the individual realizes his self; work is not confined to school nor should the kindergarten be exclusively preoccupied with play. Froebel is particularly critical of the idea that we work only to supply our material needs. Such a view is 'illusory and degrading'. On the contrary, man works 'to give outward form to the divine spirit within him so that he may know his own nature and the nature of God'. Some productive activity is essential for the healthy development of body and soul. It is a religious issue: religion without work is empty dreaming, work without religion makes man into a beast of burden. 'Work and religion are co-existent,' he concludes. 'God the eternal is eternally creative.'[21]

Work is an essential ingredient in the development of the individual. Each child, irrespective of social or economic circumstances, should be obliged to devote an hour or two each day 'to some serious activity in the production of some definite external piece of work'. Too much of children's time is spent in aimless and trivial pursuits rather than accomplishing worthwhile things. 'They dislike bodily work in the present,' Froebel declares, 'and believe they will not need it in the future.'[22] He gives us many examples of children engaged in work in the company of their parents: the carter's child 'hardly two years old' leading the horse, the 3-year-old minding his mother's goslings, the gardener's child helping with the weeding: a variety of instances of children observing their parents' occupations and wanting to participate. It is not that the children don't want to participate in the kinds of productive activities we call 'work', but that adults do not sufficiently encourage them to develop this interest in a practical way: 'the domestic and scholastic education of our time leads children to indolence and laziness; a vast amount of human power thereby remains undeveloped and is lost.'[23] This is not just an economic observation: the loss is primarily developmental, the child is denied the opportunity to become all that he can be. Schools should include instruction in the manual arts and crafts as part of the curriculum.

Political aim

Froebel's interest in education was deeply influenced by political ideals. His political vision was of a democratic commonwealth of up-right, cooperative people who would not take their responsibilities and privileges for granted and would do all that they could for the improvement of the human condition. It is therefore incumbent on the school and the family to foster the emerging individual through the experience of group relationships and activities, to prepare each for life in community: the school is the nursery for future citizens.

This provides a more practical reason for his promotion of work among the young. A crucial task of educational institutions (including the home) is to prepare the individual for specific domestic or vocational tasks. As well as being developmentally significant, work provides one of the most important links between the individual and society. Individual and society are not in opposition but in a relation of mutual dependence; what we would now call a symbiotic relationship. A community cannot thrive if the individual members are not attaining their fullest development; individuals cannot pursue full development unless the community is thriving.

Froebel's conception of the relationship between educational discipline and positive outcomes is optimistic: in true education 'necessity should call forth freedom, law arouse self-determination, external force develop inner free will, hatred from outside evoke love within'. This is the test of the success, even the legitimacy, of educational discipline. Failing these kinds of outcomes 'education has no meaning and no effect'.[24]

Froebel recognized the need for both individual and group discipline. But he also recognized that the only true discipline comes from within; if the child is not accustomed to law and order in her life then it is unlikely she will respond positively to it later: law is necessary and is our only means to true freedom. The educational task is to reconcile the need for restraint with the opportunity for freedom to develop.

Symbolism

Froebel's religious beliefs give meaning to his almost obsessive pre-occupation with symbols. Just as Nature symbolizes the essential being of God so man creates symbols as the only means to hand of expressing his inner life. 'It seems to me,' Froebel explains in one of his self-revelatory letters, 'that man's dual nature as body and mind, and above all his essential creativity, lead him to create visible expressions of his mind's activity, to see himself symbolically, as it were'.[25] It is through creating and understanding symbols that the human being can best realize his true essence. He traced his realization of the centrality of symbols to his time studying crystals at Berlin: 'for me now theory and its application, life, Nature and mathematics were all to be studied in a single formation, the crystal, and a world of symbols opened before me.'[26]

At the top of Froebel's list of important symbols is the circle or sphere which represents for him fidelity, completion and perfection. Consequently it became the first item of his educational apparatus, or 'gifts'.

The gifts

No account of the educational innovations of Froebel would be complete without making reference to his 'gifts', a series of sets of educational apparatus specifically designed to generate the child's self-active behaviour. As we have seen, Froebel believed that educational activities and materials would have to be designed to promote self-active behaviour: to lead the learner out of the inner world of infancy into the outer world of humanity. The 'gifts', a series of structured learning materials, would lead the child through play to the intuition of fundamental truths about Nature. The materials, including spheres, cubes and cylinders subdivided into various configurations, were intended to stimulate, direct and structure the play of the infant and child so that she would learn fundamental lessons about reality. They were, probably, the world's first structured educational equipment.

The sphere, for instance, was not just an object of play through which the small child could learn characteristics of the physical world. It was a general expression of the completion and unity of all things including the child himself; it was also an image of all things in general and of specific things, like heads and apples, in particular. In addition it offered the child the first opportunity to possess wholeness and completeness.

The 'plays' which Froebel prescribes for the ball/sphere and the other 'gifts' cannot be described here. Suffice to say that the prescriptions constitute a course of training: structured, systematic and detailed, they appear to be far from any reasonable conception of free play any child might spontaneously engage in.

Friedrich Froebel died on 21 June 1852. His contribution to the humanization of the education of the very young is incalculable. Despite the fact that kindergartens were for a time banned in Prussia during his lifetime (they were considered dangerous to society), Froebel's ideas, methods and gifts have spread throughout the civilized world in the century and a half since his death and have enriched the lives of children everywhere.

12 John Henry Newman (1801–1890): University Education

With Newman we turn to an exclusive concern with university education, and in particular the question 'what is a university?', and a profile of the ideal graduate of such an institution. Although firmly set in the nineteenth century, Newman's views continue to have resonance for the university of the twenty-first century.

Background

Born in London in 1801 to solidly middle-class and staunchly Anglican parents, Newman entered Trinity College, Oxford at the age of 15. He was elected a Fellow of Oriel College, the most intellectually distinguished of the Oxford colleges, in 1822. In 1824 he took Holy Orders and became an active member of the so-called Oxford movement which advocated deep reform in the Anglican Church and a renewal of its common apostolic origins with the Roman Catholic Church. In 1845, following two decades of often bitter controversy, and much spiritual turmoil, Newman was received into the Roman Catholic Church. He was ordained as a Catholic priest the following year.

In 1852 the Roman Catholic hierarchy in Ireland decided to establish a Catholic university in Dublin. Ireland was then part of the British Empire and was effectively ruled directly from London. Because of ideological difficulties surrounding educational developments of the day, and resultant conflict and controversy, the hierarchy hoped to establish a Catholic institution which would be quite independent of the government. They invited Father Newman to become Rector of the new university. He delivered a series of lectures[1] which were subsequently published as the first part of *The Idea of a University Defined*.

These lectures developed ideas on the nature, scope and purpose of a university and on the definition of a liberal education.

However, the planned university was not a success, partly because as a private venture it did not have the necessary State support which such a large scheme requires. In any event, like so many educational reformers before and since, Newman lacked the administrative qualities necessary for such an undertaking.

What is a university?

Newman certainly would have had no sympathy with the view that a university is an institution dedicated to innovations in technology and to the improvement of commercial products. A university he sees as, in the first instance, a place of universal learning (from its ancient designation of a *Studium Generale*) which draws its members from far and near. 'In its simple and rudimental form,' he believed, it should be 'a school of knowledge of every kind, consisting of teachers and learners from every quarter'. This appeared to be the essence of a university, 'a place for the communication and circulation of thought, by means of personal intercourse'.[2]

Newman anticipates the objection that given the wide availability of knowledge of every kind in magazines, periodicals, tracts, pamphlets and books it should no longer be necessary to attend at a particular location in order to become educated. In our own time this objection would have even more force given the explosion in the availability of information and instruction through the mass media and computer technology. What more can we require, Newman asks, by way of intellectual education of each and every one, than 'so exuberant and diversified and persistent a promulgation of all kinds of knowledge'? Why should anyone leave their home to go in search of knowledge? Why 'need we go up to knowledge, when knowledge comes down to us'?[3] This is a crucial question for on its answer depends the continuing justification of the university, not only as an idea but as a real, complex, and expensive, institution.

Newman did not despise the popular education available through the mass media; the effects of such a wide range of information and instruction were remarkable. But education is different: for true *education* more is needed. Education requires the authentic living voice of the teacher, the professor. The written word, the book, provides us with a record of truth, an authority to which we can appeal in cases of doubt or disagreement, and an 'instrument of teaching in the hands of a teacher'. However, to become thoroughly versed in any area of expertise and scholarship we must 'consult the living man and listen to his living voice'. While the general principles of any field of study can be learned from books 'the detail, the colour, the tone, the air, the life which makes it live in us' can only be acquired from 'those in whom it lives already'.[4] Like the theory of any other activity, the theory of learning is no more than theory until one sees it in action, embodied, as it were, in a living practitioner.

'He in whom the learning lives already' might be taken as the definition of the professor, the living embodiment of his chosen discipline. The professor vivifies and articulates what otherwise would be no more than dry information. In addition, the professors represent the interests and integrity of their discipline both in the university itself and to the wider world. Who would defend and vindicate the interests of mathematics if not a mathematician, of biology if not a biologist, of history if not a historian? In cases of disputes between the sciences the professors are best fitted to resolve these disputes 'without risk of extravagant pretensions on any side, of angry collision, or of popular commotion'.[5] For professors are people for whom a liberal philosophy has become the professional habit of thought.

Now of course it is not necessary to go to a university to find such a person: there are individuals in all walks of life who have comparable knowledge, expertise and enthusiasm. They are to be found practising in several professions: medicine, law, teaching, architecture, art, music, etc., to the highest level of attainment *and* passing on their knowledge and expertise to others without the context of the university. 'The personal influence of the teacher,' Newman concedes, 'is able in some sort to dispense with an academical system.' The academical system, however, cannot fulfil its function without the personal influence of the professor. This influence is the life of the various disciplines, without it they are inert. 'With influence there is life; without it there is none.' The absence of the appropriate influence will diminish the role and function of the university. 'An academical system without the personal influence of teachers upon pupils,' Newman declares, 'is an Arctic winter; it will create an ice-bound, petrified, cast-iron university, and nothing else.'[6] It is not the teacher who needs the university, it is the university which needs the teacher.

Knowledge

Newman's views are grounded in his view of knowledge.

True knowledge is not fragmentary. However complex and varied it may be, the world is one; there is but one universe. Everything that exists and that is known to the human intellect 'forms one large system or complex fact'. This universal fact comprises an indefinite number of specific and particular events and phenomena. These, because they are parts of the whole, have innumerable connections, commonalities and all kinds of relations between them individually and collectively. 'Knowledge is the apprehension of these facts, whether in themselves, or in their mutual position and bearings.'[7]

The human mind is incapable of comprehending the vastness of reality at a glance, the universe is virtually infinite. We are like short-sighted readers who can only take in a fragment of the total at any given time. Worse, we are short-sighted readers with short lifespans. So human knowledge is a multiplicity of partial views built up over successive lifetimes of scholars: these partial views, each more or less legitimate and correct in its own sphere, are the various human sciences.

The sciences represent a division of labour in the human enterprise of attempting to come to a complete knowledge and understanding of all that exists. No one of the sciences is sufficient by itself to represent all that is known or knowable. When we take them all together they provide an approximation, no more, of the objective truth. Individually, as we master successive sciences (mathematics, physics, and biology, say) we draw closer to an accurate understanding of the truth. But no matter how much we know from the various sciences there is always more to be known.

So, no one of the sciences which the university professes can ever tell us all that is to be known about anything, much less tell us all that is to be known about everything. The sciences increase our knowledge and they enable us to communicate it, that is all. This is what Newman means by 'science as a form of knowledge': each science enables the intellect to understand existing knowledge and to add to it; each also facilitates the communication of this knowledge to others. Sciences can do this because they have structured and systematized existing knowledge so that it is more accessible and communicable.

Any of the sciences taken in isolation, without the counter-balancing influence of others, will give not only an incomplete, but a distorted picture of reality. The effect will depend on which of the other sciences is chosen to stand beside it to moderate the picture of reality it gives. So, we would return from a country walk with a distinctly different understanding if we had had the company of a geologist, than if we had been in the company of a botanist.

The student

Newman's conviction that the sciences interact with one another and supplement the picture of reality that each gives individually, means that each of the studies of the individual student should be moderated by others. A student confined to only one branch of knowledge would acquire a narrow, not to say distorted, picture of reality. Such a narrowness of study may be defended on the grounds that it allows for greater engagement with the subject in question, and a greater depth of knowledge and understanding. But the cost of such focused expertise is a loss of breadth of understanding. It is better, in the first instance, that the student engages with a number of branches of knowledge, as each will exert its own particular influence on the others and contribute to a broader understanding of reality as well as of the inter-relationships between disciplines.

As well as the effect of the mutual moderating influence on the students' chosen subjects, there is also the more pervasive influence of the general atmosphere of the university itself. Living and studying in a place where learning is valued and promoted has a cumulative effect on intellectual development. While it is not possible for each student to pursue every available subject, each will benefit from living in an ethos which values the entire range of studies which a university professes and studying in proximity to those who represent all of these branches of knowledge. Students will also, of course, mix socially and academically with their peers who are pursuing different courses of study to theirs. This being the case, they cannot but come under the influence of points of view which are different to those to which they are being exposed in their own courses. 'This I conceive,' Newman writes, 'to be the advantage of a seat of universal learning, considered as a place of education.'[8]

In short, Newman anticipates that the individual student will benefit not only from the study of his or her chosen subjects but also from living among those who pursue other subjects, both as teachers and as students. By, as it were, 'rubbing shoulders' with those whose interests and academic pursuits are different from his or her own, the student will benefit from the influence which these disparate views will have on his or her own interests and convictions.

In addition, there is the tradition of learning and of the organization of learning which the university as a whole represents. This intellectual tradition, independent of any particular branch of knowledge or of any particular teachers, will provide guidance in the student's choice of disciplines and provide an intellectual and historical context for those he or she chooses. Although the student can pursue only a small number of subjects out of the wide array available, the university, with its structures and traditions, will enable him or her to discern how these choices fit into the great edifice of accumulated knowledge, how they relate to its principles and parts, and how the parts relate to one another. Students could not do this were they following a course of study elsewhere than at a university.

Liberal education

The meaning of a liberal education is at the core of Newman's defence of university education. A liberal education is not narrow, even though the student may be required to concentrate only on a few chosen subjects: narrowness is avoided by keeping the student mindful of the breadth and depth of knowledge as a whole. The purpose is to inculcate a habit of mind which will continue throughout life. The characteristics of this habit of mind, this 'philosophical habit', are 'freedom, equitableness, calmness, moderation, and wisdom'.[9]

This habit of mind is acquired through training. The training ensures that the intellect is not subordinated to some particular or marginal purpose; that it is not, so to speak, enslaved by the particular outlook of a specific view or attitude, such as a specific trade or profession, a particular study or branch of knowledge. On the contrary, the mind is 'disciplined for its own sake, for the perception of its own proper object, and for its own highest culture'.[10] This is what is called liberal education.

The value of liberal education

So what is the use of this education? What is its practical application? What, from the point of view of the man of business, is the pay-off? What is the real worth in the market place of the article called 'a liberal education'?

Newman does not deny that such education may have measurable utility. If the knowledge derived is useful, good and well. But he does not attempt to identify what the practical results might be because his concern is not with the practical, in the sense of some kind of immediately measurable pay-off, at all. Here is how he responds to the question regarding the worth of liberal education: it 'is simply the cultivation of the intellect,' he declares, 'its object is nothing more or less than intellectual excellence.' The purpose of the liberal education is to

> open the mind, to correct it, to refine it, to enable it to know, and to digest, master, rule, and use its knowledge, to give it power over its own faculties, application, flexibility, method, critical exactness, sagacity, resource, address, eloquent expression ... [11]

For the pragmatic mind this is a difficult idea to absorb. The problem, as Newman points out, is that we have no single word in the English language which refers clearly and unambiguously to 'intellectual proficiency and perfection'. We have, in contrast, specific words to denote physical well-being ('health' and/or 'fitness') or moral well-being ('virtue', 'goodness'). But no such word for intellectual well-being. The terms 'health' and 'virtue' have a fairly clear meaning with reference to physical well-being and moral behaviour respectively. When we describe a person as 'healthy' or 'virtuous' or 'good', there is general acknowledgement of the kinds of claim we are making. Neither is it strange to consider 'health' or 'goodness' as ends in themselves: we consider being healthy, or fit, to be a good thing irrespective of the uses to which the health or fitness might be put. How do we express the same kinds of judgements with reference to the intellectual condition of the individual? We have no single word, no 'recognized term' to carry the burden of meaning.

In the absence of such a term, Newman proposes to refer to 'the perfection or virtue of the intellect by the name of philosophy, philosophical knowledge, enlargement of mind, or illumination'. Whatever term we agree on, he argues that it is the function of a university to make the development, pursuit and promotion of this intellectual well-being its principal objective. The *raison d'être* of the university is the education of the intellect, the pursuit and development of intellectual culture. When it succeeds in cultivating such an intellect among its scholars, 'it has done its work when it has done as much as this'. The university 'educates the intellect to reason well in all matters, to reach out towards truth, and to grasp it'.[12]

The object of the university, the pursuit of truth and the provision of a liberal education, is independent of the requirements of any power which may use it, be it Church, State, or economy. Newman's fundamental principle is that the cultivation of the intellect is an end which is distinct from all others; it is sufficient in itself irrespective of any practical application it might have. A university promotes the health of the intellect just as a gymnasium promotes the health of the body.

Yet there is a good, a utility, which follows from a liberal education as Newman conceives it. Although it cannot be valued or priced in market or monetary terms, it is comprehensible nonetheless.

Liberal education and the advantages it confers must make a difference to the possessor and to all of those with whom he or she comes in contact. Newman does not mean a utility in what he calls 'any low, mechanical, mercantile sense'. What he means is that a liberal education is of advantage to its possessor in that it diffuses a 'good, or a blessing, or a gift, or power, or a treasure' to him or her and then 'through him to the world'. 'I say then,' he concludes, 'if a liberal education be good, it must necessarily be useful too.'[13] But this is not very clear and Newman is forced to take recourse to the analogy with physical health to explain what he means.

There is a universal acceptance that health is desirable: it is a blessing and worth seeking and cherishing for its own sake. We do not have to be told further what health is *good for*. In the same way, irrespective of the uses to which the intellect is subsequently put, irrespective of what utility it might have in art, in business, in a profession or in a trade, the cultivation of the intellect is good in itself. Just as any physical undertaking will require physical health and an appropriate level of fitness ('as a man in health can do what an unhealthy man cannot do') so any intellectual undertaking will presuppose a certain level of intellectual acuity. This 'general culture of mind'[14] is the best preparation for any professional or scientific study or undertaking.

Priority of liberal education

Despite what might appear to the modern reader as the rather dismissive tone of Newman's reference to 'any low, mechanical, mercantile' connections for liberal education, the liberal mind is not dismissive of the utilitarian pursuits of the trades or professions, or of the specialized studies of the sciences. Newman does not deny that the university may be the proper place for utilitarian arts and sciences to be taught. But the first priority of the university is the education of the person, and only secondarily the education or training of the specialist. The cultivated intellect must be its priority. The university should not give priority to professional or vocational formation because the formation of the whole person, the citizen in the ancient Greek sense, must come first. A man or woman is first and foremost a person, only secondarily a doctor, or teacher, or scientist. A cultivated intellect should be the priority because it is, like health and virtue, 'a good in itself'. It confers 'a power and a grace' on every undertaking and enables its possessor to be more useful, to more people, than he or she would otherwise be.

Learning

Of course the university is concerned with knowledge, but not as Newman puts it, *mere knowledge*. Knowledge is no more than the indispensable means whereby the mind is nourished and expanded. It is, as it were, the instrument of attaining this expansion of mind. The aim is not simply the acquisition of information, however comprehensive it might be. Undoubtedly, in a university knowledge must be comprehensive, but this is the beginning, not the end of the matter. What is of crucial importance is the manner in which the knowledge is acquired by the student and possessed and processed by the mind.

   Education is an active, formative process. It allows us to impose order and significance on the knowledge and information we acquire. It consists in, to use a modern phrase, the *appropriation* of the knowledge, the process of making it our own. Newman illustrates with the analogy of the digestive system. Just as our digestion transforms food into the substance of our physical being so education transforms what we learn 'into the substance of our previous state of thought'.[15] If this transformation does not occur then there will have been no enlargement of the intellect, that is, no education.

For true learning is not just acquiring information; it is relating new ideas to one another and to what we already know; it is the expansion of our intellect and our understanding in accommodating new knowledge. A truly great intellect is one which

> takes a connected view of old and new, past and present, far and near, and which has an insight into the influence of all these, one on another, without which there is no whole, and no centre.[16]

Knowledge is not merely an acquirement, it is a philosophy. By 'philosophy' Newman does not mean a separate subject of study; it denotes the capacity and the tendency of the mind to integrate its knowledge into a coherent whole and to add new knowledge to it in an organic, not just an additive, way. He is arguing for enlargement of mind as opposed to narrowness of mind. Narrowness of mind is the characteristic of those who, however comprehensive their store of information or knowledge, have not developed the capacity to generalize, to associate, to fit their knowledge into a broad and balanced view. For such people nothing which they encounter causes them to make associations with other encounters, other information, other knowledge. They have not developed their capacity to see relationships between ideas, to associate new and old, or new and new. 'Nothing has a drift or relation; nothing has a history or a promise.' Everything that they know or learn stands on its own and 'comes and goes in its turn, like the shifting scenes of a show which leave the spectator where he was'.[17] The difference is between the passive possessor of information and the active processor of knowledge.

Conclusion

Newman's thoughts on the function of the university, on liberal education, and on the importance of the postponement of vocational or professional training until the individual has acquired a breadth of vision and depth of understanding in a general way, continue to challenge universities and university educators. Whatever the specificities of his answers, he has raised questions which any account of the value of education in general, and university education in particular, must address.

Newman was made a cardinal of the Roman Catholic Church in 1879. He died in 1890. His greatest educational legacy is the challenge he posed to educators to remain true to the ideal of an educated mind and not to allow the life of the intellect to become subordinated to pragmatic imperatives whether these be waging war or making profit.

13 John Dewey (1859-1952): Education for the Future

Background

John Dewey, one of the most powerful influences on educational thought in the twentieth century, if not the most powerful, was born in the town of Burlington, Vermont in 1859. His father was proprietor of the local general store where, apparently, locals would gather from time to time to discuss, with equal interest, affairs of both state and locality. According to one apocryphal story the store window carried the legend:

Hams and cigars: smoked and unsmoked.

The intimate small-town ethos of nineteenth-century Burlington played a large part in forming the young Dewey's educational outlook in two ways: one negative, one positive.

On the negative side he became convinced that the conventional, formal and desk-bound approach to schooling, typified by the small town and rural schools of his childhood, was futile. It was inadequate for the burgeoning USA, a new society emerging out of a simple agricultural economy which was being transformed by unprecedented industrialization, immigration, rapid population growth and drastic social change. The traditional education was predominantly static in subject matter, and relied on no more than rote memorization from the pupil. Since it was authoritarian in methods it required mainly passivity and receptivity on the part of the learner. Educators in this scheme could imagine nothing better than fixed subject matter which was drawn from scholarly sources remote from the experience of the pupil. The principal subject matter tended to be the conclusions of scholars rather than the experiences of learners.

On the positive side, Dewey was convinced that the ordinary experiences of day-to-day community life, be they social, economic, cultural or political, provided real and significant educational experiences. Politics was not just a matter of national and international significance removed from the interests of the ordinary citizen, but a matter of vital and immediate concern to the community. School should prepare the child for active participation in the life of the community; education must break down, rather than reinforce, the gap between the experience of schooling and the needs of a truly participatory democracy. 'The school,' Dewey wrote, 'is primarily a social institution.' Since education is a social process

> the school is simply that form of community life in which all those agencies are concentrated that will be most effective in bringing the child to share in the inherited resources of the race, and to use his own powers for social ends ... education is a process of living and not a preparation for future living.[1]

Career

Dewey graduated from the University of Vermont in 1879. After a period teaching high school he went to Johns Hopkins University where he gained his PhD in 1884. By his middle thirties he was Head of the Department of Philosophy, Psychology and Pedagogy at the University of Chicago. It was here, in 1896, that Dewey established his famous experimental school, the laboratory school.

In 1904 Dewey was appointed Professor of Philosophy at Columbia University and it was from this base that he articulated and spread the educational ideas which he had developed in Chicago. They were to make him the most famous and influential educator of the twentieth century. He wrote, lectured and travelled extensively. On his retirement in 1930 he became Emeritus Professor at Columbia. One of the difficulties that Dewey presents to anyone who would present a short précis of his career is that he lived to the age of 93, active to the end.

Educational experimentation

Dewey's laboratory school was not designed to implement a pre-structured pedagogical plan: the vision was not of implementation but of open experimentation. The laboratory school was intended as an experimental institution in two senses: first, it was intended to facilitate research and experimentation into new principles and methods of teaching and learning; second, it was designed in acknowledgement of the active participation of learners in learning and so allowed learners to take an experimental approach to their own education.

Dewey considered the laboratory school to be the testing ground for his philosophical ideas and their implementation. As a pragmatist who believed that the meaning of an idea or theory is to be found in its practical consequences, Dewey tried to eliminate the dichotomy between philosophy and ordinary experience. 'Education,' he wrote, 'is the laboratory in which philosophical distinctions become concrete and are tested.' If we think of education 'as the process of forming fundamental dispositions, intellectual and emotional, toward nature and fellow men' philosophy may even be defined, Dewey concluded, 'as the general theory of education'.[2]

The traditional classroom

The design and furniture of the traditional school tells the story of traditional education; it is a story of submission, immobility, passivity and dependency. Dewey uses the analogy of the biologist who, through the examination of 'a bone or two', can reconstruct an entire animal. In the same way consideration of 'the ordinary school room' of the past will reveal a place 'with its rows of ugly desks placed in geometrical order', allowing for no individual differences of size, interests or circumstances, and minimizing freedom of movement. There was just enough space 'to hold books, pencils and paper'. With the addition of a table, chairs, bare walls, 'and possibly a few pictures', 'we can', Dewey concludes, 'reconstruct the only educational activity that can possibly go on in such a place. It is made for listening'. Traditional education is an on-going exercise in listening: studying out of a book 'is only another kind of listening'.[3] Excessive reliance on listening generates dependency and passivity. There could be nothing closer to Rousseau's dismissal of book-based learning.

Traditional vs. progressive

Dewey's critique of traditional school design was not a matter of whim or of arbitrary taste regarding educational architecture, but a central feature of his philosophy. He wanted his new laboratory school to replace the dependency and submission of traditional classrooms with opportunities which would allow learners to create their own experience: to experiment, to enquire, to create. He wanted a classroom where children could move about, form groups, plan and execute operational solutions to self-selected problems; in short, to learn for themselves and between themselves, under the direction and guidance, rather than the command, of the teacher. 'Guidance,' he assures us, 'is not external imposition'. He emphasizes the true meaning of guidance: 'It is freeing the life-process for its own most adequate fulfilment.'[4] In the old system it was the function of teachers to motivate children – often against their immediate interests – to learn the established subjects. This gave rise to what Dewey considered a 'demoralizing doctrine' which informed the consequent methodology: first we select the subject matter, then we look about for ways to make it interesting. On the contrary a school should be a 'society of free individuals in which all, through their own work, contribute to the liberation and enrichment of the lives of others'. This, for Dewey, 'is the only environment in which any individual can really grow normally to his full stature'.[5]

Pedagogy

In Dewey's pedagogy the teacher has two principal functions. First, the teacher must guide the young through the complexities of life and give them opportunities to learn in the natural way, that is, by solving relevant problems. Second, the teacher must enable (or in today's language 'empower') the young to cope adequately with contemporary conditions and to come to terms with the novel problems which an unpredictable future will bring.

Dewey's *Pedagogic Creed*[6] sets out a general view of the teacher's role in both positive and negative terms. The teacher's function is not to 'impose certain ideas or to form certain habits in the child'. On the contrary, the teacher 'as a member of the community' will, on behalf of the community, 'select the influences which shall affect the child' as well as assisting 'him in properly responding to these influences'. It is the teacher's business 'to determine, on the basis of larger experience and riper wisdom, how the discipline of life shall come to the child'.[7]

The old model of education placed a premium on assignments, on private, isolated study and on recitation. Dewey uses the laboratory school as the new model: the mission of the laboratory school was to find more effective ways of learning and teaching, to find ways of breaking down barriers between schools and their sustaining communities, and to find subject matter which would break the hold of traditional rote learning and symbol interpretation. What Dewey means by this is the way in which the traditional subject-centred education system fragments knowledge. It 'subdivides each topic into studies; each study into lessons; each lesson into specific facts and formulae'. It is the logic of the subject matter that determines the objectives and the method of the teaching/learning process. The principal emphasis is put upon 'the logical subdivisions and consecutions of the subject matter' rather than on the experience and response of the learner. The education system sees the child 'simply as the incomplete immature being who is to be matured; ... as the superficial being who is to be deepened; (as the one whose) narrow experience is to be widened'. The process of education requires that the child is passive and receptive: 'His part is fulfilled when he is ductile and docile.'[8]

Child and curriculum

This approach sets the pupils' experience at nought against the accumulated knowledge of the race: the pupil is made into a passive receptacle whose only function is to receive the structured subject matter which scholars have codified (the 'subjects'). It is this codification which gives shape and purpose to the traditional approach to education: knowledge is classified into discrete subjects or disciplines; history is not geography, mathematics is not art, science is not religion, literature is not history. Human knowledge is divided according to the logical and epistemological distinctions of scholars, not according to the experience of the individual child.

The psychological approach to education which Dewey advocates follows the developmental capacity of the child to engage with subjects at an appropriate level. The subject-centred approach can no more substitute for the psychological approach than a finished map can recapture the personal experience of the explorer. Yet the two are not mutually exclusive: the child is the explorer of his or her own experience of the world; the subjects are the maps he or she (and all of us) may use to guide explorations and locate them in relation to what is already known (he or she learns to read the maps/subjects through the lens of his or her own relevant experience). The good teacher matches the child's initial exploration of the world with exposure to appropriate bodies of knowledge so that the former is not repressed and the integrity of the latter is not compromised.

Dewey puts the pupil at the centre of education as a wilful, purposive and active agent in the learning process. The child cannot be other than 'the starting point, the centre, and the end'. Whatever growth or development the child is capable of is the ideal. In education, subjects should be secondary; they are purely instrumental in the service of growth. The development of the child involves more than subject matter; self-realization rather than knowledge or information is the goal. 'To possess all the world of knowledge and lose one's own self is as awful a fate in education as in religion.'[9]

The child's relation to the curriculum should not be one of subordination to established knowledge. The alternative is not the abandonment of existing established knowledge for an anarchic child-centred approach. Children do not experience the world through the medium of subject disciplines: their knowledge is integral and ranges as far and wide as curiosity leads. Interest moves readily, and without a conscious break, from topic to topic, experience to experience. The personal and social interests which comprise the on-going stream of life give unity to experience. 'Whatever is uppermost in his mind,' Dewey writes, 'constitutes to (the child), for the time being, the whole universe.' The universe of the child's experience is 'fluid and fluent; its contents dissolve and reform with amazing rapidity. But, after all, it is the child's own world. It has the unity and completeness of his own life'.[10]

The child's attitude to his or her experience should be reflected in the curriculum which, initially at least, should reflect the experience of the child in an integrated rather than a differentiated way. The differentiation of the experience into subject specialisms comes by degrees: a developmental differentiation of the child's organic experience into the traditional categories of knowledge such as geography, history, mathematics, literature, etc. The child must learn the ways in which human knowledge has been structured into subjects or disciplines, but this is not the starting point – it is a development on the journey.

This is why Dewey could write that the 'child and the curriculum are simply two limits which define a single process ... the present standpoint of the child and the facts and truths of studies define instruction'. The process moves outward from the present, subjective, and wholly personal experience of the child to the knowledge of the race 'represented by the organised bodies of truth that we call studies'.[11] It makes little sense to put the child's lived experience and the established disciplines into opposition. They are not in competition; they are not alternatives any more than logic and psychology, or reason and development, are alternatives. One represents infancy and childhood, the other the maturity 'of the same growing life'. To set them in opposition 'is to hold that the nature and destiny of the child war with each other'.[12]

Although the child must begin the process of learning the symbol systems associated with the various disciplines, there must first be something in the child's experience which requires or demands this or that symbol, this or that discipline, this or that subject, before they can mean anything to the child. The child's use of language, for instance, must spring from the child's own experience – whether this be actual or imaginative. As well as growing up, the child grows out into the world mediated by structured human knowledge.

Principles

The laboratory school operated on three simple principles which collectively informed Dewey's educational philosophy.

The first principle was that the business of the school is to train children in cooperative and mutually helpful living – to help them to grow into community. In his *Pedagogic Creed* Dewey declared that the only true education 'comes through the stimulation of the child's powers by the demands of the social situations in which he finds himself'. By meeting the demands of successive social situations the child is 'stimulated to act as a member of a unity', that is to emerge from the ego-centricity of his 'original narrowness of action and feeling'. He or she must begin to think of him- or herself in terms of the social group to which he or she belongs.[13]

The social calls the child forth through communication: society exists *in* communication. The words 'common', 'community' and 'communication' have more than an etymological connection:

community is built on commonalities, and communication is the way in which these commonalities are transmitted from person to person, generation to generation. 'The communication which insures participation in a common understanding is one which secures similar emotional and intellectual dispositions – like ways of responding to expectations and requirements.'[14] This is what makes a community.

The second principle was that all educative activity must be rooted in the instinctive, impulsive activities of the child, not in the imposition of structured, external material. 'The child's own instincts and powers furnish the material,' Dewey wrote, 'and give the starting point for all education.' Both quantity and quality of learning is determined by the child, not by the subject matter.[15]

Finally, the laboratory school promoted the child's individual tendencies and activities; these were organized and directed to promote the idea of cooperative living. The learning process should take advantage of the child's individual tendencies and activities to reproduce on the child's plane the typical doings and occupations of the larger, maturer society in which the child must finally participate.

Learning is rooted in the community. The individual and society cannot be considered in isolation one from the other:

> The individual who is to be educated is a social individual, and that society is an organic union of individuals. If we eliminate the social factor from the child we are left only with an abstraction; if we eliminate the individual factor from society, we are left only with an inert mass.[16]

The communal imperative is not a demand for collective 'sameness'. On the contrary, communal life affords the individual the opportunity to 'learn to be human', the opportunity 'to develop ... an effective sense of being an individually distinctive member of a community'.[17] Education regulates the process through which the young come to share in the social consciousness.

Purpose of education

Although education should be practical it is not the practicality of a narrowly vocational preparation. The future is unpredictable: it is not possible to foretell what the world will be like at any point in the future. Consequently it is not possible to prepare the child for any 'precise set of conditions'. To prepare children for the future is to prepare them to command themselves, to train them so that they will have full use of their capacities and faculties: 'that his eye and ear and hand may be tools ready to command, that his judgement may be capable of grasping the conditions under which it has to work, and the executive forces be trained to act economically and efficiently.'[18]

Growth

Growth is a central concept in Dewey's philosophy of education, and to this day perhaps the most controversial. He does not accept what are called 'teleological' explanations which seek the significance of human experience or effort in some future state: the eventual dictatorship of the proletariat, the attainment of the beatific vision, the New Jerusalem, or whatever. In all cases teleological explanations invoke some future perfection both to explain what is happening now and to stipulate what ought to be happening now. They are especially favoured by educational theorists: from a definition of some manner of idealized future you can determine what and how we should be teaching our children in the present. Dewey prefers an evolutionary account of human activity, one which rejects any notion of evident destiny and freely acknowledges our ignorance of the future.

Education, then, cannot be a preparation for some idealized future (since we have no way of knowing the future). It is simply a process of growth, the continuing reconstruction of experience. Human growth is not determined by any outside or independent aim or end. Educational progress consists in developing 'new attitudes towards, and new interests in, (our) experience'. Education is a process of reorganizing our knowledge, our expertise and our experience in order to confront changing circumstances.[19]

This process is best understood in Dewey's notion of enquiry. When our normal expectations are not met we have a problematic situation; our normal routines of response and behaviour are no longer adequate. We must examine the situation, identify what has changed, and develop strategies to cope with it. Solutions are always provisional because we live in an evolving world: further experience will reinforce or challenge our provisional solutions. We cannot avoid change, we must adapt.

It is difficult for traditional educators, who have always looked for the purpose and significance of education outside of the process itself, to accept this. The world is changing even as educational preparation is in progress. The growth of which Dewey speaks is not growth towards some predetermined and externally imposed ideal or end: it is growth, as it seems, for its own sake. 'There is nothing,' he declares, 'to which growth is relative save more growth; there is nothing to which education is subordinate save more education.' The educational process is its own end; it is not subject to any independent evaluation.[20]

There is no limit, in principle, to the possibilities of change, development and evolution since we simply do not know what the future holds or what demands it will make on us. The best preparation we can make for the future is to develop to the fullest extent the individual's capacity for adaptation and innovation: the capacity to respond creatively to changing circumstances.

Experience and theory

Dewey's pragmatist philosophy stresses the priority of experience over theory. We learn to think and reason by thinking and reasoning, by tackling real problems which arise in our experience. When we think, we become conscious of a problem or obstacle to our development; we analyse the situation; we identify possible solutions; we compare the implications of the different solutions and select the best course of action; we implement this in practice.

Dewey's philosophy is about dealing with problems which arise out of real situations. It aims at control. It stresses that solutions to problems are tentative and must be judged by their usefulness. The method is the method of science. It aims at the control of the environment and improvement of the environment by creative and reflective thought. The educational manifestation of the scientific method is the project method associated with Dewey and his close follower William H. Kilpatrick.

The project method certainly does *not* mean the transcription of 'information' accompanied by illustrations to be hung on the classroom wall to impress important visitors. The principal value of a project is not the outcome but the experience of the process.

In more general terms, the practical importance of the result of thinking is subsidiary to the *process* of thinking.

The control and direction of enquiry is central: knowledge begins in doing, it is active. Growth occurs in the process of putting ideas to the test of experience. Learners should be given wide opportunities for purposive enquiry. This is the value of the project method; the pupil learns by trying to solve problems:

> If he cannot devise his own solution (not of course in isolation but in correspondence with the teacher and the other pupils) and find his own way out he will not learn, not even if he can recite some correct answer with one hundred per cent accuracy.[21]

It is like the difference between studying a map and making a journey: while the map is a useful guide for the traveller it is not a substitute for the experience of travelling.

Solving a problem is making a hitherto incoherent situation coherent and integrated; it involves taking a selection of apparently incompatible experiences and transforming them into a unified whole – this unified whole is the solution to the problem. A fact or a theory is valuable only insofar as it has significant practical application measured by the contribution it makes to human growth. Without such application it is useless, regardless of its theoretical appeal.

Dewey is sometimes associated with the worst excesses of a do-as-you-please approach to elementary education, so much so that he was forced to distance himself on a number of occasions from those who claimed to be his disciples.

Dewey's contribution to the development of education in the twentieth century was incalculable, if not without controversy. His greatest contribution has been to liberate the education of children from the dead hand of tradition and from what he himself has called the 'static cold-storage ideal of knowledge'. He forged a theory and practice of education which can be relevant to contemporary industrial and social progress without becoming the slave of either.

14 Maria Montessori (1870–1952): Education for Personal Competence

Background

Maria Montessori was born in Chiaravalle, near Ancona, in Italy. She rejected the socially acceptable option of becoming a teacher in favour of a medical career, an unheard-of option for a young lady of the late nineteenth century. However, she persevered and in the teeth of the opposition of her family, the university authorities, social convention and her fellow students she graduated in 1894 with a double first in medicine and surgery: the first woman to graduate from the University of Rome with a degree as a medical doctor. Her passion, courage and determination allied with her humanity, insight and imagination were to make her a remarkable educator.

Following her graduation, Montessori was appointed assistant doctor at the university psychiatric clinic, a position which gave her the opportunity to observe the problems of mentally handicapped children and to involve herself in their education. At this time she was taking classes at the university in philosophy and experimental psychology ('which,' she recorded, 'had only recently been established in Italian universities'). She was also researching the field of pedagogic anthropology in the elementary schools; studying 'the methods in organisation used for the education of normal children'.[1] From 1900 she lectured in pedagogic anthropology at the university where she held the post of Professor of Anthropology from 1904 to 1908.

Major influences

Besides Froebel, the major influences on Montessori's educational thinking were the French medical doctors Jean Itard (1775–1838) and Edward Séguin (1812–1880). Both were dedicated to the education of children with mental and sensory deficiencies. Itard became famous as the teacher of the famous 'wild boy of Aveyron', while Séguin was a teacher who became a physician and, building on the work of Itard, developed pedagogies appropriate for the teaching of mentally defective children. Montessori's admiration for these two pioneers was immense and for years she followed their prescriptions in her own pedagogical work. Throughout *The Montessori Method* she repeatedly acknowledges her debt to these pioneers.

Her work with mentally handicapped children at the university clinic led to remarkable success: 'I succeeded in teaching a number of the idiots from the asylums both to read and to write so well,' she records, 'that I was able to present them at a public school for an examination together with normal children.' Her 'idiots' passed the examination.[2] Montessori had taken the radical decision to deal with these children as persons who needed to learn, rather than as patients who needed to be treated. 'I felt,' she wrote, 'that mental deficiency presented chiefly a pedagogical rather than mainly a medical question.'[3] As a result she was able to witness what she called 'the mental awakening' of these children who had been virtually abandoned because of their perceived inferiority.

How could children, confined with hopeless lunatics in Italian asylums, succeed at public examinations as well as normal children? Montessori turned the question on its head: how could normal children perform so poorly that they could be matched by those judged to be mentally inferior? 'While everyone was admiring the progress of my idiots,' she wrote, 'I was searching for the reasons which could keep the happy healthy children of the common schools on so low a plane that they could be equalled in tests of intelligence by my unfortunate pupils!'[4]

The answer lay in pedagogical principles: the use of comparable methods with normal children would lead to similarly startling results and 'set free their personality in a marvellous and surprising way'.[5]

An opportunity to further test and develop her educational ideas came in 1907. The director of the Roman Association of Good Building needed to make provision for the pre-school children of working parents. While parents were at work and older children at school, unsupervised pre-school children played on the stairs and corridors of the apartment blocks, generating an ethos of squalor, lawlessness and disorder. The director hit on the idea of setting aside one apartment for their care and education.

In January 1907 Maria Montessori was appointed director of this project.

Casa dei Bambini

The new institution was called *Casa dei Bambini* or 'The Children's House'. The first group comprised 60 children aged between 3 and 6. Montessori's presuppositions regarding the nature and intellectual capacity of very small children were immediately challenged. She soon made a discovery which was to revolutionize the education of the very young. She likened herself to a peasant woman who goes to plough and discovers hidden treasures.

The treasures? Montessori discovered that small children are capable of intense mental concentration, love order and repetition, are capable of informed choices, prefer purposeful activity to unstructured play, have little need for systems of reward and punishment, love silence, have a deep sense of personal dignity and are capable of spontaneous self-discipline. Such insights were completely contrary to the prevailing view of childhood.

Children develop willy-nilly. Education does not induce growth and development, it controls and directs it. Education is the active support adults give to children's normal development. There are two components, a physical body which grows, and a spiritual soul which develops. 'These two forms, physiological and psychic,' she wrote, 'have one eternal font, life itself.' Teachers should not suppress 'the mysterious powers which lie within these two forms of growth' but rather should be alert to their successive needs as they appear.[6]

Principles

Montessori began with a small number of principles based on her experience with mentally defective children. Everyone needs independence in respect of the normal practices of life; education starts with the senses rather than the intellect – the sense of touch is fundamental; and education must follow the psychological development of the child rather than the requirements of a preordained curriculum. In short, education must be child-centred rather than curriculum-centred.

Sensitive periods

Crucial to Montessori's approach is the concept of 'sensitive periods' which are brief periods in the course of development during which the child is ready to acquire a particular competence or to accomplish a particular kind of task. The course of normal development passes through identifiable periods which manifest intellectual and physical readiness for certain kinds of learning. During these periods children are oriented to the aspects of their environment which are appropriate to this sensitivity. The sensitive periods 'correspond to special sensibilities to be found in creatures in process of development; they are transitory, and confined to the acquisition of a determined characteristic'.[7] The attention involved is not just a matter of a passing curiosity, it is more like an obsession.

For example, in the normal course of development children reach the stage where they begin to realize the variety of colour in the environment and will want to be able, in their speech, to refer to the relevant distinctions: red, blue, yellow, green. They are, at that point, learning-ready with respect to colour. The observant teacher or parent will respond appropriately by naming the colours on appropriate occasions and engaging in activities involving colours. If this does not happen a learning opportunity, which will never recur with the same intensity, will have been lost. The progression of these sensitive periods is irreversible – once passed over they can never be recovered or recreated. 'If the baby has not been able to work in accordance with the guidance of its sensitive period, it has lost its chance of a natural conquest, and has lost it for ever.'[8] In general, appropriate exercises and activities must be available to the child which correspond to stages of development.

It is because of the importance of the sensitive periods that Montessori is so insistent on the method of observation; the teacher should constantly observe the children and monitor their interests, the nature of the interests, their duration, etc. She or he must be alert to the 'symptoms' of need which identify the 'sensitive periods' and respond appropriately at the time they appear.

Mastery

The highest reward for learners is a sense of mastery: the completion of the task constitutes the reward. Correction comes from the materials, not from the teacher. Children effectively teach themselves through the use of didactic material which is self-correcting, i.e. which is designed in such a manner that errors are obvious. (A universally familiar example is the common jigsaw puzzle.) It is not sufficient that educational materials should stimulate: to be educational the material must also direct the activity. Children should not only persevere in an activity over time but the material should be so designed that they will do so without making mistakes. Think of the children's toy which involves fitting wooden insets into corresponding moulds cut in a board. It is not possible to complete this activity incorrectly: the smaller shapes may fit loosely into the bigger moulds but then the bigger pieces which do not fit the smaller moulds remain. The only way to complete the exercise is to get it right. This is the essence of self-correcting materials.

Montessori's materials are, in the first instance, playthings. Buttoning, fastening, lacing and tying activities which teach the children the skills necessary for dressing and undressing are first encountered as play. More sophisticated, but no less fun or less interesting to the child, are the mathematical materials – the long stair, the broad stair, solid insets of different shapes. Montessori's apparatus ensures that both learning environment and instruction are tailored to the child, not only child-centred but child-friendly. The apparatus are more detailed, more structured and much less burdened with mystical and symbolic baggage than Froebel's 'Gifts'. They are more rational, more scientific and more psychologically-based.

Does this kind of self-correcting learning material render the teacher redundant? No, it allows the teacher to become 'a director of the spontaneous work of the children … not a passive force'.[9] The approach provides opportunities for teachers to observe the children so that they can individualize their educational experiences in a systematic and appropriate way.

Mastery learning and auto-education require that children can exercise a significant measure of freedom. Montessori insists on perfect freedom, not licence; but the freedom to do what is required at any particular stage of the child's psychological development. A visitor to one of Montessori's schools would have been impressed by the children's discipline. Forty children, between 3 and 7 years old, each one engaged in his or her own chosen task:

one is going through one of the exercises for the senses, one is doing an arithmetical exercise; one is handling the letters, one is drawing, one is fastening and unfastening the pieces of cloth on one of our little wooden frames, still another is dusting. Some are seated at the tables, some on rugs on the floor.[10]

And yet all is orderly and quiet because each child is engrossed in his or her freely chosen activity.

The environment of the classroom

Montessori stresses the importance of the child's environment. In the normal course of events (certainly in Montessori's time) the child's world was dominated by adult needs and adult misconceptions. All domestic furniture, for example, was designed for adult use and comfort; children had to accommodate to it. Schoolroom furniture was so designed and fixed in place as to render the child immobile: the child's environment, whether at home or at school, was not child-friendly.

Montessori changed all of this: her commitment to 'perfect freedom' would be hollow if the means were not there to exercise it. She advocates the regulation, rather than the suppression, of liberty. Special materials and furnishings are designed to give the child practice in activities which might otherwise be picked up only haphazardly or not at all. The Montessori classroom is a radical departure from the traditional classroom in which the teacher instructs rows of immobilized learners who are either listening passively or engaged on collectively assigned tasks.

In terms of practicalities Montessori's method falls into three distinct categories: exercises of practical life; exercises in sensory training; and didactic exercises.

Practical and sensory exercises

The exercises of practical life are designed to enable children to learn to take care of themselves. Freedom is as much a lack of dependency as it is a lack of restraint. It consists, in large part, in being able to do ordinary things like washing, dressing and feeding, for oneself. The furniture in the Montessori classroom is proportionate to the children, reflecting their size and strength, so that they are comfortable with the different articles and can easily handle and move them about at need. This is the beginning of independence: children can make meaningful decisions regarding their own environment.

Desks represent the notion that educational activity requires 'a special position of the body – as we believe that we must assume a special position when we are about to pray'.[11] Montessori replaced desks with child-sized chairs and tables suitable for children to work at, washstands with individualized cupboards for each child's toiletries, cupboards appropriate to the didactic materials which are accessible to children without adult assistance, blackboards at a height appropriate to even the smallest child. Giving children control over their environment increases their freedom immeasurably.

This philosophy is not confined to the practical furnishings of the classroom, however. The little round stair, for example, is a freestanding spiral stairway which allows children to practise climbing and descending. They cannot comfortably do this on a regular stairway because of the unsuitable proportions.

Such exercises in physical movement or sensory training empower children to train themselves in appropriate ways. Montessori's educational materials enable children to develop their sensory acuity and discrimination in a way which is self-motivated and individually paced. The materials are self-correcting so that using them is a process of self-education. Montessori believed that 'the education of the senses should be begun methodically in infancy, and should continue during the entire period of instruction which is to prepare the individual for life in society'. This is a matter of the greatest practical importance: consumers, for example, lack the capacity to distinguish the different qualities of various substances with their senses. 'In fact,' Montessori says, 'intelligence is rendered useless by lack of practice, and this practice is almost always sense education'. Even buying fish becomes an impossible task for one who has not learned to recognize the requisite sensory signs of freshness.[12]

The Montessori apparatus embodies the widest possible range of variable qualities: different materials, shapes, sizes, textures, colours, weights, and so forth in the widest possible combinations. As well as being self-correcting, the equipment is graded so as to lead the child through the development of a wide range of concepts and skills.

Didactic exercises: writing

Montessori's didactic exercises are related to the basic three R's: reading, writing and arithmetic. Her system won widest attention and acclaim because of its claimed phenomenal success in teaching the three R's.

Writing comes before reading: the muscular sense is more easily developed in infancy which means that the fine motor skills required for writing precede reading, which requires a much longer course of instruction and a higher level of intellectual development.

Montessori's methodology begins with the writer not with the writing: the writer should be the focus of our attention in the first instance; analysis of written letters or words brings us no closer to understanding the human behaviour necessary to produce them. 'Let us observe an individual who is writing,' she says, 'and let us seek to analyse the acts he performs in writing.'[13] Examine writing, in other words, from a developmental point of view; what specific mechanical operations are involved?

Such analytical observation allowed her to identify the component skills of writing and to separate the formation of letters from the skills required to manipulate the writing instrument. These skills could be practised individually up to a high level of proficiency. Then, when it comes to the actual physical act of writing, the child, having mastered them, is capable of all of the motor acts necessary.

Once the writing process has been analysed and reduced to its component parts, these are then practised independently before all are eventually assembled into the act of writing. In addition, Montessori developed a system of learning the shapes of letters through tactile experience rather than through visual analysis. Letters are cut out of sandpaper and the children trace the shape with their fingers. The roughness of the sandpaper provides the only control of the accuracy of the movements. At the same time the phonetic sounds of the letters are taught. Once the preparatory stages have been completed the children begin to write as if by some spontaneous process.

Montessori has recorded how this process worked in the earliest days in the House of Childhood. She was on the roof of the tenement with the children on a sunny day. She asked a boy to draw a picture of the chimney. She gave him a piece of chalk with which he made a sketch of the chimney on the roof tiles. She praised his work. The child then

> looked at me, smiled, remained for a moment as if on the point of bursting into some joyous act and then cried out 'I can write! I can write!' and kneeling down again he wrote on the pavement the word 'hand'. Then full of enthusiasm he wrote also 'chimney', 'roof'. As he wrote he continued to cry out, 'I can write! I can write! I know how to write!'[14]

The other children were attracted by his excitement. They gathered round and began to imitate him. It was as if floodgates had been opened. Once the realization of their ability dawned the children were unstoppable. 'With a species of frenzied joy' they continued to write all over the place. They began to cover the surfaces of their homes with words to such an extent that their parents gave them paper and pencils to save their floors and walls![15]

Montessori remarks, correctly, that learning to write is not quite the same as learning to speak. The latter is much more gradual and developmental whereas with writing, once it begins the child is capable of writing *any* word. Montessori and her colleagues were astonished at the outcome which was quite unexpected. 'Those first days we were a prey to deep emotions,' she said. 'It seemed as if we walked in a dream, and as if we assisted at some miraculous achievement.' Which, in a sense, they had.

Didactic exercises: reading

Learning to read follows a similar pattern. The child begins with the phonic rendering of a word – the phonics have been learned in the process of learning to identify the letters. The child repeats this phonic rendering faster and faster until the natural sound of the word is arrived at. But this is not reading. What constitutes reading is the act of *interpretation*, inferring or deducing a meaning from the written signs alone. The real test is the child's capacity to recognize and read a word that he has not heard pronounced. 'The word which he reads has the same relation to written language that the word which he hears bears to articulate language.' Until the child reads a transmission of ideas from the written word, he does not read.[16]

Montessori abandoned the traditional reading primers in favour of a variety of literacy games which engage children with meaning.

'Truly,' she declared, 'we have buried the tedious and stupid ABC primer side by side with the useless copybooks.'[17] It is claimed that her approach works not only for Italian and for other languages which are phonetically regular but also for English which, notoriously, is not.

Didactic exercises: number

The teaching of number is accomplished principally through the use of perhaps the most famous of all the Montessori apparatus, the 'long stair': a set of ten rods measuring from one to ten decimetres. Each rod is marked off in decimetre lengths of alternate colours. When arranged in order from one to ten decimetres the rods resemble a set of ten equal steps; the 'long stair'. Through the manipulation of these rods the child learns progressively to order, count, add and subtract. Once again the method is experiential. The rods correspond to the natural numbers and gradually increase in length unit by unit. In this way they not only represent individual numbers but also give the clear visual impression of their relative values. So when a child is asked, for example, to select the representation of *five* he or she will first do so visually before verifying the selection by counting the coloured portions. This in itself is an instance of sound arithmetical method: estimation followed by verification.

By playing with the long stair the children teach themselves in a positive and satisfying way. The long stair embodies Montessori's two fundamental principles: readiness to learn and self-instruction. Once the children have become familiar with the long stair they are ready for the symbolic representation of the numbers.

The Montessori teacher

Montessori's ideal teacher would have substantial training in child psychology; her system is deeply rooted in experimental pedagogy and experimental psychology. She realized that positive intervention in the development of children requires a thorough understanding of this development. 'The broader the teacher's scientific culture and practice in experimental psychology,' she wrote, 'the sooner will come for her the marvel of unfolding life and her interest in it.'[18] However, she insisted that the scientific relationship between psychology and pedagogy be properly appreciated:

'we do not start from the conclusions of experimental psychology.' It is not the understanding of general laws relating to the 'average sense conditions according to the age of the child' which determines educational applications. On the contrary, 'we start essentially from a method, and it is probable that psychology will be able to draw its conclusions (from that) and not *vice versa*'.[19]

In fact the role of the teacher in the Montessori system is quite different from that of the conventional classroom; so much so that Montessori refers to the classroom practitioner as 'directress': her job is not, in the first instance, instructional; she must listen and observe and on that basis judiciously direct the learning activity of the child. 'Indeed,' Montessori tells us, 'with my methods, the teacher teaches *little* and observes *much*, and, above all, it is her function to direct the psychic activity of the children and their physiological development. For this reason I have changed the name of teacher into that of directress.'[20]

Montessori's system allows the individual child to develop at his or her own rate without the stress of induced rivalry, imposed competition, or the false incentives of extrinsic rewards and punishments.

Perhaps the most telling endorsement of the life work of Maria Montessori is the fact that she was forced by Mussolini's Fascists to leave Italy in 1934. By 1936 all official Montessori schemes in Italy had been abolished. The German Montessori Society was suppressed by the Nazis in 1935; in Berlin and Vienna Montessori was burned in effigy on a pyre of her published works. There could have been no greater endorsement of Montessori's system and its aim of strong, free and self-governing individuals.

15 Martin Buber (1878–1965): Education for Relationship

Background

Martin Buber was born in Vienna in 1878 into the rich intellectual tradition of European Jewry. As a student at Leipzig he became involved in the Zionist movement. There, and subsequently in Berlin, he advocated the political advancement of Jews, the renewal of Jewish culture and the establishment of a Jewish University in Jerusalem. He saw in World War I a sign of failure of communication between different traditions. His political leanings were towards community socialism, as exemplified in the Kibbutzim of the Jewish settlements in Palestine. In 1923 he was appointed to the Chair of Jewish Philosophy of Religion at the University of Frankfurt, a position he was forced to relinquish following the rise of Nazism.

Throughout his life Buber had a deep interest in education as a process of dialogue. He promoted the education of the embattled Jewish community in Nazi Germany until 1935 when he was prohibited from lecturing in public. In 1938 he emigrated to Palestine and took the Chair of Social Philosophy at the Hebrew University in Jerusalem. Although his sympathies were Zionist he consistently advocated Jewish/Arab partnership in Palestine and criticized the terrorist campaign which was waged against the Palestinians and the British prior to the establishment of the state of Israel in 1948.

Metaphors of education

Buber identified two contrasting conventional approaches to education: the progressive, child-centred approach and the traditional, subject-centred approach. According to the first 'to educate' means to draw out of the child that which is already there. This view does not consider that the educator brings anything from the

outside, but merely arranges matters so that influences pre-
venting full development are eliminated. The educator's task is
'to overcome the disturbing influences, to set aside the obstacles
which hinder (the child's) free development', to allow the child to
'become himself'.[1]

The metaphor of the gardener typifies this 'child-centred'
approach. The teacher, like the conscientious gardener, prepares
the soil, controls the environment, nurtures the growing plant, and
trusts to the plant's natural powers of growth to do the rest. The
teacher is a facilitator of growth and no more.

This approach 'indicates the care given to a soul in the making'
so that 'the natural process of growth may reach its culmination'.[2]
Those using the gardener's approach are likely to do so in the
understanding that each individual's learning future is predetermined by his or her innate ability and aptitude (if not heredity).

The predominant metaphor for the traditional, subject-centred
approach is the sculptor who approaches the raw material with a
pre-determined idea of what it is to become. Concessions may be
made to the natural features of the material, the grain and flaws of
the wood or stone, but ultimately the material is shaped to the
sculptor's will and vision. Such an educator brings a preconceived
idea of what the child will become to the educational encounter,
an idea based on some tradition or general theory of education. This
view regards the pupil as possessing diverse potentialities which are
malleable and can be changed to conform to the educator's blueprint. Education in this tradition 'means shaping the child into a
form which the educator must first visualise, so that it may serve as a
directive for his work'.[3] It is not the task of the educator to promote
the child's natural capacities but to determine how individual
endowments will be made to fit with the preconceived idea.

The approach of the gardener, the progressive approach, lays
greatest emphasis on the individuality and freedom of the child.
The approach of the sculptor, the traditional approach, lays greatest emphasis on the authority of the teacher and of the tradition
of learning which he or she represents.

Relationships

Buber identifies two kinds of human relationships – I–It relationships and I–Thou relationships. I–It relationships are relationships

with people or things in the world seen simply in terms of a fixed meaning or function: plants, animals, objects, tools, machines and people in certain roles or capacities, for example bus conductor, plumber, doctor; or as categories, Jews, Blacks, Gypsies. These are people seen in terms of a function or a classification. We do not see them, or expect them to emerge in our relationship with them, as persons: when they do, it can be disconcerting, embarrassing, even shocking; we don't visit the doctor to hear his problems, we don't really want to be reminded of the humanity of the Gypsy.

In I–Thou relationships, by contrast, we relate to the other person as a subject, a person like ourselves: we accept their uniqueness without the limitation of a label or function. This other, this 'Thou' whom we address directly as another person reflects a value and a relationship which goes even beyond human relationships: the possibility of relationship with God, in Buber's term, 'the Eternal Thou'.

Child-centred education

In many spheres of human activity ostensibly small contributions can have a totally disproportionate effect: Einstein's short paper on relativity published in 1905, Edison's primitive recording of 'Mary Had a Little Lamb' in 1877. Buber's address to the 1925 International Educational Conference in Heidelberg is one such. Entitled 'The Development of the Creative Powers of the Child', it set out his views on education; views which to this day challenge our understanding of teaching and learning.

Buber was critical of the preoccupation of child-centred rhetoric and theory (the gardener model) with the development, or liberation, of the creative powers of the child. He acknowledged that the natural creativity of the child is more than a basic instinct: children have a primal desire to participate in making meaning in the world, what he calls the 'originator' or 'originative' instinct. Human beings are makers and it should be no surprise that human children inherit this instinct. It is not just a matter of imposing form on the formless, or organizing random elements. 'What the child desires,' Buber declares, 'is its own share in this becoming of things: it wants to be the subject of this event of production.' What is important to the child is to bring into existence something that was not there before through 'intensively experienced action'.[4]

That is, the child wants to be creative, to put order and co-herence on the world, not out of greed, acquisitiveness, or as an exercise of power, but out of the primal desire to express oneself to the world. But creativity on its own is not the centrally significant event in education: there is much more than the originative instinct. Even at its most advanced the instinct for creativity will lead only to an individual achievement: an act of creation, a work of art. The experience, and the achievement, is isolated, solitary: it is an I–It relationship, a relationship with the world as an object to be used and have our will imposed on it and nothing more. No matter how valuable this kind of experience may be in itself, it is not sufficient to build a true human life (which is the professed purpose of education). It cannot create meaningful relationships with others. Relationship derives from a different origin, not the instinct to create, but the instinct for communion. I–Thou relationships, relationships with the world as person, arise from the instinct for communion with other people. In such relationships the being of the world is presented to us not as an *object* which can be formed, controlled and manipulated, but as a subject; not as a thing, but as a person.

> Only if someone grasps his hand ... as a fellow creature lost in the world, to be his comrade or friend or lover beyond the arts, does (the child) have an awareness and a share of mutuality. An education based only on the training of the instinct of origination would prepare a new human solitariness which would be the most painful of all.[5]

When we share in an undertaking with others, for instance, more is involved than simply making or creating something on our own. We participate; we discover and practise a *community* of work with others. In such participation the child goes beyond the originative instinct alone by forming relationships with others – I–Thou relationships. This instinct for communion Buber describes as 'the longing for the world to become present to us as a person, which goes out to us as we to it, which chooses and recognises us as we do it, which is confirmed in us as we in it'.[6]

The Master

There are two parts to what happens in education. First of all there is the child's spontaneous creativity which arises from the originative instinct; then there is the encounter with the human teacher. It is the encounter with the teacher, who embodies a relevant scale of human values, which is decisive; the teacher provides the educative force. Left to itself the child's spontaneous expression, whether in movement, speech or art, is an unrealized beginning. Creativity-focused approaches, which promote and celebrate the child's freedom, misunderstand the role of the educator, 'this other half'. In a similar way the traditional subject-centred approach which promoted and celebrated authority misunderstood the significance of the child's creative spontaneity, 'the first half'.

Traditional authoritarian education can be symbolized by the image of the funnel: predetermined material is poured into the learner with little active participation or engagement. This symbol is being replaced in the modern child-centred theory by the symbol of the pump: the teacher's role is to draw, or pump, out the powers which are latent in the child.

In a true educational relationship, Buber argues, the spontaneity and creativity of the child must meet the criticism and instruction of the teacher. The relevant scale of values is not just *represented* by the teacher as dogmatic or necessary but is *embodied* in the teacher. The proper mode for teaching is influence, not interference. The influence must be concentrated in the humanity of the teacher and be absorbed by the pupil as a result of the relationship between the two: an I–Thou relationship between two beings equal in their humanity, not an I–It relationship in which the teacher dominates and manipulates the pupil for purposes known only to him- or herself.

Consequently, Buber's preferred model for the teacher is that of the 'Master'. By using this word Buber means to convey someone who is in charge, certainly, one who is Master of the situation, but also Master of the matter to be learned, whether this is knowledge or a skill. But there is more. Those who study under the Master are disciples: the disciples learn from the Master not just the cognitive or technical instruction he or she has to offer ('handwork or brainwork') but, almost incidentally, the way of life which gives this meaning: 'the mystery of personal life', the spirit of the pursuit, whatever it may be.

'The Master remains the model for the teacher.' The teacher must intervene in the learning and experience of the pupil in an unobtrusive way. Through the teacher 'the selection of the effective world' (curriculum) reaches the pupil: the teacher is the conduit. He or she fails in their task 'when he presents this selection to (the pupil) with a gesture of interference', that is, when he or she imposes the matter to be learned. The curriculum (not just the substance of the various subjects but the associated values and attitudes) 'must be concentrated in (the teacher)'. Perceived interference causes division in the pupil between obedience and rebellion. But 'a hidden influence proceeding from (the teacher's) integrity has an integrating force'.[7]

What is to be learned and known is presented to the learner not as 'object' (i.e., information, rules, processes, etc.), but as embodied in the teacher, the Master. The teacher has lived the world he or she teaches. The pupil learns the teacher's world not by rote learning of 'objective' information but through dialogue with the teacher, as in the ongoing, often unconscious, dialogue between the Master and the apprentice or disciple.

The Master/disciple model of the teacher/pupil relationship is in sharp contrast to the traditional form in which the teacher was in possession of all the right answers. The Master/disciple model is also in contrast to the progressive form which is based on a belief in the 'unfolding' of dispositions which are already there in the pupil awaiting release. According to Buber's view there is nothing 'there' except capacities.

Without human community and human culture we are nothing more than a bundle of unengaged capacities. If it were possible to examine the soul of a new-born child, and we were to do so, we would not find dispositions (which are formed habits or tendencies) but capacities (potentials, possibilities) 'to receive and imagine the world ... the whole environment, nature and society'. No one can learn everything that is to be known, so that what we term 'education', that is, formal education, 'conscious and willed', means a selection. To educate means 'to give decisive effective power to a selection of the world which is concentrated and manifested in the educator'.[8] The world engenders the person in the individual.

The decisive encounter

Buber illustrates the difference between the old and the new with the example of a drawing lesson. In the old school the teacher demanded strict compliance with the rules and conventions. There was no room for individual initiative or personal perspective. In the new school the pupils are not hindered by imposed rules. They are free to render their own impression of the object to be drawn without the restrictions of conventional models.

The teacher of the old traditional approach, the 'compulsory' school of thought, began with rules and conventional representations. Once you were instructed as to what constituted beauty 'you had to copy it; and it was copied either in apathy or in despair'. The teacher of the 'free' or progressive school, on the other hand, presents a theme or arrangement and allows the pupils to draw it as they please. 'If the pupils are quite unsophisticated soon not a single drawing will look the same.'[9]

It is the latter, the 'free' approach, which provides the basis for the true educational encounter. In the first case, the traditional (sculptor) approach, 'the preliminary declaration of what alone was right' generated, not enthusiasm, but 'resignation or rebellion'. In the case of the progressive, child-centred (gardener) approach the pupil is allowed to give free rein to his or her capacity to confront the world imaginatively, to engage his or her 'originator instinct' and attempt to render *his or her* view of reality. The pupil must have freedom to encounter and engage with the world in his or her own way. But this freedom is not the end or objective of education; it is the beginning.

This is where the 'decisive encounter' must take place between the teacher and the learner. The child's spontaneous and unsophisticated effort to engage with the world, in this case through drawing, must be met by the values of human culture, the knowledge of what is appropriate and proper, personified in the 'criticism and instruction' of a sensitive and loving teacher, 'the delicate, almost imperceptible and yet important influence'. The children are brought to engage with 'a scale of values' embodied in the teacher. However unsystematic this scale of values may be, it is 'quite constant, a knowledge of good and evil that, however individualistic it may be, is quite unambiguous'.[10] And so the child begins, or continues, the process of subjecting his or her creativity to the demands of human culture. Such subjection should not be a subjugation. In the hands of the kind of teacher Buber is describing it would be an empowerment.

Freedom

Freedom is merely possibility. There are two kinds of freedom: a higher or inner freedom which is moral freedom ('the soul's freedom of decision'), and an outer freedom, the freedom for development, which consists in not being hindered or limited. Particularly in the latter case, which has become a preoccupation of child-centred education, it is important to remind ourselves that it is only a *capacity* for growth and development, not the growth and development itself. In either case freedom is the beginning, not the end, of education.

Freedom is a functional good, a means to an end; it is not a substantial good, or end in itself, it is a means to something else. Nor is it simply the opposite of compulsion. It is a presupposition, a possibility, nothing more. It is a necessary prerequisite to education, not a sufficient condition for education. Only in an age when the coherence of traditional certainties is breaking down can we consider freedom as a value in itself.

Compulsion in education will not lead to true engagement. Communion on the other hand allows for the child's opening up to the world and its possibilities, and being drawn in to the world of human culture through voluntary engagement. Freedom simply means the possibility of communion, no more than that. On its own it is useless but without it nothing of worth is possible. 'Without (freedom) nothing succeeds, but neither does anything succeed by means of it,' Buber declares, 'it is the run before the jump, the tuning of the violin ...'[11]

Dialogue

The relation between the pupil and the teacher must be a 'dialogical' relation. In dialogue we are addressed by the thought and speech and action of another human being. By accepting their otherness as human beings like ourselves we are able to respond. For there to be true communication, genuine speaking and listening, we need to eschew abstract codes or established procedures. For example, teachers cannot use abstract generalizations or rules of thumb to impose their will upon the pupil: each engagement with a pupil is particular, unique and unprecedented. As the Master, the teacher must fully realize the reality of the learner's life experience. Each one of us wishes to have our value and potential as a human being confirmed by others and we have the reciprocal capacity to confirm others in *their* humanity. It is only as this capacity unfolds that we become truly human.

Learners must be addressed as whole persons. If the teacher overlooks the real otherness of the learner, the teacher will not be able to help him or her. If the teacher sees learners not as they are in all their reality but as the teacher would wish them to be, or as they are defined in ready-made categories like age, class, social background, family connections, test scores, examination potential, and so forth, then addressing him or her 'in her wholeness as a person' becomes impossible: he or she becomes a function of a system of thought or administration, not a person.

The doctor/patient relationship is similar: such a relationship requires that the relationship 'should be a real human relation experienced with the spirit' by the patient. As soon, however, as the doctor is tempted by the desire to manipulate or exploit the patient, or to succumb to the patient's wish to be dominated or exploited, and loses sight of the true basis of the relationship, the patient's need to be treated to health, then 'the danger of falsification arises, beside which all quackery appears peripheral'.

In other words it is not the doctor's job to dominate the patient or to use the patient for his or her own purposes (as an experimental subject, say, or for sexual gratification or professional aggrandizement) but to address the patient as a fellow human being in need of help. In the same way, pupils are not in the relationship as a unit of attendance, a potential consumer/producer or as a statistic in a research programme. The pupil is a unique person waiting in good faith for the intervention of the teacher which can deepen their personhood.

More is required than empathy. Dialogue requires real listening as well as real talking: the learner has a mouth as well as ears, has a story to tell, an insight to give, a question to ask. Responses are not preordained or predetermined and the teacher's reaction to the learner's contribution cannot be prepared beforehand any more than the doctor's diagnosis. Each encounter is unique as it is unpredictable. The goal of the dialogue is the dialogue itself in which each of the participants, pupil and teacher, learns more of him- or herself in the encounter. And they also learn more of what is of value to the reality of the other. The teacher cannot be indifferent to the needs of the learner but the response to those needs is *influence* not interference or imposition.

The learner

The teacher does not choose the pupil. The pupil is already there and must be accepted in the totality of his or her reality. This is vividly described by Buber:

> The teacher sees them crouching at the desks, indiscriminately flung together, the misshapen and the well-proportioned, animal faces, empty faces, and noble faces in indiscriminate confusion, like the presence of the created universe; the glance of the educator accepts and receives them all.[12]

The teacher must understand the reality of the learner's experience. The teacher carries to the pupil, from the human community, an assurance of trust, of meaning and of love. The complete realization of the pupil is a necessary, constitutive element of education. What Buber calls 'the innermost work of educational relationship' is that the pupil learns to trust the world through the intervention and influence of the teacher. He or she trusts the world because the teacher exists and stands as guarantee, as it were, that 'meaninglessness, however hard pressed you are by it, cannot be the real truth'. There is light in the darkness, salvation in fear, 'and in the callousness of one's fellow men the great Love'.[13]

Such realization cannot be mutual: the teacher and pupil do not meet as equal participants or equal contributors. They are mutually present to one another but the exchange between them is 'one-sided': the teacher can experience their shared experience from the point of view of the pupil, but the pupil cannot experience it from the point of view of the teacher; if he or she could there would no longer be any need for a teacher. This is not to say that the teacher gains nothing from the engagement. Through concern for, responsiveness to, and responsibility for the pupil teachers are directed to their own self-education, to a deeper recognition of human need, experience and growth.

The trust and duty placed upon the teacher to care for the pupil, 'this living soul', provides a unique possibility for 'that which seems impossible and yet is somehow granted to us', self-education.

Self-education cannot take place through self-concern, but only through being concerned with the world, with others. The self-education available to the teacher is not professional development, or in-service training. It is more profound: it is the possibility of self-transcendence which can give the teacher a deeper understanding of the world that he or she and the pupil explore together.

The ultimate aim

Finally, Buber asserts that there is no norm or 'fixed maxim' for education. That is, there is no essence of education which we can identify as being universally valid. What appears at any given time to be the essence of education only appears so because it is rooted in stabilities and certainties which appear to have permanence: it only appears that there is a complete set of educational objectives in a static context, a stable society, a uniform culture, an orthodox church, an enduring era. In such circumstances education, like 'all stirring and action of the spirit', is submissive to the prevailing mores and values. Education has autonomy only 'in an age which is losing form'.

> Only in it, in the disintegration of traditional bonds, in the spinning whirl of freedom, does personal responsibility arise which in the end can no longer lean with its burden of decision on any church or society or culture, but is lonely in the face of Present Being.[14]

Such an age calls forth ultimate personal responsibility on the part of the teacher who can invoke no 'norm or fixed maxim' to justify educational decisions and practices. The authoritative source for such standards is, for Buber, the one true direction, the Eternal Thou, God.

16 Alexander Sutherland Neill (1883–1973): Education for the Liberation of the Psyche

Background

It might be said that the revolution in child liberty initiated by Rousseau in the eighteenth century culminated in twentieth-century England at Summerhill school. The founder of this extraordinary school was a Scottish teacher called Neill, 'A.S.', or simply 'Neill' to his pupils who often teased him with the cry 'Neill, Neill, orange peel!'

Neill was born in Scotland in 1883. His father taught in the one-teacher school at Kingsmuir. It was here that Neill received his education and where he became an apprentice schoolmaster at the age of 16. While he tended to copy his father's methods it was not the teaching itself he enjoyed: to the end of his life he would deny that he ever *was* a teacher! What attracted him was the enjoyment of the company of the pupils who were still close to him in age. In a sense, whatever his subsequent achievements, he never grew beyond that simple camaraderie with children so that, despite his denial, he could write, 'I think that a teacher is born and that all the training in all the colleges will not make one a good teacher'.[1]

He spent some time as an unqualified teacher before he finally graduated from Edinburgh University with a degree in arts. He was less than flattering about university education. It never required the students to engage with the respective arts in any creative way at all. 'I held then and do now,' he wrote, 'that it is better to write a bad limerick than to be able to recite *Paradise Lost* ... but the university never asked us to compose even a limerick.'[2]

Following his graduation (all he knew was that 'I didn't want to teach'![3]) he spent a spell in journalism. At the outbreak of World War I, much to his relief, he was initially exempt from service because of a minor medical condition. The magazine he was then working for folded and he took a job as temporary headmaster at Gretna Green village school in Scotland. It was here that he wrote his first book *A Dominie's Log*, an account of his experiences in the school. ('Dominie' is a Scottish word for schoolmaster.) In the spring of 1917, when physical requirements for recruits had been made significantly less stringent he was recruited but he never saw active duty.

After the war Neill spent two years in an experimental school and then took a job as an assistant editor with a progressive journal, *The New Era*. Whether he was sacked or abandoned the job because of his divergent views is not clear. But by this time he was thoroughly disillusioned with the conventional education system and in 1921 he co-founded a progressive school in Dresden, Germany, with Lilian Neustätter who was to become his first wife. The education programme was based on the arts, crafts, music and dance as the principal means of self-development. After several moves the school settled on a small property called Summerhill near Lyme Regis on the south coast of England. It retained the name Summerhill even when it moved from Lyme Regis to Leiston in Suffolk. Apart from a five-year period in Wales during World War II, the school has been at Leiston ever since.

Summerhill

Freedom is central to the ethos of Summerhill: it is as if the central pedagogical rule of the school was that there should be no pedagogical rules. Neill wanted a school which would fit the child rather than forcing the child to fit the school. 'I knew the other way well', Neill wrote referring to conventional early twentieth-century schools, 'I knew it was all wrong. It was wrong because it was based on an adult conception of what a child should be and of how a child should learn'.[4]

In order for the children to have freedom to be themselves Neill and his colleagues adopted an extremely radical policy of non-intervention: 'to renounce all discipline, all direction, all suggestion, all moral training, and all religious instruction.' This required 'a complete belief in the child as a good, not an evil, being'.[5]

Neill is particularly critical of conventional schooling and his description of conventional schools is almost a negative definition of the kind of school he wanted Summerhill to be. The conventional school 'makes active children sit at desks studying mostly useless subjects' and is considered a good school only by those 'who want docile, uncreative children' for 'a civilization whose standard of success is money'. Summerhill, on the contrary, accepted people for what they were, not for what they might become. It was to be a place where people could develop whatever innate abilities, and achieve whatever aspirations, they had. Those, he wrote, 'who have the innate ability and wish to be scholars will be scholars ... those who are only fit to sweep the streets will sweep the streets'. Summerhill has not 'produced a street cleaner so far' and Neill explained that this was not a matter of snobbishness but that he would 'rather see a school produce a happy street cleaner than a neurotic scholar'.[6]

Often referred to as 'the man who loves children', Neill denies the charge: 'one cannot,' he says, 'love masses, only individuals, and all individuals are not lovable.' He would prefer to be thought of simply as being on the side of the child, offering approval, sympathy and kindness. It is more important to 'understand children than to love them'.[7]

Although Neill wrote a great deal he never fully systematized a philosophy of education as such. But certain features of the Summerhill ethos are central. The first and most important is freedom. Neill had very clear views on freedom. In the first place, it cannot be conferred on children. Freedom is the child's natural state and all that adults can do is to refrain from interfering, keep out. It is not the teacher's business, he believed, to form, or train, or prune, but simply to refrain. 'The bestowal of freedom,' he wrote, 'is the bestowal of love'.[8]

What does this mean in practical terms? It is one thing to advocate freedom in the abstract, quite another to implement this abstraction in the rough and tumble of the real world. Neill first defines freedom in terms of limits: it is always subject to the freedom of others. It means doing what you like so long as you don't interfere with the freedom of others to do what *they* like. Neill's position is no more than a restatement of the classic liberal principle: individual liberty consistent with the liberty of others. But Neill is talking about *children* and many would have reservations regarding the capacity of the individual child to make free decisions, and to take responsibility for the consequences of such decisions for themselves and for others.

A common adult misconception is that free children will do nothing, or, worse, only harm. This was not the experience at

Summerhill. In fact the children, once they became accustomed to the opportunity to do nothing, began to look about for something to do. But this time *they* were in charge, they chose their activities based on their own interests and motivation. 'It is interesting to know,' Neill commented, 'that free children take to mathematics. They find joy in geography and in history.' Free children, in fact, choose from the subjects on offer only the subjects in which they are interested. Most of the rest of their time they devote to other interests, woodwork, metalwork, painting, reading fiction, acting, playing out fantasies, playing jazz records.[9]

There is a significant difference between forcing a child not to throw stones and forcing him to study Latin. The former activity involves other people and so the community may intervene to restrain a child because he is interfering with others' rights. Learning Latin, on the other hand, or anything else for that matter, concerns only the individual himself. 'Forcing a child to learn,' Neill declares, 'is on a par with forcing a man to adopt a religion by act of Parliament.'[10]

He distinguishes very clearly between the physical health and the psychic health of the child. There are, of course, certain things which must be insisted upon: nourishing food, warm clothing, appropriate bedtime, and so forth; but these are all matters pertaining to the *physical* health of the child. In relation to the psychic health of the child nothing should be imposed, and this entails that nothing should be demanded in relation to learning. Every child should have total freedom of choice whether to learn or not to learn. Of course children will learn willy-nilly because that is their nature: but they should not be subjected to adult preconceptions of what should be learned at any particular time. Compulsion alienates children from learning itself and diverts them from learning what interests them.

Without compulsion the children of Summerhill learned enough to pass entrance examinations and to get A-levels. They did these things because they wanted to, not because someone else wanted them to. The free child learns important things: sincerity, independence and a genuine interest in people and things. In conventional ('unfree') education 'only the head is educated'. Unfree education makes a full life impossible because it disregards or downplays the emotions. Because they are dynamic, if emotions are denied opportunity for expression and repressed, the result will be 'cheapness and ugliness and hatefulness'. Summerhill tries to invert the process: 'if the emotions are permitted to be really free, the intellect will look after itself.'[11]

Neill stresses over and over that the disciplined child is an insincere child, whose self has been subordinated to an imposed model of what he or she should be. This child can never be him- or herself because the imposed model of what he or she should be keeps getting in the way, it has never been integrated with the real self. Compulsion on the psychic development of the child contradicts the principle of liberty; things learned under compulsion are not integrated into the self.

Teachers

A school like Summerhill demands a very special kind of teacher, one who is prepared to accept the children on their own terms and at their own level. Above all, the teachers must have such a secure sense of their own identity that they do not need to have their egos pandered to by the children. Neill made it very clear in all that he wrote about Summerhill that an expectation on the part of adults that children should treat them differently or defer to them was unacceptable. Respect and fear are part of the same attitude. In order to deal with free children the teacher should be on the child's level. Disapproval of children's behaviour should be communicated, as it is by their peers, through attitude rather than by intervention otherwise the option of authoritarian control is retained. If the child is to have the opportunity to develop inner freedom then the adult teacher must refrain from any form of domination.

The teacher must not only have faith in the child's nature but also faith in the child's intelligence and innate wisdom. Teachers must be conversant with child psychology so that they know especially when to refrain from intervening in the affairs of the child: it is better to do nothing than to do the wrong thing. The staff in a free school must themselves be free from any impulse to authoritarianism, in fact Neill demands that they should have neither dignity nor authority. What they must have is sincerity and they must never use their position, their age or their experience to gain any advantage of privilege over the child. Just as the proper home is one in which 'children and adults have equal rights' so in the free school no-one has any advantage because of age or position.[12]

Ultimately, Neill demanded of teachers that they empower children to resist the dull conformity and mass psychology characteristic of contemporary, industrialized societies. Conventional education fashions children into accepting the status quo. This is necessary for a society 'that needs obedient sitters at dreary desks, standers in shops, mechanical catchers of the 8:30 suburban train – a society, in short, that is carried on the shabby shoulders of the scared little man – the scared-to-death conformist'.[13] He variously compares the educational process to herding sheep or training dogs ('as we train our dogs to suit our own purposes, so we train our children') and identifies the sinister outcome that can result: 'I saw a hundred thousand obedient, fawning dogs wag their tails in the Tempelhof, Berlin, when in 1935 the great trainer Hitler whistled his commands.'[14]

Regard for the child should not be confused with sentimentality and possessiveness: Neill was contemptuous of the horticultural metaphors which dominated much 'progressive' education in the late nineteenth and early twentieth centuries. Children are not fruits or flowers, and should not be the objects of a romantic sentimentality.

Liberty or licence

Summerhill, based on a belief in the innate goodness of the individual child, was a boarding school. There was no uniform, there was not even a dress code of any kind: pupils were free to dress as they wished, or not at all. Social and status distinctions between teachers and pupils were non-existent. There was no discipline as the term is usually understood, i.e. requiring certain forms of behaviour, codes of conduct, attendance and standardized work practices; only teachers had timetables, pupils were free to come and go as they pleased. There was no religious education or moral training, apart from the basic principle of liberty consistent with the freedom of others to enjoy their liberty – but that principle was fundamental. Neill illustrates the point very tellingly:

> I spent weeks planting potatoes one spring, and when I found eight plants pulled up in June, I made a big fuss. Yet there was a difference between my fuss and that of an authoritarian. My fuss was about potatoes, but the fuss an authoritarian would have made would have dragged in the question of morality ... I did not say that it was wrong

to steal my spuds; I did not make it a matter of good and evil –
I made it a matter of *my spuds*. They were *my* spuds and they should
have been left alone. I hope I am making the distinction clear.[15]

To develop uniquely as an individual one needs one's own
property. Neill is perhaps disingenuous to deny that this is a
moral matter, but he is frequently at pains to make the distinction
between morality which is necessary for the well-being of individuals and morality which is imposed for purposes of social,
political or economic control. 'It is,' he agrees, 'important for a
child to learn that one cannot ... damage someone else's property
or someone else's person.' Letting the child do as he or she pleases
without regard to the persons and property of others is 'bad for the
child, and the spoiled child is a bad citizen'.[16]

Neill is always careful to make this qualification: the freedom he
advocates is *not* absolute, it is always subject to respect for others.
It is this other-regarding aspect of Neill's liberty which differ-
entiates it from licence. Freedom and licence are not the same
and it is important to be able to distinguish where one ends and
the other begins. Licence is a form of behaviour which ignores the
rights of others: it is wilful, selfish and self-centred. No child lives
in isolation. No child can be allowed to behave in such a way that
his or her actions constitute an infringement of the freedom of
others. Where no one else was affected the child could do as he or
she pleased. And Neill meant it!

> I recall the military gentleman who thought of enrolling his nine-year-
> old son as a pupil.
>
> 'The place seems all right,' he said, 'but I have one fear. My boy may
> learn to masturbate here.'
>
> I asked him why he feared this.
>
> 'It will do him so much harm,' he said.
>
> 'It didn't do you or me much harm, did it?' I said pleasantly. He went
> off rather hurriedly with his son.[17]

Self-government

A central feature of life at Summerhill was self-government; a form
of participatory democracy whereby everything connected with
group life, including punishment for social offences, was settled by

vote at the Saturday night General School Meeting. Each teacher and each pupil, irrespective of age, was free to attend and each had one, and only one, vote. At these meetings the rules for the governance of the school were made, and repealed, sometimes at the same meeting. Rule-breakers were charged, tried and if found guilty, had punishment assigned. Grievances, against other pupils, or teachers, frequently against Neill himself, were aired and judged. It was a practical exercise in civics and an ongoing experiment which gave pupils control over their own social affairs and provided them with a working model of a democratic society. According to Neill 'the school that has no self-government should not be called a progressive school. It is a compromise school'. 'When there is a boss,' he declared, 'there is no real freedom.' It matters little whether or not the boss is a strict disciplinarian. On balance, Neill thinks that the disciplinarian is preferable; it gives the children something specific to rebel against: 'the soft boss merely makes the child impotently soft and unsure of his real feelings.'[18]

The system of self-government depended heavily on a firm conviction, a deep faith even, in children's innate sense of justice and fair play. Self-government was not anarchy. Children were not, in fact, allowed to do as they pleased for their own laws constrained them. As mentioned, certain crucial material matters were dealt with exclusively by Neill and his wife: selection of food, allocation of bedrooms, collection of fees and payment of bills, as well as the appointment and dismissal of teachers.

One of the weaknesses of the system of self-government, however, was that it depended heavily on a cadre of older pupils who took it seriously. Although the younger children participated they were incapable of running the system on their own. They were, Neill admitted, 'only mildly interested in government'. He did not think that younger children left to their own devices would bother with it: 'their values are not our values, and their manners are not our manners.'[19] But through participation in a real system the younger children learned; and in turn they became the older students who were committed to the ideal of self-government.

Play

Play is central in the development of the well-balanced individual. For Neill, childhood is playhood. Play is the means whereby growing children develop a balanced and healthy psyche which enables them to undertake the tasks of life. Too frequently it is seen as a break from the more serious side of life which we call work. Too early insistence on the centrality of work prevents the individual from developing the inner security which is needed to cope with life's problems. Generally adults consider play to be, if not a waste of time, then certainly of lesser value than work. As evidence, Neill directs our attention to large city schools with lots of rooms for all kinds of learning activities and abundant expensive apparatus for teaching and learning. More often than not 'all we offer to the play instinct is a small concrete space'. He complains that 'the evils of civilisation are due to the fact that no child has ever had enough play. To put it differently, every child has been hot-housed into an adult long before he has reached adulthood'.[20]

Officialdom

Summerhill was not proof against the attentions of officialdom. His/Her Majesty's Inspectors visited it regularly, as by law they were obliged to, although Neill could not understand why teachers as a professional group tolerated a system of intrusive inspection that would have been anathema to other professions. He was sceptical about the purpose or effectiveness of such inspections, remarking that 'the Ministry is primarily interested in efficiency, and I fear that this efficiency applies to learning rather than to living, to tidy rooms rather than to happy children, to the number of water closets rather than to the absence of illness'. While an inspector can evaluate the level of children's learning and whether the various teachers are doing their jobs well, he or she cannot inspect the things that really matter: 'tolerance or happiness or balance.'

The report of one pair of visiting inspectors at least is very favourable – though Neill's comments on that report – which he reproduces in full in *Summerhill* – might lead to the suspicion that the visits were not always so cordial. On this occasion the inspectors' report stated that 'it would be difficult to find a more natural, open-faced, unselfconscious collection of boys and girls and disasters which some might have expected to occur have not occurred in all the twenty-eight years of the school's existence'.[21]

This was in 1948 and at that time there were 70 children between the ages of 4 and 16 enrolled. Of Neill himself the inspectors commented:

> He is a man of deep conviction and sincerity. His faith and patience must be inexhaustible. He has the rare power of being a strong personality without dominating. It is impossible to see him in his school without respecting him even if one disagrees with or even dislikes some of his ideas. He has a sense of humour, a warm humanity and a strong common sense which would make him a good Headmaster anywhere ...[23]

All in all this inspectors' report was extremely favourable. But it is difficult to escape the suspicion that whatever the merits or otherwise of Neill's ideas it was his open, robust and unfailingly optimistic personality which made Summerhill such a success. He denied it; he claimed that his approach was based on a general theory. Central to this general theory was the unique personality of each individual: the self. The goal of education is the achievement of selfhood. 'It is the idea of non-interference with the growth of the child and non-pressure on the child that has made the school what it is.'[24] Yet it is not the persuasiveness of any general theory that one takes away from his writing but his palpable passion, the utter conviction which Neill brought to the task.

All his life Neill fought against the phenomenon of the unfree child and against the hypocrisy and fear which kept the souls of children from blossoming as he believed they should. The unfree child is the contrary of the ideal graduate of Summerhill:

> The moulded, conditioned, disciplined, repressed child ... who lives in every corner of the world ... He sits at a dull desk in a dull school; and, later, he sits at a duller desk in an office or on a factory bench. He is docile, prone to obey authority, fearful of criticism, and almost fanatical in his desire to be normal, conventional, and correct. He accepts what he has been taught almost without question; and he hands down all his complexes and fears and frustrations to his children.[22]

Summerhill continues to operate under the direction of Zoë Readhead, Neill's daughter.

17 Paulo Freire (1921–1997): Education for Freedom

Background

Paulo Freire was born in Recife, Brazil, in 1921 and was the son of a well-to-do banker who suffered a fateful reversal of fortunes as a result of the Wall St crash in 1929. The family circumstances changed radically and they were forced to move to the countryside where they witnessed the predicament of the impoverished peasantry.

The young Paulo saw at close quarters that the ignorance and lethargy of the peasants was rooted in their political, economic and social powerlessness. They were not architects of their own fate but victims of systemic oppression. They were submerged in what he came to call a 'culture of silence': accepting their situation as part of the natural order and lacking a voice to speak out against the injustices which dominated their daily lives. By internalizing their oppressors' image of them they came to share a view of themselves as good for nothing, ignorant, idle, lazy and unproductive. Once convinced of their own worthlessness they never realized that 'they, too, "know things" that they have learned in their relations with the world and with other men'.[1] These kinds of self-evaluations are true of any group which is the object of prejudice and which has allowed such prejudice to dominate them.

Freire learned an unforgettable lesson about the inescapably political nature of education and its role in the process of oppression.

Education

Education is never neutral. Every educational system has the effect of transforming the people who pass through it in certain ways. In the case of the oppressed, Freire has no doubt that the educational transformation is deliberately contrived by dominant groups that use education to encourage others to be passive and to accept oppression; to develop a 'submerged' state of consciousness. The oppressive groups exploit the passivity to 'fill that consciousness with slogans which create ... fear of freedom'.[2]

By looking at education in this way Freire highlights its ideological or political function: generally, education is used to make the oppressed see their oppression as natural and necessary; to see it as a function of the 'natural' or 'unchangeable' order of things and of their own lack of worth.

The fatalism which is induced by fear of freedom and lack of worth is not a natural characteristic of the behaviour of the people affected, even though they themselves attribute it to 'the power of destiny or fate or fortune ... or to a distorted view of God'. They interpret their subservience and suffering, this 'organized disorder', in reality the effect of exploitation, as the will of God.[3]

Oppression

Who are the oppressed? What is oppression? An oppressive situation is any situation 'in which A objectively exploits B or hinders his self-affirmation as a responsible person'.[4] Oppression requires control. The most effective and efficient means of control is not physical force or coercion, or even the threat of them. It is control of the consciousness of the oppressed: the most effective control makes people's own minds the instrument of the control; the most effective control is mind control.

The oppressed are fatalistic about their situation because they fail to see that the interests of the status quo are not their interests. Convinced of their own lack of worth as individuals they deprecate their own knowledge and experience. Emotionally dependant on the oppressor they look to the oppressor for validation of their existence. They aspire to share the way of life of the oppressor, that is, to become oppressors themselves. They aspire to be human in the fullest sense, but to them the fullest sense, the highest form of achievement, is to be an oppressor: 'their ideal is to be men; but for them to be a "man" is to be an oppressor. This is their model of humanity.'[5]

Pedagogy of the Oppressed

Pedagogy of the Oppressed, Freire's major and most influential educational work, can be read as a manual of resistance to the kind of mind control that keeps oppressed people in a state of submission. What *is* a pedagogy of the oppressed?

Humanization is the vocation of human beings: their most important life task is to maximize their humanity. Developing an education *for* people, no matter how well intentioned or inspired, simply reinforces helplessness and dependency. If educators are to help the oppressed to achieve their humanity they must do so in partnership with them. The resulting pedagogy would make the phenomenon of oppression, its causes and the subjective experience of oppression, matters to be studied by learners themselves. Engagement with, as it were, the theory and practice of oppression would be a first necessary step in liberation. A pedagogy of the oppressed is a process of enabling – of empowering – oppressed people to see the realities which are keeping them in a state of subordination.

The oppressed must first of all *see* their condition and alternatives to it. Education empowers the oppressed to discover alternatives in situations which have been taken as natural, necessary and unchangeable. It is only when they see alternatives that they can begin to transform their own world and experience. From the educator's point of view this is a process of humanization. From the point of view of the dominant group, the oppressor, it is 'subversion', for it challenges their control and their power.

The 'banking' concept of education

Conventional schooling systems illustrate the process of oppressive domination. They embody what Freire calls the 'banking' concept of education.

Education is suffering from what Freire calls 'narration sickness'. The teacher–student relationship at any level, elementary, secondary or tertiary, whether inside or outside the school, is largely a *narrative* relationship. It comprises 'a narrating subject' (the teacher) and patient, listening 'objects' (the students). The teachers' function is to fill students with the contents of their narration: the teacher speaks, the students listen. Knowledge is bestowed by those considered knowledgeable upon those considered ignorant. The more teachers can accomplish the narrative task, the more completely they fill the students' minds, the more successful they are. For their part students are judged on their capacity to be filled with, and retain, the relevant material: it is largely a memory exercise.

Whatever the subject, the experience of learning loses vitality and relevance in the narrative process for two reasons. First, irrespective of whether the subject contents are values or facts, the process of narration itself renders them 'lifeless and petrified'. 'The teacher talks about reality as if it were motionless, static, compartmentalized, and predictable.'[6] The contents of the narration have become disconnected from the human experience that engendered them and gave them their original significance. Real experience has been replaced by words, and the words in turn have been 'emptied of their concreteness and become a hollow, alienated and alienating verbosity'.[7] Second, teachers' narration expounds on topics which are removed from the students' lived experience. By being excluded from students' learning programmes their lived experience is devalued and alienated. As a consequence students accept the knowledge that is bestowed upon them passively: it never becomes their knowledge because it has no immediacy to their lived experience.

In a metaphor which echoes Dickens in *Hard Times*, Freire describes the work of the conventional teacher as filling learners full of knowledge, as we would fill jugs, bottles or other receptacles. The entire process reduces the learner to nothing more than a container to be filled.

In the banking concept of education only the teacher takes an active role: the teacher thinks, chooses, talks, disciplines, etc., while the students' participation is passive. Students do not determine their own learning experiences. Their life experience is set at nought, diminished and trivialized by the imposition of the belief that *only* what the schools teach is worthwhile knowledge.

Education, then, in the banking metaphor, becomes 'an act of depositing'. The students are the depositories into which the teacher lodges instalments of learning. Students' participation extends only as far as submissively 'receiving, filing and storing the deposits'.[8]

Oppressive education

The banking concept mirrors oppressive society as a whole and perpetuates its dominating values and attitudes. Students are deprived of opportunities to become more human through the process of learning. As collectors and cataloguers of knowledge imparted by teachers, they are alienated from their own experience. As learners they become objectified, their capacity for creativity is denied and they lack opportunities for taking initiatives on their own behalf. Ultimately, it is the learners themselves who are filed away through their lack of meaningful participation in the process of their education. For it is engagement in enquiry that makes it possible for human beings to be truly human. 'Knowledge emerges only through invention and re-invention,' Freire declares, 'through ... inquiry men pursue in the world, with the world, and with each other.'[9]

As students' creative power is nullified, their credulity is re-inforced. The imposition of predefined units of information and ready-made learning programmes limits their curiosity and their engagement with the world. They are indoctrinated to adapt to the world of imposition and integrated into the structure of oppression. As teachers regard students as passive receivers of 'deposits' of knowledge, their role is to regulate the way in which the world 'enters into' the students. The entire educative effort robs students of the responsibility of thinking and acting for themselves.

Critical consciousness can only emerge when a learner actively engages with the world so as to transform it. While learners devote their time to storing the deposits entrusted to them by narrating teachers, they relinquish opportunities to develop critical consciousness. By accepting a partial and fragmented view of the world, and the passive role assigned to them by the system of education, they are accepting passivity as their normal state of being. As a result they are more likely to adopt a fatalistic attitude towards their own experience and to adapt to the world as it is rather than seeing the world as it could be.

The manner in which the educational enterprise is conducted, the process of education itself, carries its own message. We learn not just what we are taught, but about ourselves and others and the world in which we live from the *way* we are taught and the structure of the institutions in which we are taught. The banking concept of education helps to perpetuate and reinforce a culture of silence. This is a condition in which the learner, convinced that he or she knows nothing of value, accepts unquestioningly the account of the world sanctioned by the system and conforms to the received orthodoxy. True education should equip people to know and respond creatively to the concrete realities of the world in which they live, *their* world.

Domestication

This process of indoctrination, or domestication, is not irreversible. The deposits of the banking concept of education contain contradictions which the students may discover for themselves.

In time such contradictions may lead hitherto submissive students to begin to question the system and to challenge the attempt to domesticate their reality, to nullify their life experience, and to turn them into compliant creatures of the system. 'They may discover through existential experience,' Freire says, 'that their present way of life (as students) is irreconcilable with their vocation to become fully human.'[10]

It may become apparent, for example, that the explicit values being promoted by the school are contrary to the messages being communicated by the practices of the school as an organization. Many schools which teach about democracy and justice will be organized as autocracies (how many school principals are elected by their students?) and be regulated according to administrative imperatives rather than principles of justice. Such contradictions become the means of turning formerly passive students against their domestication and of generating protest against their alienation from their own lived reality in and out of school. Such an important matter should not be left to chance.

Liberating education

Educators inspired by humanist and revolutionary principles cannot wait for pupils' realization of the real state of affairs to happen fortuitously. Such educators must promote processes whereby students are given encouragement and opportunity to engage in critical thinking in the quest for the humanization of both learner and teacher. Such efforts must be firmly based on trust in students and in their creative capacity to transform their experience. This pedagogy requires partnership, not domination.

Humanization and its opposite, dehumanization, are radical alternatives. To be fully human is to act upon and transform the world; humanization is man's vocation, his 'great humanistic and historical task'.

Although humanization is constantly denied by those who would dominate, its very denial reaffirms its existence. It may be frustrated by injustice, exploitation or domination and associated violence. But even so, 'it is affirmed,' Freire believes, 'by the yearning of the oppressed for freedom and justice, and by their struggle to recover their lost humanity'.[11]

It is learning itself, the seeking, the process of becoming educated, which should be of paramount importance and not the accumulated knowledge, as life is a succession of problems to be worked on and solved.

Advanced industrialized societies promote the objectification of people; the schooling systems (which embody the banking concept of education) reinforce a passive consumerist mentality by transmitting prepackaged information. This dehumanization can be opposed by a liberating philosophy of education that transforms the human experience from passive/receptive to active/creative.

Freedom

Freedom is central to humanization.

Freedom is something we must pursue and acquire for ourselves, something we must continually struggle for. It is not something which can be bestowed on us by another: for what can be given can be taken away and if it can be taken away it is not true freedom. It is 'acquired by conquest, not by gift'; it is not something outside of us which can be acquired on a once-for-all basis, like a possession or an object; it must be constantly reaffirmed. Freedom is the prerequisite to humanization, it is 'the indispensable condition for the quest for human completion'.[12]

The experience of schooling either enslaves or liberates, it cannot do both. Students cannot achieve freedom through the agency of a system which disempowers them by alienating them from their own life experience. The denial of freedom is central to oppression. Denial of freedom is often disguised as paternalistic concern for the 'welfare' of people who cannot be trusted to pursue their own interests.

The banking concept of education does not operate in a vacuum. It is reinforced by paternalistic social apparatus which views the oppressed as 'welfare recipients'. This designation locates them on the periphery of society and defines them in terms of their difference from the norm in what is otherwise a 'good, organised and just society'. The oppressed are defined, and treated, as deviants, 'the pathology of the healthy society'.[13] Instead of addressing the needs of the oppressed by changing society, the oppressor attempts to change the oppressed to preserve the status quo.

Praxis

Human activity comprises two dimensions, thought and action, theory and practice. Either without the other is incomplete. When thought and action are appropriately combined they constitute a transformation of the world. The transformation must be informed by theory but theory must equally be built on the experience of practice. Neither is sufficient without the other. Action without sufficient critical analysis of the real situation is a mindless activism: engaging in action simply for the sake of doing something. Reflection without action leads to an impotent verbalism.

Teaching and learning should be a two-way process. Knowledge is not the property of teachers to begin with but the end result of true teacher/student dialogue. This dialogue must engage with the world as it is for the participants; meaning their experience, their needs, their developing aspirations.

Students must learn how to perceive their world and their experience, including the way they are treated and required to behave, critically. They must be empowered to come to see their world as a process and not as a static reality; it is in a state of transformation. Through their thought and action, their praxis, they can influence this transformation. The form of action which they adopt will be largely determined by the way in which they perceive themselves as beings in the world: whether active or passive, engaged or submissive, involved or manipulated.

The point of departure of liberating education is not the communication of established knowledge. It begins from the situation in which the learner is submerged: his or her life situation. Problem-posing education transforms this life situation through praxis. Problem-posing education cannot serve the interests of the oppressor because it encourages the oppressed to question: to ask 'why?' The methodology poses problems through which the learners develop their power to see their own reality.

This methodology entails a radical change in the role of teachers. They are no longer just instructors, but become equal learners in dialogue with the students. Teachers and learners 'become jointly responsible for a process in which all grow'. Such a process of teaching and learning has no place for the defence of positions based on authority. On the contrary, 'in order to function,' Freire writes, 'authority must be on the side of freedom, not against it . . . no-one teaches another nor is anyone self-taught. Men teach each other mediated by the world'.[14]

The word

Language delimits an important distinction between human beings and animals. Animals are 'beings of pure activity' unreflectively immersed in the world. They do not think about their situation. Human beings, on the other hand, 'emerge from the world', they are able to detach themselves from their immediate experience, objectify it, and reflect on it through the medium of language; they are able to name the world, and, in naming it, transform it.

Freire reminds us of an ancient realization regarding naming: a word is not just a verbal noise or a visual symbol, but a significant instrument of power: to be able to name something is to begin to exercise control over it. 'Human existence cannot be silent,' he explains, 'to exist humanly is to *name* the world' and naming is part of the process of control: to say the true word is transformative, 'saying that word is not the privilege of some few men, but the right of every man'.[15] We transform the world by naming it, by identifying in it those contradictions which subvert the process of humanization. Hence, dialogue is the medium of liberating education.

It is important to remember that, in Freire's terms, action is an important dimension of the word 'naming'. When naming, reality loses its dimension of action then reflection also deteriorates, and 'the word is changed into idle chatter, into verbalism, into an alienated and alienating "blah"'. The word becomes empty, and though it can sound as if it is denouncing the world (reality) it cannot really do so, 'for denunciation is impossible without a commitment to transform, and there is no transformation without action'.[16] So merely *saying* what we think is wrong, or needs to be changed (transformed), is insufficient, a matter of 'empty words'. This is a phenomenon with which we are all familiar: when we challenge someone who is finding fault to say what they intend to do about the situation, we are prepared to dismiss them as being 'all talk', empty verbalizers without any commitment to action.

Dialogue

Dialogue is the medium of transformative education. It is the opposite of the banking concept of education.

Dialogue occurs when human beings come together for the express purpose of naming the world with a view to changing it. It can never be reduced to an act of 'depositing' ideas for passive acceptance by others. Dialogue is possible only when all concerned share the aspiration to name and transform the world. 'Without dialogue there is no communication,' Freire insists, 'and without communication there can be no true education.'[17]

In identifying the conditions for dialogue Freire manifests the deep Christian roots of his educational philosophy. Dialogue requires the traditional Christian virtues of faith, hope and charity (love) as well as an attitude of humility.

Faith is the faith of men and women in their shared vocation to be more fully human. A prerequisite of dialogue is an 'intense faith in man' and in his or her power to 'make and remake, to create and recreate, faith in his vocation to be more fully human (which is ... the birthright of all men)'.[18]

Hope is the opposite of submission and apathy. In order to engage in humanization in cooperation with others it is necessary to be optimistic regarding the chances of success. This hope is 'rooted in men's incompleteness, from which they move out in constant search – a search which can be carried out only in communion with fellow men'.[19]

Love is commitment to others. If we do not love our fellows then dialogue cannot exist. 'The naming of the world, which is an action of creation and re-creation, is not possible if it is not infused with love.'[20]

But these virtues are insufficient without the associated willingness to learn from others and from their naming of the world; this is humility.

To these Christian virtues, from a parallel humanist tradition, Freire adds critical thinking. Critical thinking is based on the understanding that reality is not static; it is a process of transformation. It is constantly engaging with reality in the pursuit of influencing change through action, despite associated risks. Critical thinking is the opposite of naïve thinking. Naïve thinking holds fast to received accounts of reality and of our place within it: it is dehumanizing. Critical thinking resists and challenges conformity to received accounts of normality and reality; it requires the continuing transformation of reality for the sake of the continuing humanization of man. In conventional education systems teachers and students are in a contradictory relationship. True education aims at resolving the contradiction between teacher and learner by involving both authentically in a shared effort to understand aspects of their world.

Liberating education is not a one-way process, *for* the student or *about* the student. It is a process which is undertaken by the teacher and the student jointly on significant themes which reflect the concrete situation given in the experience and the aspirations of those involved. Authentic learning cannot be imposed on one person by another. Ready-made programmes of learning are inadequate and must be replaced by a pedagogy which, through dialogue, engages the learner in the formulation of his or her own programme of learning, a programme which addresses issues of genuine interest. Education can be either an instrument of enslavement, which induces unquestioning submission and conformity to the present system, or an opportunity for liberation.

Paulo Freire died in 1997. He worked throughout his life for the liberation of the oppressed, promoting education which enhances the power of critical thought, challenges conventional limits to freedom, and aims at the liberation of teachers and learners everywhere.

18   Ivan Illich (1926–2002):
Education Without Schooling

Background

In the 1960s and early 1970s there was an upsurge of vehe-
ment and articulate criticism of the educational establishment in
industrialized countries which challenged not just the technical
efficiency of formal schooling but its very *raison d'être*. Through
his book *Deschooling Society*, Ivan Illich became the best known
of the anti-school critics. It was first published in 1971, and
immediately caught the imagination of a worldwide readership.

Illich was born in Austria in 1926. He later became a naturalized
citizen of the USA. He studied at the Gregorian University in Rome
and at the University of Salzburg. In 1951 he was ordained and
served as curate in an Irish-Puerto Rican parish in New York. From
1956 until 1960 Father, and later Monsignor, Illich was Vice-Rector
to the Catholic University of Puerto Rico. He subsequently resigned
his priestly functions. He was cofounder of the Centre for Inter-
Cultural Documentation in Cuernavaca, Mexico and from 1964 to
1976 he directed research seminars on 'Institutional Alternatives
in a Technological Society' with a special focus on Latin America.
Subsequently he held academic and research posts at a wide range of
universities and institutes of higher education. Illich died in 2002.

Formalized schooling

Deschooling Society had an explosive effect on the educational
establishment in the early 1970s. The 1960s had been a time of
unprecedented optimism in the power of schooling to promote
social cohesion and equality, economic development and personal
freedom. Formal education had been perceived as the principal
panacea for many of the social and economic ills of industrialized
societies: poverty, unemployment, community disintegration, racial
segregation and personal alienation. Illich disagreed. Illich argued

that the obligation to attend school places restrictions on the right to learn. Education through schooling is unlikely to succeed on a universal basis. Its unfeasibility is a function of the nature of the school–teacher–pupil nexus. Alternative institutions, based on similar premises of imbalances of power between teacher and learner, claims to exclusivity of knowledge or compulsory attendance, even with changed teacher attitudes, would not make educational outcomes any more likely. Nor would increased provision of methods or materials, or any expansion of the intervention of the teacher, be likely to make a difference. Neither the 'proliferation of educational hardware or software (in classroom or bedroom) nor ... nor the attempt to expand the pedagogue's responsibility until it engulfs his pupils' lifetimes,' he declared in the introduction to *Deschooling Society*, 'will deliver universal education'.[1]

Why such a negative reading of formal schooling? Because formal education, the school as conventionally understood, is riven by irreconcilable contradictions. Schools are 'age-specific, teacher-related processes requiring full-time attendance at an obligatory curriculum'.[2] Despite professed educational objectives, schools promote anti-intellectualism; they substitute rote learning and obedience for true learning and intellectual freedom; they are expensive bureaucracies which reinforce the inequalities which learners bring to the learning situation; they reward conformity and submission and blur distinctions between morality, legality and personal worth. School pupils are convinced that when they break a school rule they have not only broken a rule but behaved immorally and 'let themselves down'.[3]

Illich asserts that schools reflect the assumption that there are secrets to be learned, that to have an acceptable quality of life we need to know the secrets. These secrets can be accessed only by submission to teachers who reveal their orderly successions. Those who are schooled conceive of the world as 'a pyramid of classified packages accessible only to those who carry the proper tags'.[4]

General critique

Illich's critique of contemporary industrialized society spreads across a wide range of established service industries: health, transport, welfare and psychological healing. But the school is the paradigm.

Like all bureaucratic agencies, schools appear to work by systematically misrepresenting what they actually do. Pupils are habituated to the belief that learning occurs because of teaching, that true education is reflected in grade advancement, that acquisition of a qualification corresponds to the possession of competence, that fluency is evidence of the ability to say something interesting. Pupils are 'schooled' to accept service in place of value.[5] 'What counts,' Illich declares, 'is that education is assumed to be the result of an institutional process managed by the educator.'[6]

This applies not only to schooling but to other socially dominant secular institutions: hospitals, transportation systems and professions generally. Institutions succeed by convincing consumers (pupil, passenger, patient) that they meet consumer needs: what the consumer needs (education, transport, health) is defined in terms of what the institutions can offer. As a result, 'medical treatment is mistaken for health care, social work for the improvement of community life, police protection for safety, military poise for national security, the rat race for productive work'.[7] Socially and personally desirable goals of health, learning, dignity, independence and creative endeavour are defined generally in terms of the performance of associated institutions: so, medicine 'defines what constitutes disease and its treatment'.[8] Hospital-based health care, like modern school systems, 'fits the principle that those who have will receive even more (health)'. In medicine the rich will get more high-cost treatment for avoidable diseases while the poor will just suffer from them. In schooling this means that those who are most successful in meeting the demands of the system will succeed best 'while dropouts learn that they have failed'.[9] Improvement becomes an issue of increasing allocation of resources to bureaucratic management systems.

Universities

Universities provide a telling example. University institutions have lost their central purpose as 'liberated zone(s) for discovery and the discussion of ideas both new and old'. In the traditional university ('a community of academic quest and endemic unrest') masters and students met to study the works of the past masters. Such study 'gave new perspective to the fallacies of the present day'.[10] Contemporary universities, however, create elites 'for selective service among the rich of the world' and domesticate talent by co-opting 'the discoverer and the potential dissenter'.[11] While universities, with traditions of academic freedom and apparently untrammelled research, appear to promote social, cultural and political critique, they do so only in relation to those 'who have already been deeply initiated into the consumer society'.[12]

Schools teach us to need institutions, especially the university, the culmination of the schooling process, 'the final stage of the most all-encompassing initiation rite the world has ever known'.[13] Formalized education, through to university level, reinforces the belief that what is educationally important can be delivered in pre-prepared programmes, modules and curricula. This commodification reduces educational research to the mechanistic task of amassing 'scientific evidence in support of the need for more educational packages and for their more deadly accurate delivery to the individual customer'.[14] Above all, however, schools teach 'the need to be taught'.[15]

Institutionalization

Institutionalization, while growing more expensive, has come to rule our lives in increasingly intrusive and debilitating ways. Organizations and social practices which appear to exist to help us really disempower us by making us dependent on them. Birth and death provide examples: not too long ago it was normal to be born and to die at home among friends and family. Now these events have been institutionalized by doctors and undertakers: being born or dying at home become 'signs either of poverty or of special privilege'.[16] Has the institutionalization of birth and death, in maternity 'hospitals' (is anyone sick?) and funeral 'parlours' (is anyone at home?), led to anything other than a significant impoverishment of family and community life?

Institutionalized service in industrialized countries now affects everyone, rich or poor. Schools, universities and hospitals guide people's lives, form their world view and define what is and is not legitimate for them to do. So, for schools and teachers, for example, the possibility of educating oneself, being *self-taught*, is not just unreliable but contradictory, for how could the ignorant teach themselves? 'Once the self-taught man or woman has been discredited, all non-professional activity is rendered suspect.'[17] The notion of treating one's own illness is equally objectionable to the medical profession: clearly the lay person has not the expertise to make a reliable diagnosis, much less prescribe treatment. People no longer have the right to declare themselves sick. 'Society now accepts their claims to sickness only after certification by medical bureaucrats.'[18]

Domination of service

Service institutions like schooling and medicine evolve in two stages. First, new knowledge (pedagogy, medicine) is applied to clearly stated problems and scientific criteria are formulated to measure the efficiency of the solutions. The resultant success is then used to establish and perpetuate an elite claiming to be the sole provider of the relevant service. Now these elites can be kept satisfied only through the constant escalation of their expenditures: 'more' means 'better'. Increasingly, needs are transformed into demands for services and commodities that can only be provided by the institutions which have set up a monopoly on the relevant needs.

Modernized poverty, for instance (i.e. most poverty in industrialized nations), not poverty in the absolute sense of a life or death struggle for survival, is more likely to be defined in terms of some bureaucratically defined norm, for example, 'a fraction of the average industrial wage'. Such 'poverty' is treated with technology and money. But all of the money is not given directly to those defined as poor. Rather it is used to provide services through the agency of expert professionals who have convinced everyone that their ministrations are morally necessary as well as being practically efficacious. In the long term such treatment generates dependency on the relevant professionals. Since the self-interest of the relevant professionals demands that it continue, then the long-term interests of the recipients of the service become a secondary issue: the professionals have more political power than the poor, the sick and the uneducated. So the incapacity of the poor, the sick and the uneducated continues and their natural communities become less able to help them.

Schools

Schools are complex places. They provide 'education' to individual learners but they also have related, and not always obvious, functions: providing custodial care, indoctrinating children with values, self-assessments and aspirations and controlling the selection of social roles.

Schools are inappropriate places for compensating individuals who are culturally, economically or intellectually disadvantaged. Money spent on schools tends to have an unequal distributive effect. The relatively privileged gain at least as much from any intervention as the disadvantaged; and so the gap between the two, the gap which defines the disadvantaged, is no narrower than it was before. Consider, for example, the allocation of resources to improve learner/teacher ratios: clearly *all* pupils, and not just those in most need of intensified instruction, will benefit from such an intervention. Neither do new technologies provide a solution: they reinforce the advantage to the well-to-do. The already established economic and social advantages of the well-to-do gives them material and cultural advantage in conventional educational systems, whatever the arrangements.

Poorer children will 'fall behind as long as (they) depend on the school for advancement of learning'. The starting line in the race between advantaged learners and their disadvantaged peers is not straight. The disadvantaged learner child, who is handicapped in the race for educational attainment due to cultural difference, intellectual inequality or linguistic unsuitability, is already behind at the start. The middle- or upper-class learner begins with all the advantages of culture, language, aspiration, parental interest, and so forth. Poorer pupils do not learn what they need to know: they merely 'get certified for the treatment of their alleged disproportionate deficiencies'.[19]

One effect of schooling is the creation of a demand for more schooling. Schooling generates the belief that those who have some schooling are inferior to those who have more. People are discouraged from taking control of their own learning: this is a systemic anti-educational outcome of compulsory education. School is the recognized agency, the specialist institution, for the distribution of education. A significant part of this ideology is the belief that when schools and school systems fail it is not the *idea* of institutionalized schooling which should be questioned, but that resources need to be increased. It becomes a simple arithmetical equation: more money equals more education. Only questions of a technical nature have legitimacy; should money be spent on teachers, gadgets, new programmes, increased supplementary supports such as psychologists, social workers, counsellors, and so on?

What Illich calls the 'escalation of schooling' is destructive. Increasing dependence on school systems further defers the possibility of finding effective alternatives. Since the lion's share of the finance available for education is being put into formal schooling and universities there is little motivation for those who wish to explore non-school alternatives. To the extent that school systems are successful in providing access to privilege, employment and wealth through a grading system, they increase expectations that if they were larger, more complex and better funded, they could do this more effectively.

Equality of opportunity

Illich is not anti-educational. His point is that compulsory schooling in formal, bureaucratized institutions is not the way to achieve goals of equality of opportunity and universal education. Obligatory schooling contradicts its own aims. Equal educational opportunity is 'both a desirable and a feasible goal, but to equate this with obligatory schooling is to confuse salvation with the Church'.[20] Education should be disestablished just as religion has been disestablished. The state should no longer enforce the ritualism of education.

One aspect of the problem is the way in which it is not one's knowledge which is of paramount importance but the way in which that knowledge was acquired. If it was not acquired through the conventional system of schooling and credentialling then it does not qualify as proper knowledge. Once schooling becomes established as the exclusive route of social and economic mobility all other routes are eliminated. Individuals acquire social and economic roles by meeting a predetermined 'curriculum of conditions'. It is not the qualities or competences which are relevant but the process 'by which such qualities are supposed to be acquired'. This is neither liberating nor educational: schools simply reserve 'instruction to those whose every step in learning fits previously approved measures of social control'.[21] It's not what you know it's the way that you have come to know it. It is not the destination, but the route taken, which is important.

Universal schooling has failed in the most central of its historic aspirations: to establish a fair and equitable meritocracy whereby status would attach to those who, irrespective of personal background or social class, showed most ability. It was meant, Illich argues, to separate role assignment from personal life history; this is what meritocracy means. Everyone should have equality of opportunity. However, rather than promoting equality of educational opportunity, formalized school systems became the monopoly distributor. The equalization of opportunity through the agency of schooling was an illusion. The law should forbid discrimination based on schooling. Where one acquired one's knowledge or expertise is as irrelevant as one's place of birth or parentage.

Conviviality

The growing dominance of professional hierarchies (teachers and other educational professionals, doctors, social workers, therapists, psychologists, etc.) can be challenged by finding ways of channelling money away from the bureaucracies and targeting the needs of individuals and their sustaining communities directly.

In place of increasingly expensive institutional arrangements we should facilitate 'tools for conviviality'. 'Conviviality' denotes the opposite of industrial productivity; 'autonomous and creative intercourse among persons, and the intercourse of persons with their environment'. Conviviality should be considered as a fundamental ethical value which can be 'realized in personal interdependence'.

An illusion is that most learning is a result of teaching, that is, the deliberate intervention of a professional teacher. But most things that people learn are learnt accidentally and incidentally, in places outside the deliberately contrived learning environments called schools. If people learn important or significant things in school, Illich claims, it is only because they cannot help doing so as they are obliged to attend school for a significant part of their lives.

Most learning happens casually. Children learn to walk and talk and to manipulate objects and ideas without direct instruction in the first instance. The result is what counts: if you can read it doesn't matter when, where or how you learned.

Two kinds of learning

This does not mean that planned learning and planned instruction are of no value. Nor does it mean that when they occur they may not need to be improved. There are two kinds of learning. There are competences which are skills-based; these are responsive to the drill teaching associated with the old-fashioned schoolmaster. Most skills can be acquired and improved by drilling procedures: skills require mastery of definable and predictable actions (riding a bicycle, writing, doing numerical calculations). Teachers of skills can devise simulated situations where the skill can be learned and practised.

The second kind of learning comes into play once skills have been acquired: learning how to use those skills creatively. Creative use of skills cannot be learned by a drill teaching procedure. By definition, creative use of the skills is not predictable and is not amenable to drill and practice. Using skills creatively is not a skill!

Learning the creative, exploratory use of skills presumes that individuals have already acquired the skills to some extent: those who can read, cycle or speak French, for example. It also requires that such people wish to use their command of the skills creatively. And, crucially, it relies on the unexpected question which opens new doors of enquiry. The learner in this form of learning must formulate his or her puzzlement, his or her unresolved query. The answer cannot be attained by improving performance of the relevant skill, much less by learning another skill. On the contrary it will be an insight, a new understanding of what is being learned.

Purposes of education

Any educational system worthy of the name should, Illich claims, have three related purposes: to make resources available to all who want to learn; to allow those who want to share knowledge or expertise to establish contact with those who want to learn it; and to facilitate access to opportunities for those who wish to present an issue to the public. Such a system should use 'modern technology to make free speech, free assembly, and a free press truly universal and, therefore, fully educational'.[22] For these purposes four related resources must be made available to learners: things (machines, objects, artefacts), models (people who embody skills and values), peers (for argument, competition, cooperation, understanding) and elders (who embody standards and values).

So skills, for example, can be acquired by matching learners with those who already have the skill and wish to teach it. Understandings – the creative application of the skills – can be facilitated by matching partners of similar interests or by apprenticeship to those who have the experience of creative application of skills. But while matching for skills-acquisition is relatively innocuous (since it leads only to the acquisition of the skill, not its substantive application) matching for exchanging understandings is fraught with danger for the educational establishment: it opens up opportunities for radical groups to emerge and pose challenges to the educational, cultural and political orthodoxy.

Learning the creative use of skills is politically significant. If people are empowered to define their relationships in terms of mutually identified problems then the political establishment is under threat since standard responses to social, economic or cultural situations are no longer reliable. For this reason the most radical alternative to school would be a network which allowed each person the opportunity to share his or her thoughts and concerns with like-minded others.

It doesn't matter what your interest is: a book, a movie, political subversion, whatever. All that is needed is a way to bring those with mutual interests together for mutual support and enlightenment. In this way learning becomes separated from social control. Suddenly, all is permitted in terms of educational experience which becomes decoupled from considerations of race, ethnicity, social class, age, gender, education, etc. Such learning is truly educational because it is chosen to match the learner's present needs and purposes. (In universities it is often personal contacts with like-minded people which provide most opportunities for personal and intellectual development.)

The educational establishment will not like such arrangements: it will, Illich prophesies, generate a contempt based on the presumption that the likely participants are ignorant. Such learning webs, for the orthodox educator, would be no more than instances of the ignorant meeting the ignorant 'around a text which they may not understand and which they read *only* because they are interested in it'.[23]

'Edu-credits'

Unfortunately Illich's solution, to a very radical analysis of a problem, is surprisingly right-wing. He proposes an 'education credit' system whereby everyone is given credit, 'edu-credits', to be spent on education in a setting of choice: *laissez faire* education. Such a system would promote competitiveness and consequently (so Illich's theory goes) benefit the educational consumer. (So 'education' becomes a product to be consumed by customers rather than a service to be delivered efficiently and effectively to clients, 'pupils' or 'students'.) A radical left-wing analysis leads to a solution on the radical right! But then Illich was not a radical left thinker: his suspicion of state centralization of control and provision was nearer to the conservative right than to the radical left.

The major difference between Illich's solution and that proposed by conservative politicians is that the latter propose spending the education credits *in* the school system in the belief that the resultant competition would lead to increased standards of service across the board. Illich, on the other hand, proposes using 'edu-credits' *outside* the school system. His believes that existing schooling systems are so counter-effective that they are beyond reform. His 'edu-credits' would be redeemable at informal 'skills centres' where motivated clients could learn skills faster and more cheaply than they could in schools.

People who practise desirable skills successfully in the community are presently discouraged from teaching them independently because they lack formal certification of either their skill level or of their capacity to teach the skill. Illich intends that anyone should be able to use their 'edu-credits' to learn skills from accomplished practitioners, whether they possess certified sanction or not: why, for example, should employers not augment their financial situation by teaching workplace skills in return for educational credits?

Illich is eminently quotable: he has an ear for the ringing rhetoric of the anti-establishment; he appeals to the subversive in all of us. If you are totally unmoved by Ivan Illich then there is a part of you that has died – or has never been alive. If Illich's solution is wrong it does not mean that his analysis is mistaken. He belongs to the gadfly tradition in social critique which stretches back to Socrates. His main contribution is not in the quality of the solutions he proposes but in the effect he has of challenging and deflating the smug certainties of the educational establishment. He poses questions which we must answer.

The method advocated by Illich in 1971 anticipates the Internet which now allows the kind of matching, on a global scale, which Illich proposed, although it does not necessarily permit the kinds of *personal* contact he envisaged. Has it delivered the kinds of convivial learning that he anticipated?

Conclusion

The benefits of modernity did not come all of a sudden: in education and schooling they came as a result of the slow accumulation of ideas and the slow development of new perspectives and practices. Whatever else one may say about the teachers and thinkers dealt with in this book it is clear that they were all dedicated to a vision of a future in which the power of education to bring personal fulfilment, social improvement and political development is recognized and promoted.

Over the course of the millennia we can see certain positive trends associated with educational developments.

There has been a significant increase in esteem for the individual, including individual children, and for childhood. While this sympathy for the individual child is evident in the enlightened views of Quintilian, it was the romantic revolution in the perception of childhood which followed Rousseau that established such esteem as the standard. It led eventually to the almost universal recognition of the dignity and rights of children as enshrined in the United Nations Convention on the Rights of the Child in the twentieth century.[1] This is not to say that all children are reaping the benefits of this new perception. Unfortunately exploitation, neglect and abuse continue but there is now a template, a standard of esteem and care, against which the treatment of children can be measured, evaluated and, where necessary, identified as falling short of this standard, and condemned.

In addition to the scientific and medical innovations since the seventeenth century, which brought about major changes in health, quality of life and life expectancy, there was the undoubted growth in the understanding of human development. Understanding of developmental patterns led to the proto-psychological educational theories of Pestalozzi and Froebel and culminated in the developmental psychology of the twentieth century. Many of the findings of developmental psychology confirmed the pre-scientific intuitions of Rousseau and his successors.

Occasions of change

So what does the future hold? Where is the next major breakthrough in educational thought likely to occur? Who will be the new Rousseau, or the new Dewey? It is of course impossible to tell. If we could answer questions like these we would already in some sense know what the next major development would be. There are some indicators.

Consider, for example, the history of universal compulsory education. This is premised on the practice of legally enforcing children's attendance at school and compelling them to remain there in age-specific groups, in receipt of common learning experiences and subject to common evaluations. Is this a sustainable way of dealing with the individuality of children into the future? What differences are relevant for differential treatment and interventions? In historical terms it is only relatively recently that educational policy-makers have begun to take individual differences, particularly disadvantages, whether mental, physical or cultural, seriously for purposes of educational remediation. But we cannot continue to evade the consequences of our knowledge of child development.

Developmental psychology, as well as telling us that human development moves through certain fixed stages, has also established our intuition that individuals move through these stages at idiosyncratic rates of development is true (a child is described as 'precocious', or as a 'late developer'). Over a wide range of capacities individuals of comparable chronological age differ significantly in the development of these capacities. Thus, while we continue to implement age-specific arrangements in our schools and other social institutions, we also recognize that the range of developmental progress among children of the same chronological age can vary enormously. Increasingly, formal systems will have to take account of learners who fall below the norm and also attend to the needs of all learners on an individual basis in relation to all of their capacities. It is questionable whether this can be done in schools and classrooms as currently organized.

Is an education which is dominated by literacy and literary methodologies likely to continue for very much longer? We are on the cusp of an era in which computers will speak our texts to us and save us the labour of reading, just as palm-sized computers save us the labour of calculating. What difference will such a change make to pedagogies which are almost exclusively premised on the laborious decoding of texts?

What of psychology? Education in the twentieth century was dominated by the discoveries of cognitive, developmental and educational psychology and it is likely that psychology will continue to have a profound influence on teaching and learning. Already, for example, the influence of Howard Gardner's theory of multiple intelligences is having substantive influence on curriculum design and reform, as well as on teachers' perceptions of the educational value of alternative learning experiences. It is also likely that as psychological testing becomes more refined and reliable it will provide more directed interventions addressing specific learning difficulties and prescribing more personalized learning programmes for individual learners. The dominance of testing was reinforced with the introduction of international comparisons: adapted versions of the same tests in reading, mathematics and science are administered over a wide range of national systems. Where the results and comparisons are treated by testing practitioners with great circumspection they are grist to the mills of politicians, journalists and other controversialists who use them to motivate, cajole, frighten and threaten school systems the world over to greater efforts.

Such developments, however, are no more than refinements on what already exists. There is no longer anything remotely radical about improved psychological provision; there is even concern about its potential for hidden manipulation. There is growing suspicion that increased reliance on testing and measurement serves only to depersonalize teaching and learning and to drive teachers and learners into submission to the test instruments themselves. Ultimately, it could be argued, wide-spread testing serves primarily to protect the state's investment in education and impose uniformity of outcomes rather than to promote the specific interests of individual learners.

Radical changes rarely come from expected sources. Perhaps the next great development in education will come through novel applications of micro-chip technology: microscopic implants to improve perception, memory, concentration and expression or to enhance performance in mathematics or language or art. Such developments are no longer exclusively in the realm of science fantasy: once the technology became available to replace or enhance the performance of human organs, miniaturization makes the increased use of such interventions probable rather than merely possible. Brain implants allowing monkeys to control a robotic arm with their thoughts have already been reported[2], as have implants which make it possible to predict monkeys' behaviour.[3]

Such interventions may sound to many like a dehumanization: objectionable on vaguely moral grounds of excessive interference with the natural order. Yet nowadays we hear relatively few objections to electronically enhanced prostheses, for example, or to organ transplants or to the implantation of electronic regulators such as pacemakers in human hearts. Where will it end? Why should it end? And why, in principle, should such technology not be used eventually to enhance the quality of human learning?

Or what of possibly the greatest scientific achievement of the second half of the twentieth century, mapping the human genome? Is there a learning gene? A piece of genetic code which can be manipulated to improve learning, sharpen interest, develop concentration or to remove obstacles to learning and intellectual development? Will it be possible to use the genetic code to type individuals at, or even before, birth so that political, social and economic hierarchies will be based on scientific grounds rather than on fortuitous circumstances?

What endures?

None of these possibilities changes education. They may make learning more efficient and less demanding, they may make schooling more effective, but they do not address the fundamental questions of understanding and value which have been at the core of educational progress for over two millennia. Irrespective of the capacity of individual learners, the questions at the core of Plato's agenda remain central: the criteria for selection of those to be educated; the kinds of distinctions, based on what grounds, that will be made between learners; the need for decisions regarding curriculum content, what will be taught and when; for what purposes, and more importantly, for whose purposes will education be controlled; how are those who will teach to be selected and according to what criteria of knowledge, achievement and orthodoxy; what methodologies will be endorsed and what accomplishments will be rewarded.

The long-term effects of education are not always benign. In the first half of the twentieth century one of the most educated populations in human history participated in the rape of Europe, the decimation of its population, and in acts of barbarity on a hitherto unimagined scale, all in the name of a theory of genetic purity and racial superiority. How did this happen? In the Introduction it was suggested that there were three possible components in any educational and political programme: authority, technology and individual liberty. Where authority supported by a real or imagined technical expertise (whether philosophical, theological or scientific) becomes the dominant value, individual liberty is suppressed. When this happens the moral vision which should be at the heart of any humane system of government disappears. This was the point of Socrates' opposition to the Sophists: no amount of technical expertise is sufficient for the proper ordering of human affairs unless it is firmly based on a clear moral vision. 'Education' is an evaluative term. When we describe a system or process as 'educational' we are asserting that it meets certain moral conditions. One of these conditions must be that it enables the individual learner to assume the burden of personal responsibility for his or her own life. A system which presumes to exercise moral responsibility on behalf of individuals is not educational, it is indoctrinatory.

Schools and teachers

Where will education happen in the future? It may be that schools as we know them will disappear as new applications of electronic media and micro-technology make it easier to communicate directly with learners in their own homes. Why should public authorities have the enormous financial burden of building and maintaining schools and colleges when all that learners need to know is available instantaneously at the press of a switch and the push of a button? Schools as locations for universal education are a relatively recent cultural phenomenon and, once an individual can read, there is no compelling reason why self-initiated auto-education through the electronic media should not become the norm.

Already there are successful models such as the School of the Air programme in Australia which has been delivering education to isolated children through a combination of correspondence and electronic technology since 1950, the 'supported open learning' programmes of the Open University in the UK and a plethora of other distance learning programmes worldwide. An online search for 'distance learning' yielded more than seven million hits!

This raises again Newman's concern regarding the role of the living teacher. For what teachers have to offer to learners at all levels of education is not just pieces of information or skills which can, at least in principle, be provided by electronic or mechanical substitutes. While a certain minimal competence in instructional methodologies and classroom management are essential for professional teachers, what is of perennial importance is what teachers bring to classrooms in terms of enthusiasm for knowledge and learning. Good teachers spark imagination, vivify inert information, inspire learners and provoke curiosity. Even in principle there is no substitute for the joy in knowledge and life which good teachers engender in their students. Good teachers are not defined by their methodological exactness or their encyclopaedic knowledge. Dickens' M'Choakumchild[4] was such and he served only to repress and stifle the life of the imagination and the exhilaration of discovery. Good teachers, as well as celebrating knowledge, also celebrate learning, the acquisition of knowledge. Good teachers are as interested in the process of their students' learning as they are in the matter being learned: they share the excitement of discovery and the satisfaction of achievement. Perhaps good teachers are born and not made; perhaps they are relatively rare individuals who embody the requisite personal characteristics and idealism which provokes others to learn. But then, as Illich suggested, perhaps they can now be accessed without recourse to contrived institutions remote from the environment where learning is relevant to people's needs.

We cannot read the future but we can make sure that the progress which has been made in human dignity and freedom is not eroded. In the final analysis the quality of education is not determined by information or methodologies, it is determined by human relations, by the regard teachers have for learners as autonomous human beings who are in the process of becoming their best selves.

Notes

Introduction

1 *The Deserted Village*, Goldsmith, O., Dublin: The Goldsmith Press, 1993.
2 Durkheim, Émile, *Education and Sociology*, trans. Sherwood D. Fox, Glencoe, Ill.: The Free Press, 1956, p. 81.
3 Kuhn, T.S., *The Structure of Scientific Revolutions*, Chicago, 1962.

1 Socrates (469/70–399 BC) and the Search for Definition

1 Plato, *Crito*, trans. by J.M.A. Grube, from *Plato: Five Dialogues*, Indianapolis: Hackett Publishing Co., 1981,
2 Plato, *Apology*, trans. by Hugh Tredennick, from *The Last Days of Socrates*, Harmondsworth: Penguin Books, 1969, p. 48.
3 Plato, *Phaedrus*, trans. by Benjamin Jowett, online at: www.infomotions.com/etexts/philosophy/400BC-301BC/plato-phaedrus-351.txt
4 *Apology*, p. 49.
5 *Apology*, p. 50.
6 *Apology*, p. 67.
7 Plato, *Phaedo*, trans. by Hugh Tredennick, from *The Last Days of Socrates*, Harmondsworth: Penguin Books, 1969.
8 *Apology*, pp. 69–70.
9 Plato, *Meno*, trans. by J.M.A. Grube, from *Plato: Five Dialogues*, Indianapolis: Hackett Publishing Co., 1981, pp. 59–88.
10 *Apology*, p. 62.
11 *Apology*, pp. 62–3.
12 *Apology*, p. 70.
13 *Apology*, p. 76.
14 *Crito*, pp. 82–3.
15 *Crito*, p. 90.
16 Plato, *Phaedo*, trans. by Hugh Tredennick, from *The Last Days of Socrates*, Harmondsworth: Penguin Books, 1969, p. 183.

2   Plato (428–347 BC): Education for the State

1   Plato, *The Seventh Letter*, trans. by J. Hayward at: http://www.farid-hajji.net/books/en/Plato/se-all.html.

2   Plato, *The Republic*, trans. by Desmond Lee, London: Penguin Classics, 2003; online version trans. by Benjamin Jewett at: http://classics.mit.edu/Plato/republic.html, Book VII, p. Quotations are from Jowett translation.

3   *The Republic*, Book VII, Sec. 540–1.

4   *The Republic*, Book II, Sec. 374.

5   *The Republic*, Book III, Sec. 389.

6   *The Republic*, Book III, Sec. 413.

7   *The Republic*, Book V, Sec. 459.

8   *The Republic*, Book III, Sec. 415.

9   *The Republic*, Book V, Sec. 456.

3   Aristotle (384–322 BC): Education for Leisure

1   Aristotle, *Politics*, trans. by T.A. Sinclair (revised and re-presented by Trevor J. Saunders), London: Penguin Books, 1992, Book I, pp. 60–1.

2   *Politics*, Book VII, p. 433.

3   *Politics*, Book VII, p. 434.

4   Aristotle, *Ethics*, Book II, trans. by J.A.K. Thomson (revised, Hugh Tredennick), London: Penguin, 1976, pp. 91–2.

5   *Politics*, Book VII, p. 445.

6   *Politics*, Book VII, p. 447.

7   *Politics*, Book VII, p. 447.

8   *Politics*, Book VII, p. 446.

9   *Politics*, Book VII, p. 447.

10 *Politics*, Book VII, p. 452.

11 *Politics*, Book VII, p. 452.

12 *Politics*, Book I, p. 59.

13 *Politics*, Book I, p. 60.

14 *Politics*, Book VII, p. 454.

15 *Politics*, Book VIII, p. 462.

16 *Politics*, Book VIII, p. 456.

17 *Politics*, Book VIII, p. 457.

18 *Politics*, Book VIII, p. 457.

19 *Politics*, Book VIII, p. 466–7.

20 *Politics*, Book I, p. 97.

5 Marcus Fabius Quintilian (35–<100 AD): The Education of the Orator

1 Quintilian, *Institutio Oratoria*, Book I, Preface, paragraph 15, trans. by Bill Thayer at: http://penelope.uchicago.edu/Thayer/E/Roman/Texts/Quintilian/Institutio_Oratoria/home.html.
2 *Institutio Oratoria*, Book I, Preface, par. 9.
3 *Institutio Oratoria*, Book XII, Chapter 1, par. 3.
4 *Institutio Oratoria*, Book I, Preface, par. 9.
5 *Institutio Oratoria*, Book I, Preface, par. 26.
6 *Institutio Oratoria*, Book I, Chapter 1, par. 4.
7 *Institutio Oratoria*, Book I, Chapter 1, par. 20.
8 *Institutio Oratoria*, Book I, Chapter 1, par. 31.
9 *Institutio Oratoria*, Book I, Chapter 1, par. 14.
10 *Institutio Oratoria*, Book I, Chapter 2, par. 18.
11 *Institutio Oratoria*, Book III, Chapter 2, par. 7.
12 *Institutio Oratoria*, Book I, Chapter 3, par. 14.
13 *Institutio Oratoria*, Book I, Chapter 8, par. 2.
14 *Institutio Oratoria*, Book I, Chapter 8, par. 4.
15 *Institutio Oratoria*, Book I, Chapter 12, par. 2.
16 *Institutio Oratoria*, Book II, Chapter 2, par. 5–8.

6 Aurelius Augustine (354–430): Education for the Inner Life

1 Augustine, *Confessions*, trans. E.B. Pusey, http://ccat.sas.UPENN.edu/JOD/augustine.html 8.12.29
2 This section is largely based on: Copleston, Frederick, *A History of Philosophy*, vol. 2, Part 1, 'Augustine to Bonaventure', New York: Image Books, 1965, Chapter 4, pp. 66–82.
3 Augustine, *The Greatness of the Soul*, trans. by Joseph M. Colleran, New York: Newman Press, 1978, p. 42.
4 Augustine, *The Teacher*, trans. by Joseph M. Colleran, New York: Newman Press, 1978, p. 177.
5 Quoted in Howie, G., *Educational Theory and Practice in St. Augustine*, London: Routledge and Kegan Paul, 1969, p. 53.
6 Quoted in Howie, G., *Educational Theory and Practice in St. Augustine*, p. 72.
7 Howie, p. 48.
8 Howie, p. 83.
9 *The Teacher*, trans. p. 174.

10 *The Teacher*, p. 173.
11 *The Teacher*, p. 177.
12 *The Teacher*, p. 176.
13 *The Teacher*, pp. 185–6.
14 *The Teacher*, p. 185.
15 *Confessions* 1,14, 23.
16 Howie, p. 146.
17 Howie, p. 149.
18 Howie, p. 149.
19 Howie, p. 144.

7 John Amos Comenius (1592–1670): Education as a Human Right

1 Comenius, John Amos, *The Great Didactic*, trans. by M.W. Keatinge, London: Adam and Charles Black, 1896, p. 229.
2 *The Great Didactic*, p. 231.
3 *The Great Didactic*, p. 167.
4 *The Great Didactic*, p. 214.
5 *The Great Didactic*, p. 218.
6 *The Great Didactic*, p. 219.
7 *The Great Didactic*, pp. 242–3.
8 *The Great Didactic*, p. 220.
9 *The Great Didactic*, p. 220.
10 *The Great Didactic*, pp. 248–9.
11 *The Great Didactic*, p. 157.
12 *The Great Didactic*, p. 409.
13 *The Great Didactic*, pp. 171–3.
14 *The Great Didactic*, p. 179.
15 *The Great Didactic*, p. 182.
16 *The Great Didactic*, p. 204.
17 *The Great Didactic*, p. 237.
18 *The Great Didactic*, p. 204.
19 *The Great Didactic*, pp. 206–7.
20 *The Great Didactic*, p. 209.
21 *The Great Didactic*, p. 226.
22 *The Great Didactic*, pp. 196–7.
23 *The Great Didactic*, p. 258.
24 *The Great Didactic*, p. 268.
25 *The Great Didactic*, p. 319.
26 *The Great Didactic*, p. 408.
27 *The Great Didactic*, p. 409.
28 *The Great Didactic*, p. 417.

29   *The Great Didactic*, p. 420.

30   *The Great Didactic*, p. 422.

31   The traditional liberal arts comprise the *trivium* (grammar, rhetoric, logic) and the *quadrivium* (geometry, arithmetic, music, astronomy).

32   *The Great Didactic*, p. 427.

33   *The Great Didactic*, p. 434.

34   *The Great Didactic*, pp. 433–4.

35   *The Great Didactic*, p. 434.

8   John Locke (1632–1704): Education for the English Gentleman

1   Locke, John, 'Paternal Power' in O'Neill, O. and Ruddick, W. (eds), *Having Children: Philosophical and Legal Reflections on Parenthood*, Oxford: Oxford University Press, 1979, pp. 240–46, esp. p. 241.

2   'Paternal Power', p. 243.

3   *Second Treatise*, Chapter VI, Sec. 55, http://libertyonline.hypermail.com/Locke/Second-frame.html

4   *Second Treatise*, Chapter VI, Sec. 60.

5   *Some Thoughts Concerning Education*, with Introduction and Notes by the Rev. R.H. Quick, MA, Cambridge: Cambridge University Press, 1899, Sec. 101, Sec. 217, p. 188.

6   *Some Thoughts Concerning Education*, 'Dedication', p. lxiii.

7   *Some Thoughts Concerning Education*, 'Dedication', p. lxiii.

8   *Some Thoughts Concerning Education*, Sec. 6, pp. 3–4.

9   *Some Thoughts Concerning Education*, Sec. 32, p. 20.

10   *Some Thoughts Concerning Education*, Sec. 66, p. 40.

11   *Some Thoughts Concerning Education*, p. 82.

12   *Some Thoughts Concerning Education*, Appendix A, pp. 189–92.

13   *Some Thoughts Concerning Education*, Sec. 70, p. 50.

14   *Some Thoughts Concerning Education*, Sec. 70, p. 50.

15   *Some Thoughts Concerning Education*, 'Dedication', p. lxii.

16   *Some Thoughts Concerning Education*, Sec. 70, pp. 46–7.

17   *Some Thoughts Concerning Education*, Sec. 68, pp. 35–45.

18   *Some Thoughts Concerning Education*, Sec. 70, p. 50.

19   *Some Thoughts Concerning Education*, Sec. 1, p. 1.

20   See n. 10 above regarding his recommendations for Working Schools.

21   *Some Thoughts Concerning Education*, Sec. 30, p. 20.

22   *Some Thoughts Concerning Education*, Sec. 7, p. 4.

23   *Some Thoughts Concerning Education*, Sec. 107, p. 85.

24   'Paternal Power', p. 243.

25   *Some Thoughts Concerning Education*, Sec. 81, pp. 60–1.

26   *Some Thoughts Concerning Education*, Sec. 42, p. 28.

27 *Some Thoughts Concerning Education*, Sec. 107, p. 86.
28 *Some Thoughts Concerning Education*, Sec. 195, p. 173.
29 *Some Thoughts Concerning Education*, Sec. 46, p. 30.
30 *Some Thoughts Concerning Education*, Sec. 74, p. 53.
31 *Some Thoughts Concerning Education*, Sec. 74, p. 53.
32 *Some Thoughts Concerning Education*, Sec. 66, p. 40.
33 *Some Thoughts Concerning Education*, Sec. 52, pp. 31–2.
34 *Some Thoughts Concerning Education*, Sec. 49, p. 31.
35 Quoted in Sahakian, M.L. and Sahakian, W.S., *John Locke*, Boston: Twayne, 1975, p. 16.
36 *Some Thoughts Concerning Education*, Sec. 155, pp. 132–3.
37 *Some Thoughts Concerning Education*, Sec. 189, p. 166.
38 *Some Thoughts Concerning Education*, Sec. 168, p. 146.
39 *Some Thoughts Concerning Education*, Sec. 204, pp. 178–9.
40 *Some Thoughts Concerning Education*, Sec. 210, pp. 182–3.

9 Jean-Jacques Rousseau (1712–1778): The Education of Nature

1 Rousseau, J-J., *The Confessions of Jean-Jacques Rousseau*, trans. by J.M. Cohen, London: Penguin Books, 1953, p. 21.
2 *The Confessions of Jean-Jacques Rousseau*, p. 23.
3 *The Confessions of Jean-Jacques Rousseau*, pp. 320–22, 332–34.
4 Rousseau, J-J., *Émile or On Education*, Introduction, Translation and Notes by Alan Bloom, Harmondsworth: Penguin, 1991, pp. 266 ff.
5 *Émile or On Education*, p. 37.
6 *Émile or On Education*, p. 92.
7 *Émile or On Education*, p. 39.
8 *Émile or On Education*, p. 97.
9 *Émile or On Education*, p. 49.
10 *Émile or On Education*, p. 78.
11 *Émile or On Education*, p. 86.
12 Rousseau, J-J., *Julie ou la nouvelle Heloïse*, 'Lettre III: a milord Edouard', www.C18.org/pr/Rousseau/Julie/5002.html
13 *Émile or On Education*, pp. 79–80.
14 *Émile or On Education*, p. 84.
15 *Émile or On Education*, p. 90.
16 *Émile or On Education*, p. 89.
17 *Émile or On Education*, p. 91.
18 *Émile or On Education*, p. 92.
19 *Émile or On Education*, p. 125.
20 *Émile or On Education*, p. 104.
21 *Émile or On Education*, p. 125.

22 *Émile or On Education*, p. 116.
23 *Émile or On Education*, p. 117.
24 *Émile or On Education*, p. 161.
25 *Émile or On Education*, p. 162.
26 *Émile or On Education*, p. 165.
27 *Émile or On Education*, p. 41.
28 *Émile or On Education*, p. 167.
29 *Émile or On Education*, p. 168.
30 *Émile or On Education*, p. 172.
31 *Émile or On Education*, p. 184.
32 *Émile or On Education*, p. 59.
33 Rousseau, J-J., *Considerations on the Government of Poland* and on its Proposed Reformation, www.constitution.org/jjr/poland.html Chapter IV, 'Education'

10 Jean Heinrich Pestalozzi (1746–1827): The Education of the People

1   'The Method: a Report by Pestalozzi', Appendix to *How Gertrude Teaches Her Children*, trans. by Lucy E. Holland and Francis C. Turner, London: George Allen and Unwin, 1915, pp. 199–200.
2   Quoted in Curtis, S.J. and Boultwood, M.E.A., *A Short History of Educational Ideas*, London: University Tutorial Press Ltd., 1970, p. 322.
3   Quoted in Rusk, Robert R., *The Doctrines of the Great Educators*, New York: St. Martin's Press, pp. 212–3.
4   Quoted in *A Short History of Educational Ideas*, p. 327.
5   *How Gertrude Teaches Her Children*, p. 78.
6   *How Gertrude Teaches Her Children*, p. 74.
7   Quoted in *A Short History of Educational Ideas*, p. 341.
8   *How Gertrude Teaches Her Children*, p. 98.
9   *How Gertrude Teaches Her Children*, p. 87.
10 *How Gertrude Teaches Her Children*, p. 88.
11 *How Gertrude Teaches Her Children*, p. 124.
12 *How Gertrude Teaches Her Children*, p. 51.
13 *How Gertrude Teaches Her Children*, p. 55.
14 *How Gertrude Teaches Her Children*, p. 26.
15 *How Gertrude Teaches Her Children*, p. 57.
16 Quoted in *The Doctrines of the Great Educators*, p. 211.
17 *How Gertrude Teaches Her Children*, p. 173.
18 *How Gertrude Teaches Her Children*, p. 176.
19 *How Gertrude Teaches Her Children*, pp. 160–1.
20 *How Gertrude Teaches Her Children*, pp. 182–3.

21 Quoted in *The Doctrines of the Great Educators*, pp. 227–8.

22 'The Method: a Report by Pestalozzi', p. 199.

23 Pestalozzi, Heinrich, *The Education of Man – Aphorisms*, Introduction by William H. Kilpatrick, New York: Philosophical Library, 1951, p. 27.

11 Friedrich Froebel (1782–1852): The Garden of Education

1 Froebel, F., 'Letter to the Duke of Meiningen', in Irene M. Lilley (ed.), *Friedrich Froebel: a Selection from His Writings*, Cambridge: Cambridge University Press, 1967, p. 33.

2 Froebel, F., *The Education of Man*, quoted in Lilley, I. (ed.), *Friedrich Froebel: a Selection from His Writings*, p. 48.

3 Froebel, F., 'Letter to Karl Christoph Friedrich Krause', quoted in Lilley, I. (ed.), *Friedrich Froebel: a Selection from His Writings*, p. 42.

4 Froebel, F., 'Letter to Karl Christoph Friedrich Krause', quoted in Lilley, I. (ed.), *Friedrich Froebel: a Selection from His Writings*, p. 36.

5 Froebel, F., 'Letter to Karl Christoph Friedrich Krause', quoted in Lilley, I. (ed.), *Friedrich Froebel: a Selection from His Writings*, p. 42.

6 Froebel, F., *The Education of Man*, quoted in Lilley, I. (ed.), *Friedrich Froebel: a Selection from His Writings*, p. 57.

7 Rusk, Robert R., *Doctrines of the Great Educators*, New York: St. Martin's Press, 1967, p. 278n.

8 Froebel, F., 'Pedagogics of the Kindergarten', quoted in Lilley, I. (ed.), *Friedrich Froebel: a Selection from His Writings*, p. 97.

9 Froebel, F., *The Education of Man*, quoted in Rusk, R., *Doctrines of the Great Educators*, p. 270.

10 *Doctrines of the Great Educators*, pp. 270–1.

11 Froebel, F., 'Letter to the Women in Keilhau', quoted in Lilley, I. (ed.), *Friedrich Froebel: a Selection from His Writings*, p. 47.

12 Froebel, F., *The Education of Man*, quoted in Lilley, I. (ed.), *Friedrich Froebel: a Selection from His Writings*, pp. 48–9.

13 Froebel, F., *The Education of Man*, quoted in Lilley, I. (ed.), *Friedrich Froebel: a Selection from His Writings*, p. 49.

14 Froebel, F., *The Education of Man*, quoted in Lilley, I. (ed.), *Friedrich Froebel: a Selection from His Writings*, p. 57.

15 Froebel, F., *The Education of Man*, quoted in Lilley, I. (ed.), *Friedrich Froebel: a Selection from His Writings*, pp. 144–5.

16 Froebel, F., *The Education of Man*, quoted in Lilley, I. (ed.), *Friedrich Froebel: a Selection from His Writings*, p. 83.

17 Froebel, F., *The Education of Man*, quoted in Lilley, I. (ed.), *Friedrich Froebel: a Selection from His Writings*, p. 84.

18 Froebel, F., 'Plan of an Institution for the Education of the Poor in the Canton of Berne', quoted in Lilley, I. (ed.), *Friedrich Froebel: a Selection from His Writings*, pp. 167–8.

19 *Doctrines of the Great Educators*, p. 274.

20 Froebel, F., *The Education of Man*, quoted in Lilley, I. (ed.), *Friedrich Froebel: a Selection from His Writings*, p. 137.

21 Froebel, F., *The Education of Man*, quoted in Lilley, I. (ed.), *Friedrich Froebel: a Selection from His Writings*, p. 65–7.

22 Froebel, F., *The Education of Man*, quoted in Rusk, R., *Doctrines of the Great Educators*, p. 277.

23 Froebel, F., *The Education of Man*, quoted in Lilley, I. (ed.), *Friedrich Froebel: a Selection from His Writings*, pp. 88–9.

24 Froebel, F., *The Education of Man*, quoted in Rusk, R., *Doctrines of the Great Educators*, p. 277.

25 Froebel, F., *The Education of Man*, quoted in Lilley, I. (ed.), *Friedrich Froebel: a Selection from His Writings*, p. 55.

26 Froebel, F., 'Letter to the Women in Keilhau', quoted in Lilley, I. (ed.), *Friedrich Froebel: a Selection from His Writings*, p. 47.

27 Froebel, F., 'Letter to Karl Christoph Friedrich Krause', quoted in Lilley, I. (ed.), *Friedrich Froebel: a Selection from His Writings*, p. 39.

12 John Henry Newman (1801–1890): University Education

1   Newman, J.H., www.ajdrake.com/etexts/texts/Newman/works/disc_1852.pdf 'Discourses on the Scope and Nature of University Education.' Addressed to the Catholics of Dublin.

2   Newman, J.H., *The Essential Newman*, Vincent Ferrer Blehl (ed.), New York: Mentor-Omega, 1963, pp. 160–1.

3   *The Essential Newman*, p. 161.

4   *The Essential Newman*, p. 162.

5   *The Essential Newman*, p. 177.

6   *The Essential Newman*, p. 169.

7   *The Essential Newman*, p. 171.

8   *The Essential Newman*, p. 179.

9   *The Essential Newman*, p. 180.

10 *The Essential Newman*, p. 191.

11 *The Essential Newman*, p. 181.

12 *The Essential Newman*, p. 182.

13 *The Essential Newman*, p. 193.

14 *The Essential Newman*, p. 193.

15 *The Essential Newman*, p. 186.

16   *The Essential Newman*, p. 187.
17   *The Essential Newman*, p. 188.

13   John Dewey (1859-1952): Education for the Future

1   Dewey, John, *My Pedagogic Creed*, first published in *The School Journal,* Volume LIV, Number 3 (16 January 1897), pp. 77–80.
2   Dewey, John, *Democracy And Education*, Chapter 24 'Philosophy of Education', The Free Press, 1997, www.worldwideschool.org/library
3   Dewey, John, *The Child and the Curriculum; The School and Society*, Chicago: University of Chicago Press, 1956, pp. 31–2.
4   *The Child and the Curriculum*, p. 17.
5   Dewey, John, *Education Today*, New York: G. P. Putnam's Sons, 1940, p. 298.
6   Cf. note 1.
7   *My Pedagogic Creed*, Article II
8   *The Child and the Curriculum*, p. 8.
9   *The Child and the Curriculum*, p. 9.
10   *The Child and the Curriculum*, pp. 3–4.
11   *The Child and the Curriculum*, p. 11.
12   *The Child and the Curriculum*, p. 12.
13   *My Pedagogic Creed*, Article I, 'What Education Is'.
14   *Democracy and Education*, Chapter 1: 'Education as a Necessity of Life'
15   *My Pedagogic Creed*, Article I, 'What Education Is'
16   *My Pedagogic Creed*, Article I, 'What Education Is'
17   Dewey, J., *The Public and Its Problems*, in *The Later Works*, vol. 2, Jo Ann Boydston (ed.), Carbondale: Southern Illinois University Press, 1984, pp. 330–2.
18   *My Pedagogic Creed*, Article I, 'What Education Is'
19   *My Pedagogic Creed*, Article III, 'The Subject-Matter of Education'
20   *Democracy and Education*, Chapter 4, 'Education as Growth'
21   *Democracy and Education*, Chapter 12, 'Thinking in Education'

14   Maria Montessori (1870–1952): Education for Personal Competence

1   Montessori, M., *The Montessori Method*, trans. by A.E. George, New York: Frederick A. Stokes Company, 1912, p. 42.
2   *The Montessori Method*, p. 38.
3   *The Montessori Method*, p. 31.
4   *The Montessori Method*, p. 39.

5   *The Montessori Method*, p. 33.

6   *The Montessori Method*, pp. 104–5.

7   Montessori, M., *The Secret of Childhood*, trans. by Barbara B. Carter, Bombay: Orient Longmans, 1963, p. 36.

8   *The Secret of Childhood*, p. 42.

9   *The Montessori Method*, p. 371.

10 *The Montessori Method*, p. 346.

11 *The Montessori Method*, p. 83.

12 *The Montessori Method*, p. 221.

13 *The Montessori Method*, p. 260.

14 *The Montessori Method*, p. 287.

15 *The Montessori Method*, p. 289.

16 *The Montessori Method*, p. 296.

17 *The Montessori Method*, p. 298.

18 *The Montessori Method*, p. 89.

19 *The Montessori Method*, p. 167.

20 *The Montessori Method*, p. 173.

15   Martin Buber (1878–1965): Education for Relationship

1   Quoted in Murphy, D., *Martin Buber's Philosophy of Education*, Dublin: Irish Academic Press, 1988, p. 90.

2   Quoted in *Martin Buber's Philosophy of Education*, p. 90.

3   Quoted in *Martin Buber's Philosophy of Education*, p. 90.

4   Buber, M., *Between Man and Man*, London: The Fontana Library, 1961, p. 111.

5   *Between Man and Man*, p. 114.

6   *Between Man and Man*, p. 114.

7   *Between Man and Man*, p. 117.

8   *Between Man and Man*, p. 116.

9   *Between Man and Man*, p. 115.

10 *Between Man and Man*, p. 115.

11 *Between Man and Man*, p. 118.

12 *Between Man and Man*, pp. 121–2.

13 *Between Man and Man*, pp. 125–6.

14 *Between Man and Man*, p. 130.

16   Alexander Sutherland Neill (1883–1973): Education for the Liberation of the Psyche

1   Neill, A.S., *Neill! Neill! Orange Peel! An autobiography*, London: Quartet Books, 1977, p. 147.

2 *Neill! Neill! Orange Peel! An autobiography*, p. 77.

3 *Neill! Neill! Orange Peel! An autobiography*, p. 83.

4 Neill, A.S., *Summerhill: a radical approach to child-rearing*, Harmondsworth: Penguin, 1985, p. 20, 'The Idea of Summerhill'.

5 *Summerhill: a radical approach to child-rearing*, p. 20, 'The Idea of Summerhill'.

6 *Summerhill: a radical approach to child-rearing*, p. 20, 'The Idea of Summerhill'.

7 *Neill! Neill! Orange Peel! An autobiography*, p. 119.

8 *Summerhill: a radical approach to child-rearing*, p. 92, 'The Future of Summerhill'.

9 *Summerhill: a radical approach to child-rearing*, p. 43, 'What Happens to Summerhill Graduates'.

10 *Summerhill: a radical approach to child-rearing*, p. 112, 'The Free Child'.

11 *Summerhill: a radical approach to child-rearing*, p. 99, 'The Unfree Child'.

12 *Summerhill: a radical approach to child-rearing*, p. 105, 'The Free Child'.

13 *Summerhill: a radical approach to child-rearing*, p. 27, 'The Idea of Summerhill'.

14 *Summerhill: a radical approach to child-rearing*, pp. 99–100, 'The Unfree Child'.

15 *Summerhill: a radical approach to child-rearing*, p. 23, 'The Idea of Summerhill'.

16 *Summerhill: a radical approach to child-rearing*, p. 152, 'Rewards and Punishment'.

17 *Summerhill: a radical approach to child-rearing*, p. 30, 'A Look at Summerhill'.

18 *Summerhill: a radical approach to child-rearing*, p. 59, 'Self-Government'.

19 *Summerhill: a radical approach to child-rearing*, p. 60, 'Self-Government'.

20 *Summerhill: a radical approach to child-rearing*, pp. 68–9, 'Play'.

21 *Summerhill: a radical approach to child-rearing*, p. 80, 'Report of the British Government Inspectors'.

22 *Summerhill: a radical approach to child-rearing*, p. 95, 'The Unfree Child'.

23 *Summerhill: a radical approach to child-rearing*, p. 85, 'Report of the British Government Inspectors'.

24 *Summerhill: a radical approach to child-rearing*, p. 91, 'The Future of Summerhill'.

17   Paulo Freire (1921–1997): Education for Freedom

1   Freire, Paulo, *Pedagogy of the Oppressed*, trans. by Myra Bergman Ramos, Harmondsworth: Penguin Books, 1972, p. 39.
2   *Pedagogy of the Oppressed*, p. 67.
3   *Pedagogy of the Oppressed*, p. 37.
4   *Pedagogy of the Oppressed*, p. 31.
5   *Pedagogy of the Oppressed*, p. 22.
6   *Pedagogy of the Oppressed*, p. 43.
7   *Pedagogy of the Oppressed*, p. 45.
8   *Pedagogy of the Oppressed*, p. 46.
9   *Pedagogy of the Oppressed*, p. 46.
10   *Pedagogy of the Oppressed*, p. 48.
11   *Pedagogy of the Oppressed*, p. 20.
12   *Pedagogy of the Oppressed*, p. 24.
13   *Pedagogy of the Oppressed*, p. 48.
14   *Pedagogy of the Oppressed*, p. 53.
15   *Pedagogy of the Oppressed*, pp. 60–1.
16   *Pedagogy of the Oppressed*, p. 60.
17   *Pedagogy of the Oppressed*, p. 65.
18   *Pedagogy of the Oppressed*, p. 63.
19   *Pedagogy of the Oppressed*, p. 64.
20   *Pedagogy of the Oppressed*, p. 62.

18   Ivan Illich (1926–2002): Education Without Schooling

1   Illich, Ivan, *Deschooling Society*, Harmondsworth: Penguin, 1973, p. 7, 'Why We Must Disestablish School'.
2   *Deschooling Society*, p. 32, 'Phenomenology of School'.
3   *Deschooling Society*, p. 38, 'Phenomenology of School'.
4   *Deschooling Society*, p. 78, 'Learning Webs'.
5   *Deschooling Society*, p. 9, 'Why We Must Disestablish School'.
6   *Deschooling Society*, p. 73, 'Irrational Consistencies'.
7   *Deschooling Society*, p. 9, 'Why We Must Disestablish School'.
8   Illich, Ivan, *Tools for Conviviality*, Centro Latinoamericano para la Competitividad y el Desarrollo Sostenible, Alajuela, 2002, p. 2; online at: http://homepage.mac.com/tinapple/illich/1973_tools_for_conviviality.html.
9   *Tools for Conviviality*, p. 3.
10   *Deschooling Society*, p. 41, 'Ritualisation of Progress'.
11   *Deschooling Society*, p. 40, 'Ritualisation of Progress'.

12 *Deschooling Society*, p. 43, 'Ritualisation of Progress'.
13 *Deschooling Society*, p. 43, 'Ritualisation of Progress'.
14 *Deschooling Society*, p. 73, 'Irrational Consistencies'.
15 *Deschooling Society*, p. 51, 'Ritualisation of Progress'.
16 *Deschooling Society*, p. 9, 'Why We Must Disestablish School'.
17 *Deschooling Society*, p. 44, 'Ritualisation of Progress'.
18 *Tools for Conviviality*, p. 5.
19 *Deschooling Society*, p. 9, 'Why We Must Disestablish School'.
20 *Deschooling Society*, p. 18, 'Why We Must Disestablish School'.
21 *Deschooling Society*, p. 19, 'Why We Must Disestablish School'.
22 *Deschooling Society*, p. 78, 'Learning Webs'.
23 *Deschooling Society*, p. 28, 'Why We Must Disestablish School'.

Conclusion

1 Convention On The Rights Of The Child, UNGA Doc A/RES/44/25 (12 December 1989).
2 'Monkeys Control Robotic Arm With Brain Implants', *Washington Post*, Monday, 13 October 2003, page A01.
3 'Brain implants "read" monkey minds', NewScientist.com news service, 8 July 2004.
4 Dickens, Charles, *Hard Times*, London: Penguin Books, 1994.

Further Reading

Introduction, and general

Bowen, James, *The History of Western Education* (3 vols), New York: St. Martin's Press, 1972, 1975, 1981.

Bowen, James and Hobson, Peter R., *Theories of Education: Studies of Significant Innovation in Western Educational Thought*, Sussex: John Wiley, 1974, revised 1987.

Boyd, William, *The History of Western Education*, Cambridge: A & C Black, 1972.

Cahn, Stephen M., *The Philosophical Foundations of Education*, New York: Harper & Row, 1970.

Durkheim, Émile, *Education and Sociology*, trans. by Sherwood D. Fox, Glencoe, Ill.: The Free Press, 1956.

Good, Harry G., *A History of Western Education*, London: Macmillan, 1969.

Hogan, Padraig, *The Custody and Courtship of Experience: Western education in philosophical perspective*, Dublin: Columba Press, 1995.

Rusk, Robert R., *Doctrines of the Great Educators*, London: Macmillan, 1979.

1 Socrates (469/70–399 BC) and the Search for Definition

All of the dialogues of Plato which feature Socrates as the principal protagonist are available on the Internet. The following list matches Internet addresses with book publications: however useful online resources might be there is nothing to match holding a book! Further references can be found in the chapter on Plato.

Guthrie, W.K.C., *Socrates*, London: Cambridge University Press, 1971.

Kreeft, Peter, *Philosophy 101 by Socrates: an introduction to philosophy via Plato's 'Apology'*, San Francisco: Ignatius Press, 2002.

Plato, *Apology*, trans. by Hugh Tredennick, from *The Last Days of Socrates*, Penguin Books, 1969, pp. 43–76; online version is trans. by Benjamin Jowett at: http://classics.mit.edu/Plato/apology.html.

Plato, *Meno*, trans. by J.M.A. Grube, from *Plato: Five Dialogues*, Indianapolis: Hackett Publishing Co., 1981, pp. 59–88; trans. by Benjamin Jowett at: http://classics.mit.edu/Plato/meno.html.

Plato, *Protagoras*, trans. by W.K.C. Guthrie, from *Plato: Protagoras and Meno*, Harmondsworth: Penguin Books, 1956, pp. 101–55; trans. by Benjamin Jowett at: http://classics.mit.edu/Plato/protagoras.html.

Taylor, C.C.W., *Socrates: a very short introduction*, Oxford: Oxford University Press, 2000.

2   Plato (428–347 BC): Education for the State

Barrow, R., *Plato, utilitarianism and education*, London: Routledge and Kegan Paul, 1975.

Plato, *The Laws*, trans. by Trevor Saunders, London: Penguin Classics, 1973; online version trans. by Benjamin Jewett at: http://classics.mit.edu/Plato/laws.html.

Plato, *The Republic*, trans. by Desmond Lee, London: Penguin Classics, 2003; online version trans. by Benjamin Jewett at: http://classics.mit.edu/Plato/republic.html.

Plato, *The Seventh Letter*, trans. by J. Hayward at: http://www.farid-hajji.net/books/en/Plato/se-all.html.

White, Nicholas P., *A Companion to Plato's Republic*, Indianapolis: Hackett Publishing Co., 1979 (an invaluable and user-friendly reader's guide).

3   Aristotle (384–322 BC): Education for Leisure

Adler, Mortimer J., *Aristotle For Everybody*, New York: Touchstone, 1997.

Aristotle, *Ethics*, trans. by J.A.K. Thomson (revised, Hugh Tredennick), London: Penguin, 1976; online trans. by W.D. Ross at: http://classics.mit.edu/Aristotle/nicomachaen.html.

Aristotle, *Politics*, trans. by T.A. Sinclair (revised and re-presented by Trevor J. Saunders), London: Penguin Books, 1992; online trans. by Benjamin Jowett at: http://classics.mit.edu/Aristotle/politics.html.

Barnes, Jonathan, *Aristotle: a very short introduction*, Oxford: Oxford University Press, 2000.

Lord, Carnes, *Education and culture in the political thought of Aristotle*, Ithaca: Cornell University Press, 1982.

Spangler, Mary Michael, *Aristotle on Teaching*, Lanham, Md.: University Press of America, 1998.

4 Jesus (5/4 BC–27/8 AD?): Education for the Common Man

The primary texts on the life and teaching of Jesus are the four Gospels. I have used throughout the King James version, not for any ideological or religious reasons but simply because it remains the most poetic translation and contains the vivid language of the parables and analogies which have become universally familiar.

5 Marcus Fabius Quintilian (35–<100 AD): The Education of the Orator

The translation of the *Institutio Oratoria* used is that provided by Bill Thayer at: http://penelope.uchicago.edu/Thayer/E/Roman/Texts/Quintilian/Institutio_Oratoria/home.html.

Gwynn, Aubrey, *Roman Education from Cicero to Quintilian*, Columbia: Teachers College Press, 1966.

Smail, William M., *Quintilian on Education*, Columbia: Teachers College Press, 1966.

6 Aurelius Augustine (354–430): Education for the Inner Life

Augustine, *Against the Academicians: The Teacher*, trans. by M. Patricia Garvey, Milwaukee: Marquette University Press, 1957.

Augustine, *Confessions*, trans. by Henry Chadwick, Oxford: Oxford University Press, 1998: online trans. by E.B. Pusey at: http://ccat.sas.upenn.edu/jod/augustine.html.

Augustine, *The Greatness of the Soul & The Teacher*, trans. by Joseph M. Colleran, New York: Newman Press, 1978.

Bourke, Vernon, J. (ed.), *The Essential Augustine*, Indianapolis: Hackett Publishing Co., 1974.

Brown, Peter, *Augustine of Hippo: A Biography*, Berkeley, CA: University of California Press, 2000.

Howie, G., *Educational Theory and Practice in St. Augustine*, London: Routledge and Kegan Paul, 1969.

Oates, Whitney, J. (ed.), *The Basic Writings of Saint Augustine*, Grand Rapids: Baker Publishing Group, 1993.

7 John Amos Comenius (1592–1670): Education as a Human Right

John Amos Comenius on Education, Introduction by Jean Piaget, Classics in Education series, Columbia: Teachers College Press in 1967. (This volume comprises, in addition to Piaget's Introduction, excerpts from four of Comenius' books: *The Labyrinth of the World and the Paradise of the Heart, The Great Didactic, The Pampaedia, The Panorthosia.*)

Comenius, John Amos, *The Great Didactic*, trans. by M.W. Keatinge, Montana: R. A. Kessinger Publishing Co., 1992. (An earlier edition was published in London by Adam and Charles Black in 1896. An authorized facsimile of this book was produced by University Micro-films International, Michigan and London, in 1979.)

Comenius, John Amos, *School of Infancy*, Montana: R. A. Kessinger Publishing Co., 2003.

Kozik, Frantisek, *Sorrowful and Heroic Life of John Amos Comenius*, Montana: R. A. Kessinger Publishing Co., 2003.

Murphy, D., *Comenius: A Critical Reassessment of His Life and Work*, Dublin: Irish Academic Press, 1995.

Sadler, John Edward, *J.A. Comenius and the Concept of Universal Education*, London: George Allen & Unwin, 1966.

Spinka, Matthew, *John Amos Comenius; that Incomparable Moravian*, Chicago, Ill.: The University of Chicago Press, 1943 (reissued 1967).

8   John Locke (1632–1704): Education for the English Gentleman

Axtell, James (ed.), *The educational writings of John Locke: a critical edition*, with introduction and notes, Cambridge: Cambridge University Press, 1968.

Gay, Peter (ed.), *John Locke on Education*, Columbia University: Teachers College, 1964.

Grant, Ruth W. and Tarcov, Nathan (eds), *Some Thoughts Concerning Education*, Indianapolis: Hackett Publishing Co., 1996.

Locke, John, *On the Conduct of the Understanding*, online at: www.ac-nice.fr/philo/textes/Locke-ConductUnderstanding.htm.

Locke, John, *Some Thoughts Concerning Education*, Introduction and Notes by the Rev. R.H. Quick, MA, Cambridge: Cambridge University Press, 1899. Online text available at: www.fordham.edu/halsall/mod/1692locke-education.html

Sahakian, M.L. and Sahakian, W.S., *John Locke*, Boston: Twayne, 1975.

9   Jean-Jacques Rousseau (1712–1778): The Education of Nature

Boyd, William, *Emile for today: the Emile of Jean-Jacques Rousseau*, London: Heineman, 1956.

Rousseau, J-J., *Émile or On Education*, Introduction, Translation and Notes by Alan Bloom, Harmondsworth: Penguin, 1991.

Rousseau, J-J., *The Confessions of Jean-Jacques Rousseau*, Introduction and trans. by J.M. Cohen, Harmondsworth: Penguin, 1953.

Rousseau, J-J., *The Social Contract or Principles of Political Right*, trans. by H.J. Tozer, Introduction by Derek Matravers, London: Wordsworth Editions, 1998.

Rousseau, J-J., *The Reveries of the Solitary Walker*, trans. (with Preface, Notes and Interpretative Essay) by Charles E. Butterworth, Indianapolis: Hackett Publishing Co., 1992.

10 Jean Heinrich Pestalozzi (1746–1827): The Education of the People

de Guimps, Roger, *Pestalozzi: His Life and Work*, University Press of the Pacific, 2003.

Heafford, Michael, *Pestalozzi: His thought and its relevance today*, London: Methuen, 1967.

Pestalozzi, Heinrich, *How Gertrude Teaches her Children*, trans. by Lucy E. Holland and Francis C. Turner, London: George Allen and Unwin, 1915; online edition at: http://wordsworth.roehampton.ac.uk/digital/froarc/peshow/ind.asp.

Pestalozzi, Heinrich, *Leonard and Gertrude*, trans. by Eva Channing, Montana: Kessinger Publishing Co., 2004.

Pestalozzi, Heinrich, *Letters On Early Education*, New York: C.W. Bardeen, 1898; online at: http://wordsworth.roehampton.ac.uk/digital/froarc/pestlet/ind.asp.

Pestalozzi, Heinrich, *The Education of Man – Aphorisms*, Introduction by William H. Kilpatrick, New York: Philosophical Library, 1951.

Silber, Kate, *Pestalozzi, the Man and His Work*, London: Routledge and Kegan Paul, revised edn 1976.

11 Friedrich Froebel (1782–1852): The Garden of Education

Froebel, Friedrich, *On the Education of Man*, University Press of the Pacific, 2004.

Froebel, Friedrich, *The Pedagogics of the Kindergarten*, Michigan: The Froebel Foundation, 1895 (2001 reprint); online version is available at: http://wordsworth.roehampton.ac.uk/digital/froarc/froped/ind.asp.

Lawrence, Evelyn Mary, *Friedrich Froebel and English Education*, London: Routledge and Kegan Paul, 1969.

Liebschner, Joachim, *A Child's Work: Freedom and Play in Froebel's Educational Theory and Practice*, Cambridge: Lutterworth Press, 2002.

Lilley, Irene M. (ed.), *Friedrich Froebel: A Selection from His Writings*, Cambridge: Cambridge University Press, 1967.

von Marenholtz-Bulow, Bertha Maria, *Reminiscences of Friedrich Froebel*, Michigan: The Froebel Foundation, 1892 (2001 reprint).

12 John Henry Newman (1801–1890): University Education

Gilley, Sheridan, *Newman and his Age*, London: Darton, Longman and Todd, 1990.

Martin, Brian, *John Henry Newman: His Life & Work*, New York: Continuum International Publishing Group, 2001.

Newman, John H., *The Essential Newman*, Vincent Ferrer Blehl (ed.), New York: Mentor-Omega, 1963.

Newman, John H., *The Idea of a University*, London: Longmans Green, 1919; online edition can be found at: www.newmanreader.org/works/idea/.

Newman, John H., *et al.*, *The Idea of a University (Rethinking the Western Tradition)*, New Haven: Yale University Press, 1996; this edition includes commentary essays.

13 John Dewey (1859-1952): Education for the Future

Dewey, John, *Democracy And Education*, New York: The Free Press, 1997.

Dewey, John, *Dewey on Education*, New York: Teachers College Press, 1959.

Dewey, John, *Experience And Education*, New York: The Free Press, 1997.

Dewey, John and Sidorsky, D., *John Dewey: The Essential Writings*, New York: HarperCollins, 1977.

Fishman, S.M. and Parkinson McCarthy, L., *John Dewey and the Challenge of Classroom Practice*, New York: Teachers College Press, 1998.

Hickman, L. and Alexander, T.M., *The Essential Dewey: Pragmatism, Education, Democracy*, Indiana University Press, 1998.

Menand, Louis, *The Metaphysical Club*, London: Flamingo, 2002.

14 Maria Montessori (1870–1952): Education for Personal Competence

Kramer, Rita, *Maria Montessori: a biography*, Oxford: Blackwell, 1978.

Lillard, Paula P., *Montessori Today: A Comprehensive Approach to Education from Birth to Adulthood*, New York: Schocken, 1996.

Montessori, M., *Dr. Montessori's Own Handbook*, New York: Schocken Books, 1965.

Montessori, M., *The Absorbent Mind*, India: Kalakshetra Publications, 1984.

Montessori, M., *The Montessori Method*, trans. by A.E. George, New York: Frederick A. Stokes Company, 1912; online at: www.infed.org/archives/e-texts/montessori_method_III.htm.

Montessori, M., *The Secret of Childhood*, trans. by Barbara B. Carter, Bombay: Orient Longmans, 1963.

Oswald, P. and Schulz-Benesch, G. (eds), *Basic Ideas of Montessori's Educational Theory, extracts from Maria Montessori's writings and teachings*, trans. from the German by Lawrence Salmon, Oxford: Clio Press, 1997.

15 Martin Buber (1878–1965): Education for Relationship

Buber, M., *Between Man and Man*, London: The Fontana Library, 1961.

Buber, M., *I and Thou*, Edinburgh: T&T Clark, 1971.

Cohen, A., *The Educational Philosophy of Martin Buber*, Rutherford, NJ: Fairleigh Dickinson Press, 1983.

Friedman, Maurice S., *Martin Buber's life and work*, Detroit: Wayne State University Press, 1988.

Hodes, Aubrey, *Encounter with Martin Buber*, Harmondsworth: Penguin, 1975.

Murphy, Daniel, *Martin Buber's Philosophy of Education*, Dublin: Irish Academic Press, 1988.

16 Alexander Sutherland Neill (1883–1973): Education for the Liberation of the Psyche

Croall, Jonathan, *Neill of Summerhill: the permanent rebel*, London: Ark, 1984.

Hemmings, Ray, *Fifty years of freedom: a study of the development of the ideas of A.S. Neill*, London: Allen and Unwin, 1972.

Neill, A.S., *All the best, Neill: letters from Summerhill*, London: Deutsch, 1983.

Neill, A.S., *Neill! Neill! Orange peel! An autobiography*, London, Quartet Books, 1977.

Neill, A.S., *Summerhill : a radical approach to child-rearing*, Harmondsworth: Penguin, 1985; online version is available at: http://balasainet.com/arvindguptatoys/Summerhill.htm.

Walmsley, John, *Neill & Summerhill: a man and his work*, Harmondsworth: Penguin, 1969.

The Summerhill website is at: www.summerhillschool.co.uk/pages/index.html.

17 Paulo Freire (1921–1997): Education for Freedom

Elias, John L., *Paulo Freire: Pedagogue of Liberation*, Melbourne, FL: Krieger Publishing Company, 1994.

Freire, Paulo, *Cultural Action for Freedom*, Harmondsworth: Penguin, 1972.

Freire, Paulo, *Education for Critical Consciousness*, Lanham: Sheed and Ward, 1999.

Freire, Paulo, *Pedagogy in Process: the letters to Guinea-Bissau*, London: Writers and Readers Publishing Cooperative, 1978.

Freire, Paulo, *Pedagogy of the Oppressed*, trans. by Myra Bergman Ramos, Harmondsworth: Penguin Books, 1972.

18 Ivan Illich (1926–2002): Education Without Schooling

Barrow, R., *Radical education: a critique of freeschooling and deschooling*, London: Martin Robertson, 1978.

Illich, Ivan, *After Deschooling, What*, London: Writers and Readers Publishing Cooperative, 1976.

Illich, Ivan, *Celebration of Awareness: a call for institutional revolution*, Harmondsworth: Penguin, 1976.

Illich, Ivan, *Deschooling Society*, Harmondsworth: Penguin, 1973; online edition available at: http://homepage.mac.com/tinapple/illich/1970_deschooling.html.

Illich, Ivan, *Tools for Conviviality*, London: Marion Boyars Publishers, 2001; online edition, Centro Latinoamericano para la Competitividad y el Desarrollo Sostenible, Alajuela, 2002, available at: http://homepage.mac.com/tinapple/illich/1973_tools_for_conviviality.html.